DEFIANT GARDENS

DEFIANT GARDENS

Making Gardens in Wartime

Kenneth I. Helphand

TRINITY UNIVERSITY PRESS
San Antonio

All quotations from the Bible are from *The Torah: The Five Books of Moses* (Philadelphia: Jewish Publication Society of America, 1962) unless otherwise noted.

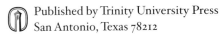 Published by Trinity University Press
San Antonio, Texas 78212

Copyright © 2006 by Kenneth I. Helphand

Jacket design by DJ Stout and Julie Savasky, Pentagram, Austin, Texas

Book design by BookMatters, Berkeley, California

♾ The paper used in this publication meets the minimum requirements of the American National Standard for Information Sciences — Permanence of Paper for Printed Library Materials, ANSI Z39.48–1992.

Library of Congress Cataloging-in-Publication Data

Helphand, Kenneth I.
    Defiant gardens : making gardens in wartime / Kenneth I. Helphand
        p.   cm.
    Includes bibliographical references and index.
    ISBN-13: 978-1-59534-021-4 (hardcover : alk. paper)
    ISBN-10: 1-59534-021-1 (hardcover : alk. paper)
    1. Gardens—History—20th century.
    2. Gardens and war—History—20th century.
    I. Title.
SB451.H45   2006
635'.0904—dc22   2005037716

PRINTED IN CANADA

10 09 08 07 06 / 5 4 3 2 1

for Margot

Contents

Preface

Gardens traverse the terrain from subsistence to the highest forms of artistry. As a landscape architect I am fascinated by the range of garden types and possibilities, and by the variety of human creativity expressed in gardens, especially when they have been created under conditions of adversity. The journey that set my feet on the path to write this book began with my encountering a single image: a photograph of French soldiers in World War I standing in front of a small vegetable garden adjacent to their dugout quarters. This evocative picture haunted me for years. Why did these soldiers make this garden? What did it mean to them? What kind of satisfaction did they derive from creating, and tending, and harvesting it? Consideration of these questions became the germ of the idea of defiant gardens.

Gardens are made all around us; some are the product of deliberate design, and others become gardens merely by our observation and insight, but most gardens are the result of a common human activity. Most gardens are at one with their settings, blending in physically and even psychologically with their surroundings. This book, however, looks at those created in extreme situations — defiant gardens. Such gardens stand not in harmony with but in opposition to their locations, asserting their presence and almost demanding response from their human visitors. This opposition provides the illumination of contrast, allowing the background to bring the central image and concept of the garden into brilliant relief.

My focus is on defiant gardens created during wartime. These include gardens made in proximity to the battlefield and death, to the sites where war is perpetrated upon civilians, to those places where people are imprisoned and imperiled during wartime. It includes gardens whose makers could safely share the fruits of their labor as well as those who resolutely planted seeds though they were in imminent danger, and never saw them flower. These gardens offer evidence of the profound meanings contained in the experience of gardens. These are all extreme situations, but there are lessons and ideas to be gleaned from these places that apply to garden making in more benign conditions.

I chose to look at gardens from the first half of the twentieth century, whose wars were the deadliest in human history: gardens built behind the trenches in World War I, on both sides of the Western Front, gardens created by Jews imprisoned in ghettos by the Nazis during World War II, gardens in POW and civilian internment camps of both wars, and gardens created by Japanese Americans held at internment camps in the United States during World War II. Sadly, these examples could easily be supplemented by many more, and as I write gardens surely are being made by individuals in the most dire circumstances.

Gardens are ephemeral. Made of natural materials and in need of maintenance, their existence is short-lived, their marks on the land quickly obliterated. Few records survive of their creation, for they have seldom been considered significant enough to be recorded for posterity. None of these wartime gardens still exist; most were destroyed or just disappeared from neglect and natural processes. There is an elusive quality to researching gardens; even when documented they rarely appear as a category in an index or catalog, and when their tales are told it is often as part of a larger story. Thus research for defiant gardens entailed journeys to diverse places. In the *Legend of Seth*, which dates from the third or fourth century A.D., Adam and Eve's son retraces his parent's footsteps, following a "green path" (*uiam uiridfem*) back to the paradise of Eden (see Patch, *Other World*, 155). In a sense I too followed a green path, looking for clues to these lost Edens found in the midst of hell. But my green path took me through the hellish landscapes of battlefields, camps, and ghettos.

I try to tell the story of these gardens through the individuals who created them and who experienced them directly. Thus I have primarily relied on first-person accounts, diaries, memoirs, testimonies, photographs, and drawings. As I shared my idea of defiant gardens with others and lectured on the topic, people told me of other examples and generously provided images and suggestions to guide my path. I am indebted to everyone who has contributed in such ways.

I began my research on trench gardens at the Imperial War Museum in London, in my opinion the world's greatest military museum, whose staff in the photo and document collection were extraordinarily helpful. I visited museums along the Western Front, including Ypres, Albert, and Verdun. In Poperinghe, Dries Chaerle, archivist of the Talbot House, provided invaluable information.

Marti Ravits introduced me to the diary of Mary Berg, starting my research of ghetto gardens. It then took me to YIVO in New York, the great repository of Jewish life in Eastern Europe, where I was assisted by Leo Birnbaum and the knowledgeable staff. At the United Sates Holocaust Museum and Memorial in Washington, D.C., I discovered the world unseen by visitors and was ably assisted by librarian Michlean L. Amir and photo archivist Maren Read. Closer to the sites of the ghettos, Dr. Eleonora Bergman, deputy director, and Jan Jagielski, photo archivist, of the Jewish Historical Institute in Warsaw shared their rare insights. In Israel, at the Ghetto Fighters House located at the kibbutz of that name, founded by survivors of the Warsaw ghetto, I was introduced to their unparalled collection ably stewarded by archivist Yossi Shavit. There I was also assisted by Judy Grossman and Simcha Stein, director. In Jerusalem at Yad Vashem, archivist Zvi Bernhardt was my guide, Rebecca Schein offered suggestions, and Sara Pechanic supplied assistance. In Los Angeles Doug Ballmann of the Survivors of the Shoah Visual History Foundation guided my exploration through the video archive there. In Eugene, Oregon, Judith Baskin introduced me to historian Michael Birenbaum, who led me along a path to survivors and their testimonies.

Yoko Okunishi of the Japanese American National Museum was my guide in Los Angeles, and in the Densho Archive, The Japanese American Legacy Project, I found rare images. Manzanar is now a National Historical Site. Cathy Gilbert of the Seattle office of the National Park Service connected me to the remarkable research the NPS has done on the internment camps, especially Manzanar and Minidoka. Anna Tamura, also of the National Park Service, shared generously her knowledge of the gardens and landscapes of Manzanar and Minidoka. The chapter on stone gardens would have been impossible without her assistance. Tim Toyama shared both his film and play, *Independence Day*.

Although the subject of gardens was new for military museums and for the archives of the Holocaust and ghettos, invariably the staff found the subject fascinating and shared generously their vast knowledge of their collections. Most of these archives now have websites, which were essential to this research, making what was once years of digging possible in an afternoon, and making the visit to the actual places even more productive. My sincere thanks to the many persons who have produced and maintain these now-essential research and communication aids.

Some of the material found here was not written in English, and I am indebted to those who were able to make these works accessible to me through translation. I am most grateful for translations from Yiddish by Roberta Newman, Sara Novoplansky, Zvi Novoplansky, and Chana Melnick, from Hebrew by the Novoplanskys, from Polish by Mischa Buczkowski, and from German by Susan Anderson. They have helped bring a literature created under unimaginable conditions to a wider audience.

Gardens are a particular product of the interaction of people and place. Thus garden research takes one to people and to places. Few of the garden makers discussed in these pages survive, but I availed myself of audio and written testimonies of scores of individuals. I thank them all, especially those individuals who shared their often painful stories with me: Janik (Jonah) Fuchs, Roman Kent, Gerda Klein, Esther Mishkin, and Elizabeth Nance. The stories of all of these individuals are the heart of this book, and the Directory of Prisoners and Internees after chapter 7 is a small tribute to their contribution and their sacrifice.

These defiant gardens have not survived, but it was imperative for me to visit as many of the original sites as was feasible. I toured battlefields and trenches of the Western Front. I attended an annual memorial event at Manzanar. I spent days walking the site of the Warsaw ghetto armed with a map of the ghetto in 1943 that located garden sites, overlaid with the modern street system. I visited the sites where many of these garden makers lie, the cemeteries of the Western Front and the death camp at Auschwitz-Birkenau. Some of my reflections on these visits are in the postwar chapter.

Many others also deserve my gratitude. Beth Diamond assisted in research in my initial article on defiant gardens, which John Dixon

Hunt, editor of the *Journal of Garden History,* subsequently published in 1997. Graduate students Kitty Davis and Suzanne Spencer-Wood provided important research assistance. Shelley Egoz supplied information on New Zealand, and Dale Gronso shared his extensive research on the Japanese American experience. Sam Helphand provided invaluable technical advice and along with Daniel Winterbottom, Rene Kane, and Don Smith donated images and artifacts. The University of Oregon Humanities Center and the Johnson Fund provided research time and financial support.

I teach garden history and theory, but I am not an expert in all the areas to which this journey took me. Thus I relied on others to help me place the stories of these gardens into their larger historical contexts. Fortunately, a remarkable collection of such persons was located nearby at the University of Oregon. David Leubke, professor of history and formerly at the United States Holocaust Museum and Memorial, read the chapters on World War I and ghetto gardens. Alex Dracolby, who teaches courses on war and military history, read the chapter on trench gardens. Francis Cogan, professor and author of *Captured: The Japanese Internment of American Civilians in the Philippines, 1941–1945,* read the chapter on prisoners of war. Anna Tamura, National Park Service landscape architect, read the chapter on internment camps. Other colleagues, family members, and friends read the entire manuscript and supplied invaluable comments. They include Liska Chan, Robert Jackson, Anne Spirn, Ben Helphand, David Helphand, and Elaine Winik. It was an honor and a humbling experience to have had my son, my brother, and my mother-in-law act as readers. Of course I take responsibility for the entire presentation and interpretation.

I am grateful to those who helped bring the book to fruition. Deborah Oliver's copyediting tightened and sharpened my prose, David Peattie provided an elegant design appropriate to the dignity of the topic, and DJ Stout added a striking cover design. Throughout the process, from conception to realization, Barbara Ras of Trinity University Press has been a perceptive reader and enthusiastic advocate of this project. These individuals were all a joy to work with and they all contributed to a result that does honor to those who created the gardens and whose stories are told in these pages.

There is one person who has been part of this work from its inception: my wife, Margot. She was my companion on this entire journey, listening to my many musings, reading the many drafts, and even witnessing my tears when the stories that I have tried to impart were too much to bear. Most important, she was my companion on the journeys from Eugene to New York, Los Angeles, Washington, London, France, Belgium, Warsaw, and Israel, in all these places enabling me to see with her eyes as well as my own.

Kenneth I. Helphand
UNIVERSITY OF OREGON

D E F I A N T   G A R D E N S

ONE ❧ War and Gardens

Small pleasure must correct great tragedies,
Therefore of gardens in the midst of war
I boldly tell.

VITA SACKVILLE-WEST, *The Garden*

THE YEAR WAS 1918, the fourth year of what was then known as the Great War, which had already claimed millions of lives. On October 3 the British poet Siegfried Sassoon met with Winston Churchill, then minister of munitions. Churchill was a hero of the Boer War, a best-selling author, and a leading politician; Sassoon was already a well-known poet of the war, a decorated and courageous soldier, and an antiwar spokesman. His statement against prolonging the war had been read in the House of Commons in July 1917. During the 1918 interview, Churchill remarked to Sassoon that "war is the normal occupation of man." Sassoon wondered, "Had he been entirely serious?" Churchill qualified the declaration with a remarkable caveat, adding "war — and gardening."[1] This can be read not only as the classic dichotomy of war and peace but also as the poles of human experience: an emotional axis mundi, the poles of destruction and violence versus creation and tranquillity. As poles, each accentuates the other. What does it mean that during war, and even in war-torn places, one can find gardens?

Gardens — even individual plants growing in bits of soil — in deserts, prisons, hospitals, highway medians, vacant lots, refugee camps, rooftops, dumps, wastelands, cracks in the sidewalk: these are examples of what I call *defiant gardens,* gardens created in extreme or difficult environmental, social, political, economic, or cultural conditions. These gardens represent adaptation to challenging circumstances, but they can also be viewed from other dimensions as sites of assertion and affirmation.

A bomb crater on the grounds of Westminster Cathedral in London was left intact and used as a kitchen garden in 1942.

Gardens are indeed many things. They're part of our homes, beautiful places, beautiful places, places for plants, leisure, and enjoyment. Gardens can evoke other places; they can symbolize belief systems, the cosmos, social status or lifestyle. Gardens are ordered. They represent in intimate ways our connections to the natural world. In virtually all languages, the etymology of the word *garden* is an enclosed piece of land. This sense of enclosure — the garden as a place apart, a different place — pervades all our garden thinking. Surely this was originally for pragmatic and practical purposes, but perhaps there are even more basic reasons. The garden defines a natural space, and as a creation with a defined center, it is bound as our bodies are bound. The English poet George Herbert wrote in the early seventeenth century, "You may be on land, yet not on a garden." We transform land into gardens in many ways, and we may attach garden values to any landscape.

Gardens also embody ideas. "Garden" is one of a set of basic environmental images such as wilderness, city, home, utopia, heaven, or hell. The garden is not only a specific type of place; it is also a remarkably elastic concept with the capacity to both generate and absorb a multiplicity of mental associations. Part of our fascination with the garden is this malleability. Gardens as physical environments employ the immutable elements, forms, and forces of nature, and they also

Garden of Mailia Husseinova and her three children in Bart Refugee Camp near the town of Karabulak, Ingushetia, Russia. The camp housed up to 6,000 refugees from Chechnya until March 2005.

bear the changing meanings we capriciously ascribe to specific aspects of nature. Gardens are frames or settings for activity and behavior; they mirror a culture's values and attitudes; they are places of ideals, aspirations, and life necessities. The garden's subject ranges from humanity's most mundane need to history's most profound questions.

Typically, in the popular imagination, gardens are thought of as sanctuaries, granting a respite from the indoors, the city, civilization, and culture, where the garden represents the nonhuman world of nature. They are desired but are rarely seen as essential, nor are they commonly plumbed for their deeper meaning. Garden scholars know well the depth and breadth of garden meaning and symbolism, but even they have not fully addressed the complexities of the garden.

The novelist and gardener Jamaica Kincaid tells about having given a talk about favorite gardens, after which her hosts chastised her for injecting conceptions of race and politics into her speech. She asks, "Why must people insist that the garden is a place of rest and repose, a place to forget the cares of the world, a place in which to distance yourself from the painful responsibility with being a human being?"[2] Kincaid demands more of the garden. Defiant gardens are a response to such challenges.

It has often been noted that the garden can be thought of in dialectical terms, viewing design as a synthesis of the basic forces, forms, and ideas of humans and of nature: control and chaos, stasis and growth, the civilized and the wild, involvement and escape, reality and ideals. Our greatest gardens span these poles in form and meaning; they encompass worlds within themselves. The Canadian literary critic Northrop Frye wrote: "There are two great structures underlying poetic imagery, the cyclical and dialectic. The cycle of nature, running through the phases of the day, the year, the circulation of water, the generations of human life, and the like, stretches like a backbone across the whole of literature. The separation of images into the contrasting worlds or states of mind that Blake calls innocence and experience, and what religions call heaven and hell, is the dialectical framework of literature."[3] Frye's observations on literary archetypes apply equally well to the garden. Its forms are an objectification of these two great structures, cyclical nature and dialectical culture.

Paradise is our formative garden image and ideal. Eden is the archetypal garden, the prototype of Western garden design, and in the tale of Eden we have condensed and concentrated the central images and ideas of gardens. Recall the attributes of Eden. The world begins with a garden. It is the territory of creation. It is where humans talk with God. It is sacred, a place of innocence, peacefulness, perfection, and complete harmony — although of course it is also flawed and contains the seeds of its own destruction. It is a microcosm of creation, where every species of the world is contained.

If we look at Eden as the formative garden idea of the West, we begin to recognize the complexity of the garden idea. Adam is the steward tending the garden of Eden, but after the Fall he is cursed and it becomes his lot to work the earth and toil in the garden. Presumably labor in Eden was not "work." One suspects that Churchill, in claiming that both war and gardening are "the normal occupation of men," was referring not to gardening for sustenance but to gardening for pleasure and beauty. Indeed, the Bible tells us that on the sixth day of the creation, "The Lord God planted a garden in Eden, in the east, and placed there the man whom He had formed. And from the ground the Lord God caused to grow every tree that was pleasing to the sight and good for food" (Genesis 2:9). Remarkably, in this first commentary on creation, "pleasing to the sight" ("good to look at" in many translations) is cited before food, which is necessary for physical sustenance. Some religious scholars note that this pairing — and its order — is significant. Perhaps the aesthetic is as essential a need as food.

The Eden of Genesis is only one example of a pervasive world myth, the myth of paradise, an ideal and perfect place. Myth defines paradise both negatively — by what is absent — and positively — that is, by what is present. It is a place without any anxieties or dangers, and certainly without death. Paradise is benificent, full of positive emotions and states of being, and, of course, immortality.

The paradisiacal environment is the setting and the physical analogue of this state of being. That the most positive aspects of the natural environment are inherent in the biblical understanding of paradise is not surprising in a mythic world of peoples intimate with and dependent on nature's cycles. In such a world, nature is continually bountiful, bearing her fruit without human labor. In our tales of paradise, the natural world is sumptuously on display, from the rocks of the earth to perfumed air to the presence of divinity. Paradise is timeless and eternal, a place of perpetual springtime, permeated with a sense of rebirth and wonder at creation. Paradise is always beautiful. It is almost always a garden.

In a sense, to be in the garden is to *be* Adam and Eve — to return to innocence. In the garden the most basic questions address the limits of knowledge, of mortality, and of immortality. In Western culture the image of paradise as a symbol of an ideal state of existence operates across the spectrum of time. At one end is a nostalgic desire to return to our origins in the ideal perfection of the past. At the other is a quest for a hoped-for future, crystallized in the image of celestial paradise.

Even if most of the industrialized world is largely removed from agricultural processes, we still think of the *essential* role of gardens as providing sustenance. But here George Eisen's *Children and Play in the Holocaust: Games among the Shadows* offers instructive parallels. Play, like the garden, isn't always taken seriously. The fact that pleasure, joy, abandon, innocence, and freedom are often present with play disguises its more profound aspects. So, too, with the garden. Ironically, that we associate the garden with the archetypal ideal of paradise and the nostalgic allure of the pastoral may account for our marginalization of garden making, where we see gardens as a luxury, frill, pastime, or leisure time activity, and not as an essential component of culture and human existence. And, the beauty of the garden may mask its deeper messages. In Eisen's examination of children's play in ghettos, concentration camps, and wartime hiding places, he discovered that play was an "enterprise of survival, a defense of sanity and a demonstration of psychological defiance."[4] Could we not think of the garden thus, too?

Maybe humans have a garden "connection," an intuitive reminder of our symbiotic ties to nature, where we are a species in mutual dependency with the world of plants.

The garden also provides mechanisms of human survival other than growing food for sustenance. The garden may act as a psychological aid, and as Jay Appleton has hypothesized, may be instinctually appealing as a symbolic landscape of sustenance. Appleton's concept of habitat theory asserts that our aesthetic responses are rooted in our species behavior. In gardens in extreme situations, we may come closer to these biological roots as our conscious appreciation of and positive response to gardens merge.

The garden's hidden or repressed possibilities may emerge in extreme situations. In a sense, the garden assumes a character or even responsibilities we didn't imagine it had but that it is willing to bear under extraordinary circumstances. In defiant situations, humans display a surprising resourcefulness in design and function, in formal arrangement, and in the appropriation of, gathering, and use of materials. Recognition of our own creativity under adverse conditions heightens our satisfaction in being in such a garden. As we know, the seeds of certain plants will germinate only when exposed to the heat of fire; the horrible inhumane conditions of the trenches of the Western Front, ghettos, and internment and prisoner-of-war camps that unlocked something dormant, allowing it to sprout as a defiant garden, are analogous to botany's fire-triggered seed germination.

Psychologists and philosophers learn about human behavior by examining people in extreme circumstances of deprivation and hardship. In the same way, gardens in extreme situations may reveal essential aspects of garden character and ideology. Gardens are always defined by their context. Perhaps the more difficult the context, the more accentuated the meaning. The horticulturist Charles Lewis suggests, "Just as the gleam of a candle is more visible in a dimly lighted room, so the human benefits of gardening are more clearly seen in impoverished environments that lack the amenities to make life pleasant."[5]

"War is hell," Civil War General William Tecumseh Sherman reportedly said. In his autobiography, *A Quest for Life*, landscape architect Ian McHarg recounts his wartime experiences and how "salubrity, the healing power of nature, came to be a major recurring theme in [his] life." He writes, "Nothing in my history, before or since, has equaled the degree of contrast I then experienced: Cassino one day — dead and dying on the battlefield, a calamitous carnage, blood, mud, sorrow, despair, bombs, rockets, and mortars — and the next waking to silence, whispers, footsteps, church bells, peace."[6] Although war may be the most dramatic example of such contrasts, a defiant perspective is an aspect of all gardens, for gardens domesticate the natural world and place it under human control. The defiant garden intensifies the meanings of landscape materials, which are the components of garden design. It reasserts fundamental aspects of the natural world as humans have imbued it with value. Cultures have often viewed nature's processes — the renewal of spring, the flow of water, fecundity, sensory richness, and growth — as life giving and hopeful. The resurgence of nature and "spring" — nature in motion or pushing through — symbolize hope and defiance. Gardens also represent an exchange between humans and the natural world, where nature neither overpowers nor threatens but becomes more subdued.

Gardens promise beauty where there is none, hope over despair, optimism over pessimism, and finally life in the face of death. Much as Eisen sees play as essentially life-affirming behavior "embodying a tenacious will and principle of existence," so too is the garden, in its eternal optimism of the promise of plants emerging from the ground, the pleasures of flowers, and the sustenance of food.[7] If the Edenic ideal of paradise is found at one extreme, its opposite is found in the landscape of hell. The polar opposites, the dialectics of the garden are at a higher pitch, perhaps highest, when hell is near.

Expulsion from the Garden of Eden by Thomas Cole, 1828.

Traditionally, the garden is associated with the Edenic, which is a respite from the city, strife, and culture. The garden is seen as equal to nature, but it is a paradoxically quintessential cultural artifact. Associated with paradise and the nostalgia of the pastoral, it is essential to look at its opposition, at hell and gardens in hell, or gardens in war.

The defiant garden accentuates the essential garden questions of the relationships among form, function, and meaning. The context of the garden structures how it is seen and experienced. Gardens either conform or do not conform to our expectations. We expect to find gardens in the domesticated landscape: the pairing of house and garden, in all its variants; gardens — largely in the form of parks and open spaces — in the city; and gardens as part of or as the agricultural and working landscape. In all of these situations the garden either is part of that domesticated environment or is the domesticating agent. But what of the garden found in a wild, undomesticated space? When we see a garden out of place — along a railroad track, or a home garden in an industrial area or a parking lot — or a garden eked out of forbidding terrain, it captures our attention and even our admiration: "I am never tired of watching and observing how plants will manage not only to exist but even to thrive in difficult circumstances," wrote English garden designer Gertrude Jekyll.[8]

The garden's diverse functions, from the most pragmatic and mundane to the most fanciful and profound, are all accentuated by the garden's circumstance and intention. Envision a garden in your backyard versus an identical garden on a highway median. When we see an improbable garden, we experience a shock of recognition of the garden's form and elements, but also a renewed appreciation of the garden's transformative power to beautify, comfort, and convey meaning despite the incongruity of its surroundings. Gardens are defined by their context, and perhaps the further the context from our expectations, the deeper the meaning the garden holds for us.

Defiance may oppose environmental conditions, the extremes of climate, difficult topography, or lack of soil, water, or even plants. Gardens in extreme environments of temperature, elevation, or water supply accentuate the material origins of the garden and its forms. This accentuation adds to their clarity of expressive form, notably in desert gardens. In the southern Sinai are gardens of the Jebalaya Bedouin, which are similar to gardens on the windblown Mediterranean island of Pantelleria, located between Sicily and Tunisia. The configuration in both places is simple: a single tree enclosed by a stone wall. The form is derived as a response to harsh circumstances: the need to create a modest piece of arable land, define territory and ownership, offer shade, collect moisture, and protect from flash flood, grazing animals, or trespassers. Physically, the Pantellerian *giardino* are almost an ideogram of a garden: an enclosed place in the landscape with plants at the center.

Another example of environmental defiance occurs in the high country of New Zealand. There shepherds such as Oliver ("Sundowner") Duff have planted gardens, he says, "since they first came over the water." Each summer when they return to the high country, the gardens need to be reclaimed. But he takes heart that plantings have survived and that "the sentimental shepherd can leave marks on

This Algerian garden in the Sahara illustrates the evolution of garden form. The fundamentals that define a garden are present, though the composition has a formal geometry, with patterns derived from agriculture, as it is an enclosed, symmetrical garden.

the landscape that neither his children nor his children's children will obliterate without atom bombs."[9]

Gardens in extreme environments are defiant, struggling to establish themselves without soil or water, or at high elevations, under high winds, or a brief growing season. Garden making in Arctic Greenland, for example, requires *tamaviaartumik* — Greenlandic for passion, ambition, and commitment.[10]

In 1831 Antonio Sebastiani published *Flora Colisea,* in which he identified 261 species growing in Rome's Coliseum, and a few decades later the Englishman Richard Deakin identified 420 species there. As Louis Inturrisi observed in the 1990s, "between the venerable cracks and crevices . . . you will notice the first brave emanations of the famous flora colisea, the Colosseum plants, which every spring despite considerable odds, make their triumphant, life-affirming appearance."[11]

Though we rarely recognize it, often the modern urban landscapes where plants (and people) live are functional deserts; trees especially are deprived of water, compacted, and straining to survive. In the

The gardens of Greenland were the subject of an exhibit at the Narsaq Museum. The images were taken between 2000 and 2002 by photographer Finn Larsen in communities on Greenland's west coast.

modern city we discover gardens in vacant lots, breaking through concrete, on rooftops, or in strips between rows of speeding, exhaust-spewing traffic.

We stop in wonder and admiration for plants surviving where they shouldn't, in the interstices of the city. But it takes careful observation and empathy to accept that gardens are not only made but can also "volunteer." As "Botanic Anarchy," a *New York Times* editorial, observed:

> The nights are beginning to chill: you can almost feel the season shifting gears under your feet. The impatiens and begonia are breathing their last around the trunks of side-street trees. But between cracks in the sidewalk, hardier things are growing with no help from humans. . . . Wherever you see green where it seems that nothing could grow, chances are it's nightshade. The green strip along the East River reveals more: horseweed and spiny-leaved sow thistle and a brave colony of delicate-leaved, snapdragon-shaped butter-and-eggs. In the impossible turf of Delancey Street strange botany develops. . . . In the

dirty median strip, nightshade covers the rubble. It may not be elegant, but then try asking a begonia to grow there.[12]

The phrase *ruderal vegetation* refers to plants that grow in waste and particularly on disturbed sites, such as garbage dumps, vacant lots, and industrial wastelands. There is a long history of constructing designed landscapes on such sites: portions of New York's Central Park were a garbage dump, and Paris's Parc de Butte Chaumont was a quarry and waste site. Contemporary horticulturist Beth Chatto's garden and nursery near Colchester, England, is built in sand and gravel on the site of a former parking lot.[13] The work of Peter Latz at Landschaftspark Duisburg-Nord in Germany is perhaps the most dramatic example, where five hundred acres of former industrial land, despoiled by smelting and manufacturing, is now a succession of gardens, many of which frame the site's ruderal vegetation. Gardens and parks such as these employ and celebrate the ability of plants to volunteer and colonize in savagely inhospitable situations. They celebrate this process by bringing it to our consciousness, intensifying its effect, and elevating it to an aesthetic.

Defiant gardens resist not only environmental difficulty but also social, psychological, political, or economic conditions. The garden can offer an assertion, a voice for the voiceless, and involvement for the disenfranchised. Gardens can defy by their chosen location and placement in unconventional places and even in defiance of the law. Guerrilla gardeners can act out protest, demonstration, or resistance. At the extreme, gardening may even be seen by authorities as a revolutionary, even criminal, act. Eventually this rogue spirit can become institutionalized; the community garden movement derives much of its energy from the garden as an assertive action.

Intuition tells us that certain landscape experiences are beneficial to our sense of well-being, and science validates that sensibility. In a simple yet profound study, Roger Ulrich discovered that hospital patients with just a view of a tree outside their window recovered more rapidly after surgery than patients without such views. The empirical health benefits of contact with elements of the natural world are real — even just pictures of nature have a salubrious effect. Practitioners of horticultural therapy exploit the beneficial effects of gardens and gardening to improve patients' social, psychological, and physical well-being. They recognize that benefits derive not only from the result — the finished garden itself — but perhaps even more so from the process of gardening.

Garden is, after all, both a noun (a place) and a verb (an action). Because most of us have a general notion of what garden work entails, even if we don't garden ourselves, it is easy for observers to imagine how something is created and then to grasp the difficulties of conception, design, logistics, the marshaling of materials, construction, maintenance, and monitoring, all of which are necessary for a successful garden: we are responding to garden as both noun and verb. Working or even just being in the garden reduces stress and can aid healing.

For decades, the environmental psychologists Rachel Kaplan and Stephen Kaplan have studied human responses to the natural world. They have given special attention to nearby nature in residential landscapes, neighborhoods, and work environments, as well as to landscape preference. They see gardening as an activity shared by millions and across all segments of society. Their work calls into question the strictly hierarchical notion of human needs described by Abraham Maslow, who hypothesized that "basic" physiological human needs must be satisfied before "higher" needs can be addressed. Kaplan and Kaplan found that people often invested themselves in activities such as growing flowers even when their most basic requirements of living were unsatisfied. Their work suggests that the definition of "basic" needs revising. Their studies of garden satisfaction show that it offers many benefits. The greatest is a sense of tranquillity, followed by the fascination with nature and the pleasure of the garden's sensory experience. But there are also the tangible benefits of food and the pleasure derived from sharing produce and knowledge. Satisfaction also derives from novelty, as well as from being in control and keeping things tidy, often in contrast to the world beyond the limits of the garden.

Research also demonstrates that the extent of a garden's positive impact is not relative to its size or scale. Very small gardens, even a single plant, can enhance people's well-being. Whether gardens are long-lived or exist only briefly, they can have an equivalent impact. By several different mechanisms they can help relieve simple mental fatigue or alleviate stress. The garden can provide a mental distraction from our usual routine, giving gardeners a sense of "being away." Imagine the power of such a feeling if you are imprisoned, confined, or awaiting an impending attack. There is also what the Kaplans call "soft fascination": the powerful aesthetic dimension that engages gardeners. There is satisfaction in having control over and maintaining order in a plot, but gardeners simultaneously feel connected to larger forces not quite under human control.[14] We could describe this reflective mode as the garden's spiritual dimension.

Garden scholars such as John Dixon Hunt have called for giving renewed attention to garden theory. In asking "what on earth is a garden," he attempts a comprehensive garden definition: they are normally out of doors; they are related to their locality but are distinct from their surroundings; time plays a central role in the life of a garden; and each garden exhibits a distinct combination of natural and cultural materials. Hunt calls for an "anthropology of the garden [that] would explore the many cultural versions of the garden."[15] This requires looking at gardens, their makers, and what gardens have meant to those who have created and experienced them. Gardens, says Hunt, are concentrated and perfected forms of place making. They are also concentrations of meaning. We may discover more about the depths of that meaning by examining the garden in its defiant guise and in looking at gardens and war.

In *The Garden,* whose opening lines are the epigraph to this chapter, Vita Sackville-West writes about a gardener's work in terms of the advance and retreat or "relapse" of an army:

> Yet shall the garden with the state of war
> Aptly contrast, a miniature endeavor
> To hold the graces and the courtesies
> Against a horrid wilderness. . . .
> So does the gardener in little way
> Maintain the bastion of his opposition
> And by a symbol keep civility;
> So does the brave man strive
> To keep enjoyment in his breast alive
> When all is dark and even in his heart
> Of beauty feed the pallid worm of death.[16]

The terrain of war is the battlefield. In a sense the battlefield, as a dystopic landscape offering no cover or pleasure and laden with terror

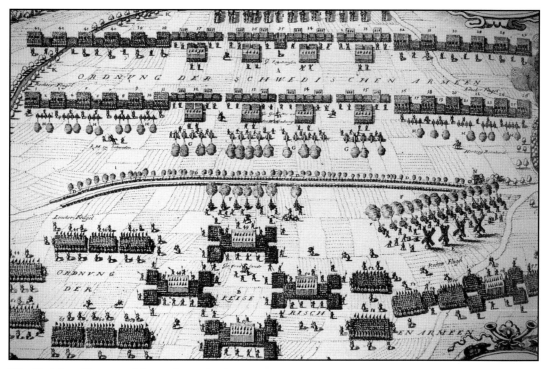

The Battle of Lutzon, November 16, 1632.

and death, is the antithesis of the garden. "War consists of actions that no man would otherwise perform . . . and it takes place in antiland-scapes that are contradictions of the landscapes that human beings live in," says Samuel Hynes. Yet the term *field of battle* has its origins in the fields and meadows of agriculture and pastoralism. These places of sustenance are transformed briefly into scenes of conflict before they resume their previous function. Jean-Henri Fabre noted that "history celebrates the battlefields whereon we meet our death, but scorns to speak of the plowed fields whereby we thrive."[17] If the agricultural landscape is often viewed as an idealized landscape, a garden, in battle it becomes an antigarden, a place of death versus life.

The transformation of a meadow into a field of battle exemplifies how action transforms the meaning and association of place. Battles and war itself are cataclysmic but transitory events. After the battle the forces of nature and human activity reclaim the land. Usually, only memory or the conscious exploration of history marks the sites of battles and the killing that took place there; most are lost to history. Throughout history, the event of the battle has primarily been short-lived and intense, but there are exceptions. Around the world are places where fields undergo conversion to battlefields, which revert to fields, only to become once again terrains of battle.

Landscape has always played a military role. The landscape is not only a passive setting but also an active agent in a war. Perhaps no one is as acutely interested in reading landscapes as are soldiers in battle, where such information can mean the difference between life and death. Knowledge of landscape is essential for the formulation of strategy and to gain tactical advantage. Machiavelli advised the prince that "he should never lift his thoughts from the exercise of war; and in peace he should exercise it more than in war . . . learn the nature of sites, and recognize how mountains rise, how valleys open up, how plains lie, and understand the nature of rivers and marshes — and in this invest the greatest attention." Once learned, this wartime skill may be irrevocable; fifty years after his experience as a World War II infantryman in Europe, Paul Fussell confesses, "I still locate in the passing landscape good positions for machine guns, antitank guns, or minefields."[18] Landscape bears symbolic weight in wartime as the site of struggle and the territory of conquest or occupation; after the war, the land embodies memories and history.

The cataclysm of war remakes landscapes. Ambrose Bierce found Shiloh to be a "smoking jungle." Forest had been reduced to blasted stumps where "all the wretched debris of the battle still littered the spongy earth as far as one could see." Until the industrial age, war was fought in an agricultural and pastoral landscape, as the names of two Gettysburg battlefields — the Wheatfield and the Peach Orchard — remind us. Indeed, throughout the Civil War, "entire campaigns hinged on how many miles soldiers could walk in a day, how much forage they could gather for their horses, how much heat or ice both man and animal could endure."[19]

On Good Friday 1917 in a letter to his wife, artist Paul Nash described the trenches of World War I:

> Oh, these wonderful trenches at night, at dawn, at sundown! Shall I ever lose the picture they have made in my mind. Imagine a wide landscape flat and scantily wooded and what trees remain blasted and torn, naked and scarred and riddled. The ground for miles around furrowed into trenches, pitted with yawning holes in which water lies still and cold or heaped with mounds of earth, tangles of rusty wire, tin plates, stakes, sandbags and all the refuse of war . . . headless trees standing white and

withered, hopeless, without any leaves, done, dead. . . . In the midst of
this strange country, where such things happen, men are living in their
narrow ditches, hidden from view by every cunning device, waiting and
always on the watch. . . . As night falls the monstrous land takes on a
strange aspect. The sun sinks in a clear evening and smoke hangs in narrow bars of violet and dark. In the clear light the shapes of the trench
stand massy and cold, the mud gleams whitely, the sandbags have a hard,
rocky look, the works of men look a freak of nature, rather the landscape is so distorted from its gentle forms, nothing seems to bear the
imprint of God's hand, the whole might be a terrific creation of some
malign fiend working a crooked will on the innocent countryside.[20]

The horrific devastation of the Great War recurred in later conflicts. At Khe Sanh in Vietnam, "Two million pounds of bombs and
whole catalogues of other weapons have torn and plowed the sterile
earth, have shattered boulders, have splintered and chewed the
stumps of trees, have pockmarked the deck with craters big enough
to be graves for tanks." As a result of seven years of bombardment,
there are over 20 million bomb craters on over 300,000 acres in Vietnam, making the war one as much against the land as against armies.[21]

In the opposition of war and gardening, the garden stands for peace.
Peace is not just the absence of war, but a positive, assertive state. Not
just "peaceful," so too the garden is not just a retreat and a respite, but
an assertion of a proposed condition, a model to be emulated.

Like gardeners, soldiers are attuned to reading the subtleties in
landscape, monitoring changes, and seizing opportunities presented
by changing situations. Soldiers seek tactical advantage, and in their
careful reading of the landscape they note anomalies.

In times of genuine aggression, however, the garden doesn't protect: it is an illusory fortress, offering resistance and respite but not
victory. According to Samuel Hynes, "war is unfamiliar, unimaginable,
insane, appalling."[22] Gardens are the opposite. They are familiar, com-
prehensible, sane, and pleasing; the sensory richness and pleasures of
the garden contrast with the sensory repulsiveness of war. There are
three instinctive and strategic responses to being attacked: running
away, hiding, or counterattacking. There are instructive analogies
between military defense and defense mechanisms, though the garden's importance as defense is often more psychological than physical: it can only provide an "escape" in the form of a hiding place. In
war we can even envision an inversion of Leo Marx's "machine in the
garden" to "gardens in the machine." Here the garden becomes an

Community garden in a Manhattan public housing project, New York City.

image for an antiwar element springing up within the machine, offering an alternative to war: a cessation of hostility, a peaceful place, a field that is not one of battle.

But human combatants are not the only enemies to be confronted in war. Civil War records, letters, and diaries are sprinkled with terms such as "used up, worn out, rattled, dispirited, downhearted, sunstroke, anxious, nervous, demoralized, badly blown, darkness, gloom . . . blues, blue days, blue and homesick" to describe the mental condition of soldiers.[23] World War I introduced "combat exhaustion" and "shell shock" to the language; World War II, "combat fatigue"; after Vietnam, "post-traumatic stress disorder" (PTSD); and prisoners of war in World War I were said to suffer from "barbed-wire disease."

Studying the intersection of gardens and war yields great rewards of understanding about humanity and about nature. Life, home, work, hope, and beauty are five attributes that lie dormant in all gardens, awaiting the catalyst that propels them to germinate and allowing us to recognize them as defiant gardens. These gardens can be of any scale, their life spans vary from that of a window box to a valley, and they may be real or imagined.

LIFE. As living beings we display biophilia, which sociobiologist E. O. Wilson argues is an indisputable, innate affinity for the natural world and especially for its life forms, flora and fauna. The products of the garden sustain us as both food for our bodies and food for our psyches. Our senses guide our behavior, provide pleasure and satisfaction, and allow us to experience ourselves as being *of* nature and as being witnesses to garden as both noun and verb.

HOME. The definition of *home* is not limited to a house or simple habitation — though these are critical — but more broadly encompasses the places whence we come, running along a spectrum from dwelling to area to nation. We have deep attachments to the places we call home, and indeed even the nomad has a sense of home. Gardens may be part of our home or reminders of homes we have inhabited. Gardens can be mnemonic devices, conjuring reminders of the place and all the associations we make with it and people, experiences, and history. Away from our desired or permanent home, a garden can be a way of transforming a place into a home, of creating an attachment to a new place and also establishing a connection to our former place.

WORK. As we have seen, *garden* is a verb as well as a noun. As both physical and mental labor, garden work can provide the particular sense of identity and satisfaction that comes from manual labor. The work represents the symbiotic relationship between human beings and the rest of the natural world.

HOPE. Gardens take time to conceive, make, develop — and grow. Hope is embodied in the temporal dimension and in the seeming miracle of the transformation from seed to plant to fruit, food, flower, and fragrance. The mere act of making a garden implies a future in which plants will reach fruition and results will be enjoyed. This is true even when we set out plants that may take generations to mature, becoming a real legacy. Gardening is inherently hopeful as a series of affirmative, assertive acts — the seeds will germinate, the plants will enjoy adequate rain and sunshine, nothing will squash or eat them . . . and we will survive to see all that.

BEAUTY. Gardens are beautiful. Our response to the natural world that we find or assemble is rooted in our instinctual response to certain conditions. Overlaid with that impulse, like an onion, are layers of experiences, memories, associations we might make, history, and culture that bind us together in groups and societies, and layers that reflect our idiosyncrasies as individuals. Beauty is in the eye of the beholder, though the beholder may have little awareness of what has created the "eye." Our awareness of our own attraction to and delight in form, pattern, proportions, intricacy, boldness, craft, and technique can be heightened by contrast and by changes in context. Thus in war, the antithesis of the beautiful — the common garden — may become the highest art. As individual soldiers can engage in heroic acts, so can there be heroic gardens.

There are many kinds of defiant gardens, but my focus is on a selection of those related to war in the first half of the twentieth century:

— gardens of World War I, built behind the lines of the Western front
— gardens built in the Warsaw and other ghettos under the Nazis during World War II
— gardens created in Europe and Asia by prisoners of war and civilian internees in both world wars
— gardens constructed by Japanese American internees in U.S. internment camps during World War II

In the final chapter, I look at gardens in more recent years, including those built in the desert by U.S. soldiers in the 1990–91 Gulf War, those created in the wake of September 11, 2001, and those of the war in Iraq.

Because gardens are inseparable from their context, I examine the setting and historical circumstances for each of these gardens. To understand these defiant gardens requires an introduction to trench warfare in World War I; ghettos and their role in the Holocaust; the experiences of prisoners of war and internees; and the causes and creation of relocation camps in the United States. I will also explore the significance of the gardens for those who created and experienced them when such gardens were living out their defiant purpose. What these individuals have said provides primary evidence for my conclusions.

In trenches, ghettos, and camps, defiant gardens attempted to create normalcy in the midst of madness and order out of chaos. During wartime, the garden represented, as Eisen put it, an "enterprise of survival, a defense of sanity and a demonstration of psychological defiance."[24]

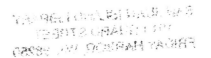

TWO ❧ Trench Gardens

The Western Front in World War I

They march from safety, and the bird-sung joy
Of grass-green thickets, to the land where all
Is ruin, and nothing blossoms but the sky
That hastens over them where they endure
Sad, smoking, flat horizons, reeking woods,
And foundering trench-lines volleying doom for doom.

SIEGFRIED SASSOON, "Prelude: The Troops"

AS WEAPON POWER INCREASED, the terrain of warfare expanded.
World War I took place on a battlefield of continental scale, the
front. Writers describing the war invariably refer to the cycle of fields
transformed to battlefields and returned again to fields, noting the
contrast between the two states of the landscape. In his war memoir,
Undertones of War, poet and author Edmund Blunden describes passing a farm and its cherry orchard. He speaks of "acres of self-sown
wheat [that] glistened and sighed as we wound our way between,
where rough scattered pits recorded a hurried firing line of long ago.
Life, life abundant sang here and smiled." He goes on, "and yet, when
war seemed for the time being left behind, belts of barbed wire again
appeared, crossing the beetfields, and wicker-lined trenches curved
along waterways and embankments."[1]

Many years ago I discovered a remarkable pair of stereoscopic
photographs titled "Shelters with Gardens Behind. In the French
Trenches." Along a hedgerow, soldiers are standing beside their
dugout shelters. A dirt pathway mimicking a walkway in a small village of houses and gardens connects the earthen hovels. Troglodyte
soldiers have emerged from these to create and work in gardens.
Visible are planting beds, vegetables, and small rails made of branches
carefully marking the boundaries and ornamenting the edges between
each soldier's plot. The caption on the reverse of the stereograph
reads: "This view tells but little of war's desolation. . . . There is a
human touch in the act of the soldiers in brightening up the spot with

These shelters in the French trenches were flanked by gardens.

growing flowers and plants. . . . It is no exaggeration to say that the soldier in the trenches digs and crawls, marches and retreats, sweats and freezes, often fights and perhaps may die. It is interesting to know that during all he is so manifestly human that flower gardens engage his spare time thought." This garden was created amid trench warfare, a world of labyrinthine horror, wet, cold, smelly, squalid, one that became a charnel house and often a tomb.

How and why would one create a garden in these places and at this time? These war gardens were surely rare, and in the front-line trenches, barely possible. Gardens behind the front lines, in reserve and supply trenches, were more common but still scarce. The act of creating any garden in these circumstances seems almost miraculous.

Soldiers did what they had to do to cope with the war. Their first goal was to survive, but they accomplished much more. These gardens offered much in addition to sustenance. They offered soldiers a way to control something in the midst of chaos. They represented home and hope, affording a pastoral escape from the war — one essential for mental health. The gardens were mechanisms of survival, but they were also a form of trench art: they were both good for food and good to look at.

Gardens are inseparable from their context. To understand the gardens of the Great War, it is necessary to come to grips with a landscape that is nearly incomprehensible. All behavior, actions, and creations, including any manipulation of the earth, for warfare or for gardening, occurred in relationship to the front and to no-man's-land, that shifting snake of land between the two seething sides of the conflict. No-man's-land was the fault line between the two massive forces, where "nature" itself was dead or destroyed. A place of horror, it had the look and feel of hell.

On August 4, 1914, the German armies marched through neutral Belgium and invaded France. In less than a month they came within twenty-two miles of Paris. The defending Belgian, French, and British armies resisted the German advance, and each side attempted to out-flank the other in what became a race to the sea. Neither side was successful, and by late September the armies stood opposite each other along what became known as the Western Front. It was 475 miles long and extended from the North Sea to the Swiss frontier. An immense human creation, the Western Front was a transformation of terrain at a continental scale. The armies literally dug in along the entire distance. Traditional military techniques to hamper the advance of enemy troops employed the construction of defensive ditches, water barriers, walls, palisades, stakes. With the development of firearms came the defense of digging into the landscape and immersing within it. The shovel became standard equipment. Trenches had been part of the American Civil War, but in World War I they reached their apogee. In time, evolving military technology, especially the development of tanks and air power, would supersede their effectiveness, but trenches epitomized the landscape of World War I. They created the conditions for the battlefield. "The war was mainly a matter of holes and ditches," wrote poet Siegfried Sassoon.[2]

The Western Front encompassed between 15,000 and 25,000 miles of trenches and in 1914–18 became the most infamous killing ground in the history of war. Millions of soldiers lived and died in a hellish city. In gruesome fashion many actually were incorporated into the trenches, as corpses were entombed into the walls. A British officer described the front to Churchill: "Imagine a broad belt . . . which is positively littered with the bodies of men and scarified with their rude graves; in which farms, villages and cottages are shapeless heaps of blackened masonry; in which fields, roads and trees are pitted and torn and twisted by shells and disfigured by dead horses, cattle, sheep and goats, scattered in every attitude of repulsive distortion and dis-memberment."[3]

The Western Front was not a single line but a series of intercon-nected bands. The location and construction of the trenches were de-termined in large part by the known distance artillery shells could fire (the most common cause of battle casualties was artillery fire) and by how fortified and dug-in the soldiers were in their trenches. The Brit-ish, French, and German trenches varied in design and strategic use.

The British system employed three broadly parallel lines: front-line, support, and reserve trenches about a thousand yards behind. These were linked by a series of communication trenches. Narrower "sap trenches" were those that extended into no-man's-land. Trench location corresponded to the firing range and type of guns, from the small arms to artillery to heavy guns. Closest to no-man's-land was the first zone of fighting, followed by a zone of ancillary services that included casualty clearing stations, followed by areas behind the lines largely populated by old men, women, and children, for all able-bodied men were at the front.

The Royal Engineers recommended that trenches be dug as zigzags six to eight feet deep and four to five feet wide; the zigzags reduced the line of direct fire in the event the trench was overrun by the enemy. However, in the north, especially in Flanders, an area with a high water table and high rainfall, such deep trenches were built up as often as they were dug in. Mud was omnipresent. Major Bernard Lewis Strauss wrote home that "mud is the keynote of our life: mud, mud, mud inches deep: on one's feet, clothes, and in one's food; mud everywhere."[4] A parapet was built up above the front edge, and beneath it was a firing step to allow soldiers a place from which they could see over and fire. The parados was the back of the trench. In most conditions the walls had to be reinforced with sandbags, timber,

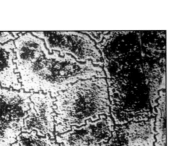

Aerial view of the trenches along the Western Front. Note no-man's-land separating the opposing forces.

or bundles of twigs called hurdles. Paths of wooden duckboards were laid. Trenches were dug, but as artillery and bombs formed new craters, additional trenches were constructed to incorporate them into the system.

Soldiers lived in cubbyholes dug into the walls of trenches, larger constructed shelters, or deep dugouts. German trenches were more elaborate than those of either the British or the French. The German strategy was literally "defense in depth," and in places the Germans had ten lines of trenches dug in. In addition, their superior trench construction burrowed deeper into the earth, affording greater protection from bombardment. Even British officer Hector Macquarrie in his wartime book *How to Live at the Front: Tips for American Soldiers* noted: "It seems that the British are not good at building trenches. You will be astonished at the beauty of construction displayed by the enemy in his."[5]

A November 1914 diary entry of British soldier Henry Willamson describes the reality of trench construction: "All trenches hereabouts were merely cast-up ridges of earth held in place by stakes, wire, hurdles, and wooden framework. Underneath their floors of boards and slats, water welled and stagnated, and an indescribable nocturnal smell,

"Battlefield of the Somme." A forest has been obliterated by warfare.

mortal, greenweedy, ratty, accompanies the tramp of our boots to and fro." He then offers his comments on digging a trench, which he ironically characterizes as "'landscape gardening' in the wood." He continues: "There is a path in the wood about half a mile behind the front which we are making into a defensive line by digging a shallow trench and dumping bundles of brushwood into it in the vain hope that they will not sink into the mud. I am sure they will. The idea is to give some foothold on the floor. We are also making corduroy paths up which rations and supplies can go." Two years later, after becoming a pilot, Willamson's viewpoint of trenches was transformed: "All you can see is a wilderness of pock-marked earth seamed with a maze of chalk lines which are the trench systems." But the view from below was different. The Germans called it a *Froschperspektive* — a frog's view.[6]

A form of trench life emerged that was experienced by millions of men. Newcomers were introduced to its protocols, which Blunden referred to as "trench education." British soldiers typically rotated two days in front-line trenches, two in support trenches, two in reserve trenches, and four to six "on billets" behind the lines. Then the sequence would begin again in some variation. On the front line, each day soldiers would stand to at daybreak, ready to mount the firing step if there was an attack; after a while the stand-down order would be issued if there were no hostilities. Every evening soldiers entered no-man's-land to man lookout stations or to retrieve the dead and repair barbed wire. In many sectors miners were busy below-ground, digging under no-man's-land to insert explosives beneath the enemy's trenches.

It was a horrible existence at the extremes of human experience and endurance. "In the trenches men lived a life of primitive instincts — fear, hunger, thirst — and with the physical extremes, deafening noises, sudden flashes, extreme cold, agonizing pain. The most innocent of natural occurrences could be the cause of intense hardship."[7] There were all manner of vermin everywhere — climbing on soldiers while they slept, and on corpses.

Despite its horror, the Western Front remained oddly accessible to the outside world, and at its northernmost point was only a seven-hour trip to London, and elsewhere only a few dozen miles from Paris — soldiers along the front had regular mail service and returned home on leave. But not all sections of the front were equal, and Tony Ashworth makes the key distinction between active and passive sectors of the front. In certain areas, and at certain times, a tacit live-and-let-live system emerged between the opposing armies.

The Western Front encompassed two great braided rivers of men and materiel. Between the armies' front-line trenches lay no-man's-land, a territory controlled not by either side but by chaos. In some places no-man's-land was as narrow as 10 yards and in others it was as deep as 500, but typically it was only 150 yards wide. Hector Macquarrie said the place was "sometimes not much bigger than a fair-sized garden." There was "a strange intimacy to the war," where soldiers could hear the coughing of their counterparts. To prevent the passage of soldiers, belts of barbed wire were strung through no-man's-land. It was a cruel, lethal, inhuman landscape. Subject to the incessant pounding of artillery, the land of Flanders became a foul, seething swamp, especially for the British, for the Germans held the high ground. Thousands of soldiers drowned in the mud. After poison gas was used, it accumulated in shell craters and the air itself became toxic. The ground was littered with the deadly junk of battle and bodies. Soldier Tom MacDonald, a member of a machine gun team who had enlisted at the age of seventeen, describes the digging of communication trenches at Guillemont: "The trees criss-cross and shattered, splintered limbs, and [the] stench was awful and we could hardly put a pick in the ground or shovel but we would strike a buried body or clothing."[8]

The world between the trenches was savagely denatured by war, and in that vacuum of nature was a pockmarked chasm separating the opposing forces. No-man's-land was a ruptured earth, a defoliated landscape of exploded trees, bomb craters filling into fetid pools, the bodies of beasts, and the rat-gnawed corpses of men. The sights, sounds, and taste of death formed its most conspicuous features. Liam O'Flaherty called no-man's-land "an unroofed tomb." The carnage was to both man and nature. As Alan Sillitoe has written, "The great trench battles of the Western Front were indeed an Armageddon for the soul of Man, a pilgrim's progress into the demolition of the psyche — and all too often of the body as well."[9] It was hell on earth, and, as Paul Fussell illustrates in *The Great War and Modern Memory,* the twentieth century's formative image of the apocalypse.

No-man's-land also occupied a symbolic position. The Western Front characterized the war, being in the trenches became synonymous with soldiering, and no-man's-land epitomized the horror and futility of the war; it came to symbolize World War I. As the territory between the opposing armies that was not occupied or controlled by either, it was literally "no-man's-land," but the appellation held another meaning: "the very negativeness of the concept hints at the utter desolation, at the uselessness of this pulverized, barren vacuum," John Ellis wrote.[10] Like a vacuum, it sucked things into it, draining the life from them and from all who entered. It was a land devoid of living men, primordial in chaos. It was not meant to be part of the human experience — it was truly no man's. Still, this most inhuman place was a human creation.

The unprecedented scale of warfare in World War I left writers and witnesses groping for metaphor and language to describe the resulting landscape. Some built on religious and mythological language, such as visions of hell, or the as-yet-unvisited face of the moon. Others stretched conventions, such as the earth as a body, while new metaphors burst into the language.

A struggle to communicate the unimaginable and unprecedented horror ensued. One soldier described the Ypres salient as "just a complete abomination of destruction." Of the Somme battlefields, Philip Gosse wrote that "nothing could live in that horrible poison-drenched shell-ploughed waste but man, and his chances of survival were but slender. Even the obsequious trench rat had disappeared." Blunden found the land "trampled, pulverized, blood-stained, its edges slurred into the level of the general wilderness." The land itself was distorted beyond recognition of its former state. Henri Barbusse described the area around Passchendaele as a "plain of lost landmarks."[11]

The land itself had become unrecognizable and incomprehensible. As Edmund Blunden approached Cuinchy, a place he called a slaughter-yard, the flowers accentuated the mental contrast he made between their natural habitat and the trenches, which had an incongruous bouquet: "Over Coldstream lane, the chief communication trench, deep red poppies, blue and white cornflowers and darnel thronged the way to destruction; the yellow cabbage-flowers thickened here and there in sickening brilliance. Giant thistles made a thicket beyond. Then the ground became torn and vile, the poisonous breath of fresh explosions sulked about, and the mud which choked the narrow passages stank as one pulled throughout, and through the twisted, disused wires running mysteriously onward."[12]

Beginning in 1986, journalist Stephen O'Shea walked the entire Western Front over a number of journeys. He found a land still "warped by a war." Climbing Verdun Hill 304, he observed: "the landscape becomes truly cataclysmic, as unearthly as anything I have seen as far as the eye can see, a heaving sea of mortified land. Not one square yard of the forest floor is level — the place is madness come to ground. . . . This is the still bleeding scar of the Great War." At Verdun he was keenly aware of humanity's destructive capabilities: "it took ten months to tear every trace of topsoil from a rolling, fertile farmland and wipe away all mark of man[,] the builder and cultivator."[13] This landscape was still lifeless nearly sixty years after the end of World War I.

Edmund Blunden wrote about his own experience in the war: "we were marooned on a frozen desert. There is not a sign of life on the

Road to Guillemont, September 11, 1916. After the battle, the landscape was a vision of hell.

horizon, and a thousand signs of death. Not a blade of grass, not an insect; once or twice a day, the shadow of a big hawk, scenting carrion." Near Aveluy with a view toward Thiepval, where the great arch — the British memorial to the Somme — now stands, Blunden described the scene: "the walk to the front line lay over the most bewildering battle-field, so gouged and hummocked, so denatured and dun, so crowded with brown shrapnel-cases and German long-handled grenades, shell-holes, rifles, water-bottles; a billowing desert."[14]

The front became an alien environment where war correspondent Phillip Gibbs said men "lived in a world which is as different from this known world of ours as though they belonged to another race of men inhabiting another planet." Yet this unnatural world was, like Frankenstein, a human creation. "On wet days the trees a mile away were like ash-grey smoke rising from the naked ridges, and it felt very much as if we were at the end of the world. And so we were: for that enemy world . . . had no relation to the landscape of life," wrote Sassoon.[15]

A new and diabolical form of forestry blasted and splintered trees. Henri Barbusse referred to the "charred skeletons of trees." Damage to trees — whose forms and life spans broadly parallel the human — and to woodland mirrored the fate of soldiers and were mute evidence of the ferocity of the fighting. Harold Macmillan thought "the most extraordinary thing about the modern battlefield is the desolation and emptiness of it all. Nothing is to be seen of war or soldiers — only the split and shattered trees."[16] Today the ruins of forests and their names — Chateau Wood, Sanctuary Wood, Shrewsbury Forest — ironically recall forests as places of repose and refuge while evoking memories of the tragedies suffered there.

At the Somme immediately after the war, John Oxenham observed that a "striking and peculiarly pathetic feature of the landscape, here and elsewhere, were those stricken forests, — great stretches of what had once been the gracious greenery of woodlands, now gaunt, naked trunks without so much as one patch of clothing bark on them; bleached and bare, hideous bony skeletons of trees, lifting their pitiful appeal to heaven; here the splintered fragment of a broken arm forking out, there the trunk half-severed . . . every hole pitted with shell and shrapnel." In a letter, Lieutenant Christian Creswell Carver described the "hideous bit of country over which the worst fighting has passed. Perhaps you imagine it as a place of broken trees and ruined houses — as a fact there is nothing — *no*thing. We live in a desolate belt . . . some five miles in depth, where no trees remain to make a show of green in the coming Spring, and the chateaux and churches are pounded to mounds of red and white dust."[17]

Poet Wilfred Owen, who would be killed the week before the Armistice, wrote in a letter that "No Man's Land under snow is like the face of the moon chaotic, crater-ridden, uninhabitable, awful, the abode of madness." It was a common metaphor among soldiers; describing the landscape as a moonscape recognized similarities between the two spheres but emphasized the lifelessness and unearthliness of the battleground. Commenting on the haunting photographs in the *Michelin Illustrated Guides to the Battlefields,* published immediately after the war in 1920 and intended for battlefield tourists and pilgrims, Winston Groom notes that in the photographs "few objects stood higher than a chimney and there were virtually no trees where whole towns had once flourished . . . the vistas . . . looked if nothing else like the landscape of the moon, so pockmarked by tens of millions of artillery-shell craters that if any one section were taken out of perspective it would appear that someone had just plowed a field or spaded up the earth for miles around for an enormous garden plot."[18] The imagery that equates war with both the lifeless moon and the peaceful act of gardening is chilling.

John Masefield described the area around Serre as "skinned, gouged, flayed and slaughtered, and the villages smashed to powder, so that no man could ever say there had been a village there within the memory of man." In his poem "The Show" (wartime slang for *battle*), Wilfred Owen wrote:

> My soul looked down from a vague height, with Death,
> As unremembering how I rose or why,
> And saw a sad land, weak with sweats of dearth,
> Grey, cratered like the moon with hollow woe,
> And pitted with great pocks and scabs of plagues.[19]

In anthropomorphizing the landscape as a body, writers now described the face of the land as deformed and disfigured and the body of the land as racked by disease and plague, ridden by the pestilence of war. Unlike the soldiers who died, the landscape survived, but it too was a casualty of the war. It was scarred, its injuries not always visible but still felt, like a shrapnel-filled body. Owen saw no-man's-land as "pockmarked like a body of foulest disease[;] . . . its odour . . . the breath of cancer." Others described the land as tortured, flayed, and dismembered. The violence against the land was so unnatural as to be deemed criminal: "the greensward, suited by nature for the raising of sheep, was all holes. . . . A whole sweet countryside amuck with murder," wrote Blunden.[20]

Having never before seen such horrors, observers resorted to a conventional image — hell. Among those finding equivalent in its most renowned literary exposition was MacDonald: "Ypres was a proper Dante's inferno. Ground churned to pulp and mire." The Germans, including law student Friedrich Oehme in a letter to home, also saw the comparison to the Italian poem: "Six weeks ago Martinpuich was [a] pretty place, inhabited and secure. Now it is a region of horror and despair. *Lasciate ogne speranza* — abandon all hope — are the words over the portals of hell in Dante's *Divine Comedy*. I kept thinking of them as we tore through the village." Surrounded by a hellish landscape, as if he himself were in hell, Oxenham found the battlefield one of "vast and cruel desolations, pitted with shell-craters full of slimy green water, from which Death and the Devil looked sullenly up at us as we passed; — vast cruel desolations which, until the curse fell on them, were rich and smiling countrysides." It was, according to Phillip Gibbs, the "devil's hunting ground."[21]

This hell was also the land of the dead, a vast graveyard. On July 16, 1915, at the Somme near Contalmaison, Henry Willamson observed that "the mile or so of grassland between was heaped with English and German dead." The Germans had a word for this: *Totenlandschaft*, "a landscape of the dead." John Masefield described the view at Thiepval on April 28, 1917: "Corpses, rats, old tins, old weapons, rifles, bombs, legs, boots, skulls, cartridges, bits of woods & tin & iron & stones, parts of rotting bodies & festering heads lie scattered about. A more filthy evil hole you cannot imagine." This was no neat cemetery, and in his poem "The Night Patrol," Arthur Graeme West wrote:

> . . . and everywhere the dead.
> Only the dead were always present — present
> As a vile sickly smell of rottenness;
> The rustling stubble and the early grass,
> The slimy pools — the dead men stank throughall.[22]

Poet Vernon Scannell, born in 1922, after the war's end, described it as the "deathscape where the iron brambles writhe."[23]

Soldiers saw, heard, smelled, touched, and even tasted daily, hourly, what in a sane world should only ever be fleeting assault on the senses by the horrific. Medical Officer Philip Gosse was haunted by the "rancid smell which pervaded all the dug-outs we occupied and worked in." Groom notes that the "ever-present odor of rotting humans, horses, mules, rats, and food mixed with the stench of excrement, lingering poison gases, the repulsive aroma of quicklime used to decompose the dead, and the acrid stink of high-explosive artillery shells. It was said that you could smell the battlefield miles before you ever reached it."[24] This was the stench of putrefaction — the decomposition of bodies human and otherwise.

Participants had particular difficulty conveying the wearing effect of noise produced by incessant bombardment from artillery: "You can't communicate noise. Noise never stopped for a moment — ever," noted Robert Graves. Friedrich Oehme wrote of the Somme that the "whole sky is lit up with flashes and flares. The air is full of the thunder of guns, the crash of bursting shells, the howling and whistling of projectile flying in both directions." Surely the most horrifying sound was the cries and moaning of the wounded reaching from no-man's-land. In such an environment, the sounds and songs of birds would have seemed miraculous. In February 1916, after fifteen months in the trenches, Roland Montfort recorded in his diary the night and morning songs of thrushes, the steadfast company of robins throughout the winter, and the owls and partridges. "Who would have imagined birds getting used to high explosives? . . . Instead of shrieking shells there floated across the wilderness of No-Man's Land that breath of old English spring time," he marveled. Medical officer Philip Gosse said he could have titled his memoirs "'A Solace of Birds,' for without the birds I dare not think how I should have got through the war at all."[25] The willingness of the birds to share the trenches with the soldiers helped stave off the men's despair at the horrors of the war.

Soldiers inevitably began to associate the mundane with the horrible, however; as anthropologist Nicholas Saunders notes, the war "broke the mold of everyday experiences. . . . New meanings were attached to the sights, sounds, smells, tastes and vibrations of war on such a massive scale." Sergeant Ernest Boughton Nottingham was able to find momentary solace in the "sound of a train . . . [and] the scent and sight of a flower." But for him, the "ecstasy of a lark" invariably conjured for him the horrors and fears of standing-to in the trenches.[26]

The contrast resulting from the juxtaposition of steady nature and the ugliness of man-produced war was sometimes staggering. On the Messines Ridge, site of the Third Battle of Ypres in 1917, Winston Groom observed: "Looking back from whence they had come, the men saw only the barren and ruined moonscape of no-man's land and the crumbling spires of Ypres and its surrounding villages. But looking eastward, down over the German rear lines, they saw a vista of pastoral scenery: tall green trees, meadows and farmlands, and here and there villages untouched by the scourge of war."[27] This battlefield view polarized what is always present in the garden, the contrast between control and chaos, but here not a "natural" chaos or "wild" with its appeals and positive associations we make to it, but of human waste and desolation.

Men lived hidden in the confined labyrinth of the trenches, with the accompanying disorientation. In an inversion of the commonplace, being out in the open was dangerous, while living belowground was secure. Yet the burrowed ground too often became a grave: sticking your head up exposed it to snipers. Daytime views of the horizon were safe only through periscopes. The safest direct view was overhead, to the sky.[28]

War, said Fussell, is the ultimate antipastoral, a perversion of the pastoral impulse and desire. War landscapes are equally perverse: they are distorted, tortured landscapes, where nature has been hideously mangled and disfigured. The actual shape of nature — or humans' expectation of her trusted, natural forms — is transformed as trees and the earth itself are rent almost beyond recognition. The war put all traditional associations of nature — innocence, tranquillity, and standing for peace and harmony, hope and beauty — to the ultimate test. For the British especially, it embodied home.

Romantic, innocent, peaceful, idyllic nature was dead in the war zone. Of course the cycles of change, including death, are part of nature. But the death soldiers witnessed hardly resembled natural death. Nature was now disturbed and disturbing. Owen's poem "A Terre" notes the change in sensibility:

> Certainly flowers have the easiest time on earth.
> "I shall be one with nature, herb and stone,"
> Shelley would tell me. Shelley would be stunned:
> The dullest time hugs that fancy now.
> "'Pushing up daisies' is their creed, you know."[29]

Yet nature still offered solace and surprises. Through a periscope Blunden observed "a rose-bush in flower" in no-man's-land. Leading trench maintenance parties in Hamel Village, he describes "old curiosities . . . I heard an evening robin in a hawthorn, and in trampled gardens among the refuse of war there was the fairy, affectionate immortality of the yellow rose and blue-grey crocus."[30]

Given their surroundings, it is hardly surprising that witnesses anthropomorphized nature, sometimes to the extreme. This is the pathetic fallacy: we imagine that nature too has emotions and that she celebrates or grieves along with us. A German soldier's trench journal of 1916 relates: "The wood which surrounds the battle lines shares its fate with that of the soldiers waiting to go over the top, and when clouds cover the sun, the pines, like the soldiers beneath them, shed tears of unending pain. The wood will be murdered just as the soldier is certain to be killed in leading the attack." He writes that the "assassinated wood . . . is my comrade, my protection, my shield against the bullets of the enemy."[31]

Despite the urgency of their immediate environment, some managed an aesthetic appreciation for and response to the battlefield. Looking across the Somme on Christmas Day 1916, Henry Willamson wrote: "Truly the painter of this war must be a landscape painter. As

The Menin Road 1919. Paul Nash's paintings became icons of the war's devastation.

far as you could see were rolling hills and valleys, brown earth pitted with upturned chalk, and battered filled-in trenches in places just discernable." As if he were watching something disturb a canvas, Blunden commented that "the evidence of a war began to gnarl the scenery."[32]

The artist Paul Nash wrote home to his wife of the "ghastly face of no-man's land. . . . the weird beauty." Samuel Hynes has traced how artists' representations of World War I helped destroy the pictorial convention and associations of landscape taste and preference. These were not landscapes, he says, but antilandscapes. Nash became an official war artist, and his paintings became the best exposition of the conflict's landscape, which Hynes called "trench-scapes." Despite his claim that "no pen or drawing can convey this country," near Hill 60 Blunden observed "the position of the proposed trench; we walked up to, through trees like black tusks, and brown clods of hillocks, blue shadows, weak sunlight, a naked poverty. Nash has drawn this bad dream with exactitude."[33]

Nash also depicted a grotesque palette: "Sunset and sunrise are blasphemous, they are mockeries to man, only the black rain out of the bruised and swollen clouds all through the bitter black of night is fit atmosphere in such land. The rain drives on, the stinking mud becomes more evilly yellow, the shell holes fill up with green-white water, the roads and racks are covered in inches of slime, the black dying trees ooze and sweat and the shells never cease."[34] The mud of the war covered everyone, and khaki-clad soldiers merged with the landscape.

Not only was the actual landscape being destroyed; the pictorial conventions for portraying landscapes were overturned as well. It is in this context that perhaps a garden, or even a flower, could restore the solace of that earlier, now dying aesthetic.

The most conventional and prosaic of landscapes, a garden, ironically became a rare and shocking sight for soldiers. Still, in the midst of these horrors, gardens were created. It is hard to understand that they were there at all. They were built and tended in all of the zones of the front. Their numbers increased with distance from no-man's-land and the front line, as the landscape of war gradually faded into the countryside. Their significance to their builders and to those who came upon them was in proportion to their scarcity and to the difficulties in creating them.

Ephemeral creations, gardens must be tended. Made from nature's materials, they are subject to cycles of growth and decay. Even those that survived the cataclysm of the war would have soon returned to a more natural, uncultivated state. Physical evidence of gardens has long been eradicated, but a few drawings and photographs survive, as do accounts in diaries, letters, and memoirs.

Touring medical facilities at the front in the spring of 1916, Carita Spencer described the trenches at La Panne (near Ypres):

> How common-place trench life has become after these two long years of habit! Nowadays men do not go to the office and the shop. They go up to the trenches for daily duties. These trenches we were in were main-line, where the enemy was not supposed to penetrate unless rude enough actually to break through. So the soldiers portioned off the rough earth beside the board walk that ran parallel to the rampart, and first they had a little vegetable garden, and next to it for beauty's sake a flower garden, and next to that a little graveyard, and then the succession repeated. Five hundred yards beyond the main line, across the inundated fields streaked with barbed wire sticking up out of the

In this December 1914 photograph, a soldier of the London Rifle Brigade poses proudly in front of the sandbags of the built-up breastwork. At his feet is his garden (and many stoneware rum jugs) at Ploegsteert Wood in the Ypres Salient, a place soon to be the scene of horrific fighting.

water, was the front line trench, a rougher rampart, mostly of earth, and when it rained, oh mud![35]

Gardens were on both sides of the line. Lothar Dietz, a philosophy student from Leipzig killed near Ypres in 1915, wrote from his dugout in the trenches on Hill 59. The remarkable garden he and his fellow soldiers created displayed imaginative use of found and scavenged materials.

As one can't possibly feel happy in a place where all nature has been devastated, we have done our best to improve things. First we built a new causeway of logs, without railing to it, along the bottom of the valley. Then from a pinewood close by, which had also been destroyed by shells, we dragged all the best tree tops and stuck them upright in the ground; certainly they have no roots, but we don't expect to be here more than month and they are sure to stay green that long. Out of the gardens of the ruined chateaux of Hollebecke and Camp we fetched

The original caption read:
"The Trench Garden."

The original caption read:
"Gardening in Regent Street
at the Front: Beauty and War."

rhododendrons, box, snowdrops and primroses and made quite nice
flower beds."

In the midst of the war, Dietz and his company also engaged in landscape restoration: "We have cleaned out the little brook which flows
through the valley, and some clever comrades have built little dams
and constructed pretty little water mills, so called 'parole-clocks,'
which by their revolutions we are to count how many minutes more
the war is going to last. We have planted whole bushes of willow and
hazel with pretty catkins on them and little firs *with* their roots, so
that a melancholy desert is transformed into an idyllic grove. Every
dug-out has its board carved with a name suited to the situation: 'Villa
Woodland-Peace,' 'Heart of the Rhine,' 'Eagles' nest,' etc."[36]

British soldiers also gave familiar names to their dugouts and
trenches. The *Illustrated London News*, which published weekly detailed accounts of the front, carried a full-page illustration in May 1915

Landscape gardening close to the German front lines in France included this woodwork structure in a trench.

of a "villa" garden on "Regent Street." It showed soldiers tending their beds of flowers and was titled "Beauty and War." The garden and shelter are set within the blasted and bare trees of the battlefield. A month later the *News* published a more romanticized drawing, from which the war seemed banished entirely. One soldier is planting tulips at the entry to a shelter. A bust sits by the bed awaiting its placement in the garden. Two other soldiers are watching a third play with a dog, while the entire scene takes place beneath the boughs of a tree in full spring flower. Later that year the *News* carried photographs of the more elaborate comforts of German trenches. From German newspapers, these surely were intended for home-front consumption, yet remarkable nonetheless. One image, captioned "Landscape gardening in the German Lines," showed decorative rustic woodwork at what appears to be the entry to an underground shelter. Another is of a walkway within a half-mile of the front line, which is a virtual village of rustic structures, complete with dooryard plantings.[37]

Letters from the front revealed the lengths to which soldiers on both sides went to domesticate — humanize, perhaps — the trenches. In February 1915, Gotthold von Rohden wrote, "A few days ago I came

French soldier laying out a flower bed at an encampment behind the lines.

upon a bit of trench which was decorated in a highly original manner: the bays and breastwork were adorned with pots of flowers, the most noticeable being some Howitzer cartridge-cases full of snowdrops, the first flowers of the coming spring. . . . When I saw the first I picked and kept them. It wasn't easy to get them, I had to crawl out on my tummy, for the Frenchie keeps a good look-out!" From France, Richard Donaldson wrote later that spring of scavenging a shelled-out village for perennial flowers and shrubs to transplant: "The village is a terrible sight, . . . and you notice the contrast more now that the fruit trees are all in blossom, and the garden beds have all their spring flowers." When the countryside yielded little, soldiers pursued other avenues to satisfy their longing. German soldier Willy Holscher wrote from the trenches in Champagne in February 1916, "Would you be so kind as to send me some flower seeds? There is nothing very nice to look at about my billet, and, as I don't know how long I may be stuck here, I want to grow some flowers. Please send me sweet-peas, convolvulus, sunflower, flax, mignonette, etc. I want to cover the unsightly earth with verdure."[38]

Among the diverse functions gardens performed were as sites for personal and collective ritual. British soldiers occupying what had been a French trench came upon "an altar built into the side of the trench, where mass was said each morning by a soldier-priest. It was decorated with vases and candlesticks, and above the altar-table was a statue, crudely modeled upon the base of which I read the word *Notre dame des Tranchees* (Our Lady of the Trenches). A tablet fastened to the earth-wall recorded in French the desire of those who worshipped here: 'This altar, dedicated to Our Lady of the Trenches, was blessed by the chaplain of the French regiment. The 9th Squadron of the 6th company recommends its care and preservation to their successors. Please to not touch the fragile statue in trench clay.' "[39] Much in this description is noteworthy, but perhaps most touching is the assumption by the careful builders of this tender altar that, literally on the front lines of a war, the "successors" would preserve rather than destroy it.

Gardens are created, but they can also be discovered or uncovered, especially where the landscape itself possesses gardenlike properties or qualities. A battalion of the British Eighteenth division, for example, gathered potatoes from a patch in no-man's-land. Despite having not been cultivated, they had survived. Paul Nash wrote from what he called the "back garden of the trenches," where "it is amazingly beautiful — the mud is dried to a pinky colour and upon the parapet, and through sandbags even, the green grass pushes up and waves in the breeze, while clots of bright dandelions, clover, thistles and twenty other plants flourish luxuriantly, brilliant growths of bright green against the pink earth."[40]

Behind the lines, conditions for garden creation were more propitious. Support facilities for front-line soldiers took the form of temporary encampments, and as one moved farther behind the lines, existing communities were essentially requisitioned as support to the front.

At bases, entry plantings or markings at tents and buildings were commonplace. Such domestication also marked territory, could signify rank, or could be a form of identification for a unit. Where plants were scarce, soldiers often laid stones to create borders. Plantings were more dramatic at headquarters sites, hospitals, and convalescent sites. At camps it was commonplace to create insignia of regiments and units, using whatever materials were available. Company gardens were more official and often created in response to orders, but their impact was sometimes significant; a photograph of the headquarters for the 244 Motor Transport Company shows an elaborate sunken

Men of the 244 Motor Transport Company in the parterre at the company's headquarters.

parterre. Gardening was a popular passion for the British, and the styles of the gardens they created on the Western Front paralleled what was popular at home at the time. Soldiers endeavored to reproduce the modest and sometimes idiosyncratic quality of English cottage and kitchen gardens, using whatever was available; the more elaborate bedding patterns characteristic of the Edwardian garden were also popular. Some battalions even sponsored garden competitions.

The most extraordinary garden behind the lines was that belonging to Talbot House. It lay on a main street of Poperinghe, Belgium, and was rented by British army chaplains Phillip "Tubby" Clayton and Neville Talbot, who had conceived the idea of a soldier's club. Named for Neville's brother, Lieutenant Gilbert Talbot, who had been killed in action, it opened in December 1915 as an "EVERY MAN'S CLUB." A sign proclaiming "ABANDON RANK: ALL YE WHO ENTER HERE" was the watchword of the house and a hopeful twist on other wartime *Inferno* references. The club's deliberate setting aside of rank was rare at the time. It became known as Toc House, using the 1904 British army's phonetic code for the letter T.

To the rear of the modest house was a conservatory and a garden with roses, pergolas, a thatched summer house, dovecote, espaliered fruit trees, and a chicken run. A sign in the conservatory beckoned vis-

The garden in Talbot House (Toc House), Belgium, has recently undergone a restoration. The monkey-puzzle tree shown in this 1916 photograph is now full grown.

iting soldiers to "COME INTO THE GARDEN AND FORGET THE WAR." It was a laudable aspiration. The house and its garden became a respite from and perhaps even an antidote to shell shock. The title of Paul Chapman's history of the house, *A Haven in Hell,* suggests its significance to the men. As a "home away from home," the house fulfilled for World War I soldiers the role served by the USO (United Service Organizations) in World War II for U.S. servicemen. A band often played in the garden, where a badminton net awaited players. Tubby called the men who lounged in the garden Khaki Basking Lizards. Tubby recalled that one soldier told him that simply lying in the garden was a welcome reminder of home.

If the upstairs chapel in Toc House offered spiritual sustenance, the garden provided its own counsel. This first house in Poperinghe became the model for Talbot Houses all over England and for an organization of Toc Houses around the world. The original house is now a museum, and the garden continues to be tended.

The French version of the Toc House was the Foyers du Soldat (hearth of the soldier), the French welfare service for soldiers. The first house opened in January 1915 near Saint Die, but it was destroyed in a bombardment. By the time of the armistice in 1919, 1,534 houses had been established, with as many as 850 in operation at one point. Located as close to the line as possible, the typical *foyer* was two "Adrian" barracks linked by a corridor; one had a club room used for recreation and the other a canteen, while the outdoor spaces were for games. The finest *foyer* was at Toulon, which boasted a winter garden, canteen, souvenir shop, lounge, showers, gym, and classrooms. According to the Taft Report, hut decoration became a key feature of the program, and the psychological value of the activities at the *foyers* was immeasurable: "it was the business of Foyers to 'chasser le cafard' — to drive away the blues — to assist in curing the homesickness, hypochondria and boredom which are always present in war experience."[41]

Also behind the lines, tent towns were built under the aegis of the International Red Cross. Philip Gosse noted in his war memoir that behind Poperinghe, a town just six miles west of Ypres, the scene of some of the war's heaviest and most persistent fighting, "a large town had grown up of tents, marquees, big and little huts, canteens and post-offices, intersected by new well-made roads and light railways. The population consisted of English speaking camp followers; R.A.M.C. [Royal Army Medical Corps], A.S.C. [Army Service Corps], miners of dumps, road makers and hundreds of men employed in the scores of occupations which went to serve the army in the trenches." In this makeshift community, "gardening had become all the rage, and everywhere you looked you saw uniformed men, from colonels to corporals, watering and tending their allotments. Some went in for growing flowers — others, more utilitarian, for vegetables. One of the doctors at the C.C.S. [Casualty Clearing Station] had dug a pit, and was trying to grow mushrooms from some spawn he had planted in a hotbed of manure."[42]

Farther from the front, the war landscape merged with the surrounding agricultural countryside of villages and fields. As the war dragged on, the British created a Directorate of Agricultural Production under the War Office specifically to establish gardens in the war zone. French and British troops already had created vegetable gardens at many locations behind the lines. The British organized a large-scale initiative to create a series of central farms. The site of one such farm was Roye, an area that had been the scene of fighting but was now three to four miles behind the lines. Potatoes and oats

Troops stacking corn in 1918.

were already in production on about 7,500 of a planned 45,000 acres when a 1918 German offensive overran portions of the area. With fields and trenches merged together, harvesting at times was done during the lulls in artillery fire. Elsewhere, former battlefields were reclaimed and returned to fields even as fighting raged just a few miles away.

The cycle of field yielding to battlefield and being reclaimed as field was enacted on both sides of the line. In Flanders, Kurt Rohrbach, a theology student, reported coming upon German soldiers harvesting grain with scythes in a battlefield as if the scene were utterly natural in the landscape of war: "So much corn had sowed itself . . . that, thanks to the rich soil and fine weather, there was quite a good crop. One must own that it contained a good many weeds, not only in the shape of thorns and thistles, but also of barbed wire, bits of entanglement-frame, and telegraph wire, and now and then the scythe got caught in one or other of these or struck the case of a shell, with a sharp, rasping noise."[43]

While the war was still raging, soldiers were growing celery along the bottom of an old communications trench near Vimy Ridge.

Who made the law that men should die in meadows?
Who spake the word that blood should splash in lanes?
Who gave it forth that gardens should be boneyards?
Who spread the hill with flesh, and blood and brains?

SERGEANT LESLIE COULSON, killed in France in October 1916

Trench gardens reveal something about the character of soldiers in World War I, as well as about the nature of gardens. First, that the line of trenches at the front remained stable long enough to plant and even harvest a garden. Second, although their primary purpose was to yield fresh produce for the troops, gardens also assuaged the horrific conditions under which the men lived.

Nearly a century later, gardens in that landscape present natural questions for us. Why were they made, how were they made, what did they mean to their makers, what did they mean to others who witnessed them, and what do they mean to us now?

Most people even now, and surely most soldiers in World War I, understand what it takes to create a garden: the process stretches from a vision and design to selecting a site, marshalling materials, actually putting hand to plow or shovel, monitoring, and maintaining. Such actions are part of the creation and maintenance of every garden. The extreme setting of the war, however, exacerbated each task in every dimension.

Soldiers created gardens as a response to their basic needs and as an aid to their physical and mental survival. They also represented desire, a wish for the comforts of home, a concrete expression of hope, and the desire for life, peace, and a future. But the paradox of the garden is that, although we associate gardens with the natural world, gardens only exist as human creations; they are places where we have exerted control over the natural world. At the front — a profoundly chaotic and unnatural situation — human success in exerting control over anything is extraordinary in itself, and a powerful reminder of our humanity.

In the trenches, even as soldiers fought for survival, their actions and preoccupations often transcended that essentially human struggle for basic comforts, which were well beyond the reach of these men: palatable food, a reasonable toilet, protection from artillery and bullets, and a dry, vermin-free place to sleep. With none of the essentials available to them, they were free to reach for the impossible; why *not* wrest control of the war-torn environment to create a square foot of beauty? Their gardens were a manifestation of the soldiers' transcendence of their environment.

Gardens in the war offered a mechanism of survival and exemplified the struggle to create something normal in the most abnormal conditions. By their mere existence, defiant gardens were extraordinary. John Oxenham found that the "amazing self-adaptation to these new conditions of elemental life and death fill one with the supremest wonder."[44] It could be said that the war-zone garden softens a harsh situation, but it does so by forcing nature into an otherwise distinctly human creation — the war itself. As nature transformed, it humanizes the place, much as the ancient agricultural traces on the shores of Rhodes announce that people are here and that they are domesticating this place. In a sense, gardens help make such places a home or, in this situation, perhaps something more akin to a nest.

At and behind the lines, many soldiers fashioned what became known as trench art, objects made by soldiers and civilians during and after the war. The ephemeral garden could be thought of as trench art as well. Trench art was constructed from the materials and waste of the war environment. Its most characteristic object was the decorated artillery shell, often embossed with the juxtapositional ornamental pastoral patterns of leaves and tendrils. Anthropologist Nicholas Saunders finds them to be "a testament to the skills and fortitude of human beings under the almost unbearable pressures of modern war. Each item, however humble, is a potential symbol of the human spirit in extremis."[45] Created out of the waste of war, these arts — and gardens may be their most fleeting form — alleviated boredom, provided an outlet for soldiers' emotions, and allowed soldiers to express their creativity and skill. Such trench arts celebrate human adaptability and resilience and the persistence of the creative impulse. Gardens also functioned as a form of cultural expression, a way of declaring that this is an English, a French, or a German place.

The following sections briefly cover the themes that emerge when we examine meaning for the World War I soldiers who created or claimed, and cared for, gardens in war-torn areas. A garden could be a combination of the task of the moment and a hope for the future.

As we have already seen, soldiers were continually presented with the extreme contrasts in their war-torn world along the front. The incongruity of nature surviving alongside the devastation of the trenches offered soldiers a way to reclaim their humanity in that bit of normalcy and to separate themselves from the chaos of the war. Pleasure was more intense amid such pain, beauty more vivid when confronted with unbearable ugliness, and hope desperately wished for in such despair.

Ludwig Fink, a law student from Freiburg, wrote from a village in the range of heavy guns, but where snowdrops were in bloom and farmers were plowing. He described his experience as "a queer mixture of joy in life and proximity in death." On a Sunday, Georg Stiller wrote from the front, "elsewhere there is rest and peace; here the murdering goes on — everlasting shells, shrapnel, and rifle fire. Nature wears its most beautiful soaring dress, the sun laughs from the brown tent of heaven, but through the blossoming, green-growing Nature fly the shells, destroying trees and fresh bushes, tearing deep holes in the earth, and annihilating young, blossoming human lives." Having accepted the incongruity in their nightmare world, soldiers found that nature offered solace. "Greenness was our dream scenery," said Blunden.[46]

The garden was a palliative, not a cure for the soldier's plight. They were living in another land, a place of strange sensations, where Blunden is surprised by the incongruity of "a garden gate, opening into a battlefield," and where they could only imagine what one soldier described as the "garden over the wall" of the nightmare.[47]

Major R. S. Cockburn reflected on his experience and response to these dramatic juxtapositions, noting in his diary the simple pleasures he now felt in watching the sun rise in the woods or hearing the birds sing, and marveling that "nature [seems] to take on a new aspect for the first time. There [is] something almost miraculous in the way of contrast between the peace and loneliness of Haurincourt Wood and the filthy slaughter-ground not far away."[48]

In a letter, Paul Nash described to his wife, Margaret, the particular contrast of nature and war that surrounded him: "Ridiculous mad incongruity! One can't think which is more absurd, the War or Nature; the former has become a habit so confirmed, inevitable, it has its grip on the world just as surely as spring or summer. Thus we poor beings are doubly enthralled." For a French soldier writing to his parents, the beauty of autumn in the Vosges, and the proximity of the most awful and degrading destruction manifested "life and death side by side."[49]

Farther from the front, soldiers found solace and refuge from the war in gardens. As a modest antidote to shell shock — the war's name for the various forms of debilitating psychological trauma afflicting soldiers — gardens were an oasis in the war's desert. The dramatic contrast between the green watered life-giving interior of the oasis and the harsh world around it accentuates its meaning. In a world of omnipresent death, nature in any form represented life.

The horrific conditions of the trenches acquired their own normality, but in their struggle to cope with their new world, soldiers experienced a palpable desire to create a new "normal." Lieutenant Robert Sterling was "longing for some link with the normal universe detached from the storm." He found it in seeing a pair of thrushes building a

Nature was a common theme in trench art. In this example, oak leaves and acorns are battered into a British shell case.

nest; "they seem to repeat in some degree the very essence of the Normal and Unchangeable universe carrying on unhindered and careless amid the corpses and bullets and madness."[50]

Soldiers tried to create an alternative reality by engaging in activities familiar from home. The accoutrements of everyday life such as trench newspapers, boxing matches, music, gardens, the creation of art, and writing letters were critical in this endeavor — a half million letters were sent weekly by British soldiers from the front. Even in military terms, all these activities and actions were good for morale. The garden thus became one more weapon in the arsenal against the enemy, a paradoxical and surprising warrior, a counterattack to the war itself.

When life, human and not, dies, it decays and returns to the body of the earth. A garden, and especially a plant emerging from the ground, is a sign of regeneration and an indication of the continuation of life. War magnifies our awareness of our human connections to these forces of life and death.

Farther behind the lines and away from the battlefield, soldiers found solace in the basic conveniences denied them on the front: a bath, a mattress, a toilet. A female presence — the ministrations of a nurse, the fleeting pleasures of prostitutes, or even the mere sight of women — was another reminder of home that also countered the unnatural, exclusively male world of the trenches.

Gardens near or at the front were a powerful reminder to soldiers that their home world still existed. The word *Blighty* (unrelated to the word *blight*), was synonymous with England. John Brophy and Eric Partridge describe Blighty as "a sort of faerie, a paradise which [soldiers] could remember, a never-never land."[51] A garden could even be a miniature Blighty landscape, where sights, smells, flavors, or flowers could remind soldiers of Blighty — home.

On life back from the line, Phillip Gibbs found that "it was good to go into the garden of a French chateau and pluck a rose and smell its sweetness, and think back to England, where other roses were blooming. England!" Near Armentières on Christmas Day 1914, Henry Willamson wrote in his diary: "Even the German shells and our axes have not yet spoilt the beauty of these great woods. . . . one cannot help thinking of the high woods of home."[52]

The men also constructed reminders of home. Trenches were named after actual streets back home, and there were crudely made signposts designating Trafalgar Squares or Piccadilly. On the walls of the Talbot House, Tubby Clayton posted maps of England, Canada, and Australia.

Soldiers hoped to be spared from death, and they hoped for peace. The familiar cycle of life — birth, growth, maturity, and death — is perhaps nowhere more visible than in a garden, where the cycle plays itself out each season and over years. But the cycle cannot be ignored in battle, where perhaps the strongest emotion is the soldier's fear of dying. By immersing themselves briefly into a garden world, however small, soldiers maintained contact with the most immediate part of their humanity: that of being alive.

For Tubby Clayton, part of the significance of the Talbot House garden was the beauty it offered: "how far a little beauty went amid such surroundings as ours. To live day after day not only in danger but in

squalor; . . . to be homeless amid all that is hideous and disheartening, habituated not only to the filth and to a horizon of apparently
invincible menace; to move always among the wreckage of men's
lives and hopes, haunted not only by a sense of being yourself
doomed to die, but by an agony of mind which cried out at every step
against the futile folly of the waste of time and of treasure, of skill
and of life itself — this is what war meant to a soul sensitive to such
impressions."[53]

Their responses to the war landscape and situation fit into a tradition
and a set of conventions many soldiers on the Western Front knew
well: those of the pastoral. The hellish landscape of no-man's-land had
a paradisiacal parallel in poetry and literature, an imaginative green
literary escape in which British soldiers expressed a longing for the
modest pastoral pleasures of the English landscape. These literary
landscapes had a counterpart not only in imagined gardens and landscapes, but also in actual gardens created on the war front. The literary responses were an imaginative resistance to the circumstances of
war. The retreat into the comforts of the pastoral is intuitively com-
prehensible, but there were defiant acts of gardening that combated
despair.

   In the literary landscape of the pastoral, there are interludes or pastoral oases in the narrative. These too had actual counterparts on the
war environment. Friedrich Georg Steinbrecher wrote home, "When
one has seen how brutal, how degrading war can be, any idyllic interlude comes like a reprieve from the gallows." Many soldiers' memoirs
recalled brief pastoral interludes, breaks from horror. They could
occupy these short-lived physical and emotional oases only for a brief
period. Henry Willamson's description recalls a classical pastoral
interlude. "We are having a peaceful happy rest away behind Albert,
at Baisieux, in lovely unspoilt country, cornfields, woods, leafy trees,
and streams." Rudolf Moldenhauer, a high-school student who died
in the first months of the war, wrote, "When we have the treat of a
beautiful sunset over the watery marshes of the Somme; when a beautiful, cold, December morning breaks through the mist of dawn and
the red clay of the trench glows in the sunshine; then we are happy and
rejoice like children in the beauty of it."[54]

   It did not take much. Major R. S. Cockburn described the pleasures away from the line; fresh fruit and vegetables, the comforts of a

Two Australian soldiers near Allonville, in a field of wildflowers. The village lay at the center of a rest area for troops engaged in the Amiens sector.

soft hat versus a steel helmet, and the trees that were not scarred and broken stumps. In Liam O'Flaherty's wartime novel, he describes a platoon crossing no-man's-land. "The men caught sight of a green slope, far off on the left, beyond a hollow. 'Look,' said Jennings, 'there's grass there. Astonishing.' With the exception of Lamont, none of them had seen a blade of grass in five months. . . . They became quite cheerful at the sight of green grass."[55]

Since the Industrial Revolution, the garden and nature had assumed new meaning as forces in opposition to the world of technology. The most terrifying technology of war emphasized this contrast. Blunden often notes the dramatic contrast in the visible evidence of war and peace. Even in the trenches, some respite was possible: "Still, in daytime, we sometimes got out of the trench into the tall grass behind, which the sun had dried, and enjoyed a warm indolence with a book. . . . The war seemed to have forgotten us in that placid sector." In a country that was "raving mad," occasionally "that bad spell was broken. Here we saw life in her rural pretty beauties." At the headquarters at Ypres, the men "enjoyed a kind of Arcadian environment," a garden with ponds and bridges and a château.[56]

The contrast was stark and complete, the associations of war with hell and nature with heaven explicit. Describing an artillery shelling of a Château Coupigney where they had been, seemingly safe behind the lines, Gosse wrote, "hitherto we had been left entirely alone by the enemy, but Satan was now about to ravish our Garden of Eden."[57]

Nothing quite expressed both the nationality and the individual significance of the fallen soldiers as movingly or as permanently as the cemeteries that sprang up along the Western Front. Cemeteries are sacred gardens, spaces cut out of the surrounding landscape for ornamentation and special care, which carry a specifically human and tragic meaning. The first graves of World War I were dug in the battlefield where soldiers fell. Whenever a respite from fighting permitted, permanent graves were prepared and crosses erected. As one German soldier noted, "The battlefield is really nothing but one vast cemetery. . . . One sees little white crosses scattered all over the ground — in front of us, behind us, to right and left."[58] Often the cross indicated only a general location for bodies that had been obliterated. Almost instinctually, the ground around haphazardly erected wooden crosses was made into gardens and became the foundation for what would later be designated as war cemeteries, with their neat rows of simple stone markers.

In a letter, theology student Hans Spatzl described the gentle care that accompanied a German grave. The body had been lowered into one of the craters produced by shell fire and covered. Atop the grave was "a pretty cross with a 'penthouse.' Two candlesticks stand at the foot. A big 7-in. shell dominates the grave, and flowers are planted in it. Nature runs wild all around — ears of corn and flowers of every color hang over the shell hole. An atmosphere of peace seems to reign there." Max Bassler described the adornment of graves at Polygon Wood: "We fetched some glazed tiles from the roof of a summer-house to put round the graves, and picked some lilac-blossom and branches of red and yellow leaves to decorate them. . . . The lilac gave out its lovely scent and the colored leaves glowed on the fresh sods, but the earth crumbles as it were impatiently."[59] As suggested by Spatzl's description, adorning many battlefield graves was trench art, which was constructed from the materials and waste of the war environment.

Tending the graves of the fallen, near Blagny, May 3, 1917.

Touring the battlefield in 1917, Sir Edwin Luytens wrote home to his wife of the sight of hastily dug graves: "The graveyards [are] haphazard from the needs of much to do and little time for thought. And then a ribbon of isolated graves like a milky way across miles of country where men were tucked where they fell." He also describes the crosses as forming white ribbons bespattered with blossoming annuals; "the effect is charming, easy and oh so pathetic. One thinks for the moment no other monument is needed."[60] Back in England, Luytens, along with Sir Herbert Baker and Sir Reginald Bloomfield, was chosen to design cemeteries for the Imperial War Graves Commission (now the Commonwealth War Graves Commission). Their design would set the pattern and standard for British Military Cemeteries around the world.

The fallen soldiers would be buried where they fell. The uniform headstones would represent "equality in death."[61] Luytens, Bloomfield, and Baker decided on white headstones, undifferentiated by rank. In each cemetery there is a Cross of Sacrifice designed by Bloomfield — the sword of war sheathed by the cross. There is also the

Members of the British Women's Army Auxiliary Corps tend graves in a
cemetery at Abbeville in February 1918.

sarcophagus-like Stone of Remembrance, inscribed "Their Name
Liveth for Evermore." The quotation from Ecclesiastes was chosen by
Rudyard Kipling, whose son fell at the Second Battle of Loos. The
inscriptions on the identical white stones identify the soldier's name,
rank, age, and date and place of death, along with the appropriate religious symbol (cross, Crescent, Star of David, and even Sikh, Hindu,
Buddhist, or Confucian symbols). Kipling had also written the most
common identification, "A Soldier of the Great War/Known Unto
God." Families were permitted to submit a short statement for inclu-
sion on the grave.

These cemeteries for the war dead are, as Sir Luytens instinc-
tively felt, stunning monuments; almost a thousand lie across the
Western Front. They are found mostly in fields, as battlefields were
restored to their immemorial productivity. A typical cemetery is
surrounded by low walls, with a gate allowing entrance to a meticulously maintained enclave. They vary in size from a few score of
graves to tens of thousands. Smaller cemeteries are particularly
poignant, for you know that the soldiers here fell within sight of the

place you are standing. The rows of headstones align in perfect formation.

At Normandy, American graves are set in an immense lawn, the most classic American "garden." The cemeteries for fallen British are miniaturized English gardens; they display the idealized version of a cottage garden. In a 1918 report by Sir Frederic Kenyon, the director of the British Museum suggested that "the cemetery will have the appearance of small park or garden." The report also suggested that "the graves themselves [be] leveled to a flat surface and planted with turf and flowers."[62] Even today the lovingly tended plantings and the miniature herbaceous borders of plants amid perfect green lawns echo the work of Sir Luytens and Gertrude Jekyll.

In Geoff Dyer's *The Missing of the Somme,* a rumination on the meanings of the Great War, he found World War I cemeteries strange because they look the same sixty years later as when they were created. In a sense that continuity mirrors our image of the soldiers, cut down in their prime and deprived of the right to grow old, perpetually youthful in surviving photographs. Veterans and spouses, parents, and children of the dead were the first generation of visitors to the cemeteries. Later, grandchildren or great-grandchildren made their own pilgrimages. On our visit to one such cemetery eighty-four years after the end of the war, we were joined by British army recruits who were retracing their historical legacy. So, in the experience of the visitors, the meaning of the cemeteries is not static but changes with each new generation.

Standing in one of the cemeteries on Redan Ridge in the Somme, Dyer reflected:

> I have never felt so peaceful. I would be happy never to leave. So strong are these feelings that I wonder if there is not some compensatory quality in nature, some equilibrium — of which the poppy is a manifestation and symbol — which means that where terrible violence has taken place the earth will sometimes generate an equal and opposite sense of peace. In this place where men were slaughtered they also came to love each other, to realize Camus' great truth: that "there are more things to admire in men than to despise." Standing here, I know that some part of me will always be calmed by the memory of this place, by the vast capacity for forgiveness revealed by these cemeteries, by this landscape.[63]

Dyer's thoughts imbue the landscape with a power and meaning, as do the builders of gardens. Indeed gardens are exactly the places where they are built wishes, hope made material.

THREE ❧ Ghetto Gardens
Nazi Europe, 1939–44

LIFE IN THE GHETTO has been studied by many, but no one has investigated how a commonplace aspect of the landscape, the garden, in both its practical and profound aspect, was sustained. But Jan Jagielski, the photo archivist at the Jewish Historical Institute in Warsaw, intuited what I meant when I told him I was looking at gardens: I was interested not only in ornamental gardens or just plantings, but in any sign in the ghetto of nature or any sign of the natural world. In response, he pulled out photo after photo of all manner of vegetation from the Warsaw ghetto's early period (1940–41), before the ghetto was compressed and death was omnipresent. In that early period, the struggle to stay alive included the making of gardens.

In the spring of 1942, a few young children in the orphanage of the Lodz ghetto, about seventy-five miles southwest of Warsaw, turned a piece of forlorn ground into a garden. The ground was hard, and "whatever their little hands could get hold of they used; spoons, forks, sticks and so on." As the garden grew, the children were awed by the first shoots, but the plants, like the children, looked malnourished. As their teacher, Sheva Glas-Wiener, tells in her memoir, every day the children waited "to see the fruit of their labor. Every morning I would see them looking at the sky and at their little garden waiting for the beets to grow larger and to ripen but they waited in vain."

When the children of the Lodz ghetto learned they were to be deported, a spontaneous fury seized them. They went to their gardens and, in a burst of anger, trampled the few beds of pathetic beets. With the toes of their shoes they kicked every clod of earth and, in a rage of frustration, tore the plants out by the roots.

"Nothing will grow after we have gone! Nothing will bloom in this garden!" a girl about ten years old screamed in rage.

"Nothing will grow! Nothing will bloom!" the others repeated and trod everything into the ground even more passionately.

This protest burst forth from the depths of their souls and they knew no other way to express their sense of betrayal and anger. They had no one to cry out to, in the moment of their pain, so they turned on the earth itself, for it had failed them. They had loved it, nurtured it and watched over it and it had not heeded them or responded to their loving care.[1]

As if to thumb their noses at their inevitable fate, these small children stamped out what they intuitively knew the gardens represented: hope and life. As they destroyed the beets, so too would their own lives be extinguished.

Today we find gardens in the Jewish ghettos of World War II an amazing proposition. How were they possible? Still, there were gardens in the four major ghettos of Warsaw and Lodz in Poland, and Kovno and Vilna in Lithuania; in this chapter we examine primarily the first three. Gardens, like other aspects of life that could be considered "normal" — going to school, park, or concert, praying, taking a walk, or having enough for dinner — were all present in the ghetto, but only through extraordinary effort. Ghetto residents carted away rubble and scratched into the earth to plant vegetables, nurtured meager trees in the Jewish prison, and created garden sites at Skra, the Warsaw stadium that yielded its playing field to vegetable gardens and ultimately to mass graves. Though short-lived, like the ghettos themselves and their prisoners, ghetto gardens were mechanisms of resistance to the horrific conditions under which people lived. They were acts of hope and defiance. By attempting to create conditions for their survival by creating the gardens, ghetto residents also made for themselves work, relief, solace, and food. To begin to comprehend these gardens, we must first understand the social, material, and psychological conditions under which they were created.

The fate of those imprisoned in ghettos is known: a large proportion died from disease and starvation, and those who survived were shipped to extermination camps, where most of them perished. But when the ghettos were first established, the ultimate fate of those imprisoned there was still unknown. Indeed, ghetto inhabitants had no reason to suspect they would *not* survive: in 1930s Europe there was no precedent for modern, industrialized mass murder, and in their long history, Jews had endured much persecution. So, the early, natural response of ghetto residents was to form organizations to try to retain the continuity of life and society under Nazi rule. Among the various organizations that arose in the ghetto were those that would create gardens.

The Nazis had a practical interest in disguising to the outside world the ghettos' more horrific aspects, so German records of ghetto life are unreliable. Our most accurate sources of information about ghetto life are memoirs by survivors, oral histories by survivors, diaries, and other material archived by ghetto organizations and individuals.

Remarkably, in the ghettos of Warsaw and Lodz, the Jews themselves designated official archivists and historians to create archives of the ghettos. In the Warsaw ghetto, resident and historian Emmanuel Ringelblum organized a staff of dozens of workers to create a ghetto archive, which was named Oneg Shabbat, including accounts of street traffic, religious life, humor, and the school system in the ghetto. When it gradually became clear to residents that they would not survive, Ringelblum wrote, "the keeping of the records became meaningful as a gesture for posterity — a pure historical act," with the hope that "the future would avenge what the present could not prevent."[2] The Oneg Shabbat archives were to be buried in milk cans and tins before the Warsaw ghetto uprising in the spring of 1943. One set was recovered in September 1946, another in December 1950. Today the archives are part of the collection at Yad Vashem, Israel's Holocaust memorial and research center in Jerusalem.

In the Lodz ghetto, which the Germans renamed Litzmannstadt, a ghetto archives office was created. Oskar Rosenfeld, Oskar Singer, Josef Zelkowicz, and others worked as official ghetto chroniclers. An inmate in the ghetto from 1940 to 1945, Nachman Zonabend also worked on the archives. In August 1944, after the last Jews were deported to the death camp at Chelmno, the Germans assigned Zonabend to a work unit whose task was to clean up the deserted ghetto. He hid portions of the archives, along with photographs and art works. He retrieved these after Lodz's liberation in January 1945 and in 1947 donated them to the YIVO Institute for Jewish Research (formerly Yidisher Visnshaftlekher Institut), where they form the Zonabend Collection.[3]

As human endeavors, eyewitness testimonies tell only a fragment of the whole, unfathomable ghetto experience, a fact that some diarists and memorists recognized. While in hiding in Warsaw, Stefan Ernest wrote in his dairy in May 1943: "They will ask if this is the truth. I will answer in advance: No, this is not the truth, it is only a small part, a tiny fraction of the truth. The essential truth, the real truth, cannot be described even with the most powerful pen." In late 1944 an unknown young Lodz diarist wrote: "It is now five years that we have been tortured in the most terrible way. Describing all our pain is as impossible as drinking in all the ocean's water or lifting the earth. I don't know if we'll ever be believed."[4]

After their invasion of Poland in September 1939, Nazis immediately began to implement the Nazi program to make Europe *Judenrein,* a continent free of Jews. Within three months, anti-Semitic statutes were in place curtailing basic rights for Jewish citizens: Jewish businesses were marked, Jews were required to wear armbands, schools were closed, restrictions were placed on professionals, and Jews were banned from certain public places. As had been the practice in Germany, in July 1940 Jews were banned from public parks, from sitting on benches, and from walking on the "better streets."[5] Jews were herded into restricted, impoverished areas, or ghettos, where they were forced to work in factories (as in Lodz) or made to eke out a living as best they could on ever-diminishing resources. The Germans controlled all access to the ghetto of food, water, and other essentials. Although ghettos had existed in Europe for centuries, the German ghettos were unlike the earlier incarnations. Whereas previous ghettos had been physical manifestations merely of residential segregation and discrimination, the Nazi ghettos were urban prisons set up to deliver their residents, ultimately, to extermination.

The prevailing landscape of the Holocaust was a man-made one. Claude Lanzmann, the director of *Shoah* (titled after the Hebrew word for Holocaust), said it was "a film about topography, about geography." That geography included the creation of ghettos, places that W. A. Douglas Jackson has called "pariah-scapes" — or places to which people have been banished.[6] Because they were existing urban areas that were walled in, each ghetto had a unique character and topography. In addition, the various German authorities themselves disagreed about whether the ghettos should be places of willful death of

Sign in German and
Polish forbidding Jews to
enter a public park in
Warsaw, 1939.

Jews by attrition through disease and starvation or whether they
should be sources of labor pools and work forces — and, as a result,
ghettos did not all have the same policies in force. For example, Lodz
was essentially an urban slave labor factory. Ultimately these distinctions were temporary, for all the ghettos were essentially holding
stations where the inhabitants died of hunger and disease or were
deported to extermination camps. Everyone there shared a common
fate; the ghettos were death traps.

Typically, ghettos were created in areas that already had high concentrations of poor Jews. Non-Jewish residents were moved out, and
Jews from other parts of the city were moved in. They were soon
joined by Jewish refugees from other communities, dramatically
increasing the density.

In the 1930s Warsaw was the largest Jewish city in Poland, with
more than a quarter of a million Jews, about one-third of the city's
population. In October 1940 the Warsaw ghetto was established in
the Jewish section of the city, which was also the area most heavily
bombed when the Germans invaded. Within a month the authorities
sealed the ghetto. About a thousand acres (1.3 square miles), or about
100 square city blocks, it originally housed 390,000 people in what
were mostly two- to four-story apartments built around courtyards.
Within six months another 70,000 refugees were transported into
the ghetto, living six to seven persons to a room. The ghetto population ballooned to almost a half-million people. The horrific conditions made death by disease and starvation omnipresent. According

to Michal Grynberg, the Warsaw ghetto was the product of "perverse civic planning, as the blueprints and annihilation were mapped into a real world of schools and playgrounds, churches and synagogues, hospitals, restaurants, hotels, theaters, cafes, and bus stops. These loci of urban life . . . acquired new associations: Residential streets were changed into sites of executions; hospitals became places for administering death; cemeteries proved to be avenues of life support."[7] Its most infamous location was Umschlagplatz, situated between the railyard and the wall, where during an *Aktion,* the periodic roundups, Jews were collected and assembled for deportation to extermination camps.

Poland's second largest city, Lodz had a population of 700,000, including 233,000 Jews. The ghetto was established in the Baluty neighborhood, a very poor slum. About 164,000 persons were shoved into about 1.5 square miles when the ghetto was sealed on May 1, 1940. Lodz was located in a part of Poland the Germans absorbed into the Reich.[8] Lodz was a textile center, the "Manchester of Poland," and more than any other ghetto it became a forced labor camp. One comparatively rural area on the east side of the ghetto, the Marysin, became the location for the ghetto's orphanage, old-age home, schools, villas for elite Jews, and gardens. When the Russians liberated Lodz in January 1945, only about 800 persons remained in the ghetto — the rest had perished in the ghetto or had been sent to death camps.

The Jewish community in the city of Kovno (now Kaunas) thrived during Lithuania's short-lived independence between the world wars. The Soviets annexed the country in June 1940 and closed down most Jewish institutions. The Germans conquered Lithuania the following June, and in mid-August the Kovno ghetto was sealed. It was located opposite the city center on the banks of the Vilija River, on whose floodplain the Jews would create gardens. The ghetto was burned to the ground in July 1944.

Ghettos were walled or fenced with restricted entry at gateways. Bridges were built to link different sections of the ghetto and to allow non-Jews to pass through on passages and the streets below. The intent was to create an impermeable boundary between Jew and non-Jew, between *Todesraum* and *Lebensraum* — death space and living space. Warsaw had ten miles of walls eight to ten feet tall topped with broken glass. But boundaries and dimensions constantly shifted. The walls that defined the Warsaw ghetto were a prison wall, a band that limited food and communication to the community, a vise that slowly squeezed the life out of the inhabitants through systematic starvation and by cutting off access to the outside world. Holocaust historian Raoul Hilberg estimates that a half million Polish Jews died in ghettos from disease, starvation, and execution. This accounts for nearly 10 percent of all Holocaust victims.

Today only a few remnants of the Warsaw ghetto's brick walls remain in place, hidden in courtyards and behind parked cars. A few bricks have been removed as tokens (icons, perhaps) and reestablished at Yad Vashem, the U.S. Holocaust Museum and Memorial, and another memorial in Australia (they too are memorial stones, like those placed on Jewish graves). The wall is not high, but it is a powerful reminder of the basic division of inside and out, and for most persons it was the boundary between death and life. It is the extreme opposite of a garden wall that is intended to circumscribe a paradisiacal and idealized environment. The ghetto wall was an inversion; the other side held at least a potential of life, all that gardens signify. A view out over the wall was a view to hope.

Peretz Hochman, thirteen years old when the ghetto was created, recited the lyrics from a scornful Polish song from 1940:

> In Saski park where fountains play
> No Jewish mother comes today;
> Rebecca, Hanna, Esther — gone
> To live in ghettos every one.
> The street where once they spent their lives
> Seem to them all like Paradise . . .
> Once little Moyshe came to play
> Now he's behind walls all day.[9]

The diaries of Chaim Kaplan, Abraham Levin, Emmanuel Ringelblum, and others record the deterioration of living conditions in the Warsaw ghetto, from its creation to its destruction after the uprising in April 1943. There was a daily struggle for the basic necessities of life, especially food. Kaplan wrote that "our constant song was potatoes! It is our whole life." By 1941 death in the streets by starvation, disease (typhus), random beatings, and killings was commonplace. Fear was omnipresent. In her memoir Helena Szereszewska wrote, "there wasn't a day or a single hour free of trouble." By the winter of 1941, "children's bodies and crying serve[d] as a persistent background for the Ghetto." Marek Stok found "the hunger and misery . . . so shocking it's beyond imagining" and the streets were filled with beggars "looking more like phantoms than human beings." Walking down any street, one stepped over corpses. "Almost daily people are falling dead or unconscious in the middle of the street. It no longer makes so direct an impression," wrote Ringelblum. But an alternative life existed parallel with the omnipresent horrors: in the same entry, he writes about a "large conference on Jewish cultural activity."[10]

In what were called the "grand *Aktions*" between July and September 1942, over 300,000 Jews were assembled at Umschlagplatz and deported from Warsaw. Natan Zelichower, survivor of the ghetto and Buchenwald extermination camp, described the grand *Aktion:* "I go out on the street: an unforgettable moment and an unforgettable sight that nothing can erase. I've never seen a battlefield, but this is what it must look like after a hurricane or fire. The streets and sidewalks are littered with corpses. . . . And strewn among the corpses that are crying out to heaven for vengeance are torn window frames, broken tables and chairs, pillows, . . . books torn to shred. Here is where the human beast guzzled blood until its maw was full."[11]

Unbelievably, tragically, conditions only worsened. Jan Karski, an emissary from the Polish underground to the ghetto, made two secret visits to the Warsaw ghetto in 1942. Passing through the ghetto wall "was to enter a new world utterly unlike anything that had ever been imagined. The entire population of the ghetto seemed to be living in the street. There was hardly a square yard of empty space. . . . Everyone and everything seemed to vibrate with unnatural intensity, to be in constant motion, enveloped in a haze of disease and death through which their bodies appeared to be throbbing in disintegration."[12]

As the fate of the Warsaw ghetto moved toward its inexorable end, it transformed into both a battlefield and a place hidden from the outside world. All vestiges of an urban community disappeared. Life became restricted to apartments and courtyards, bustling streets became deserted, and public squares were used as execution and deportation sites. Death was everywhere. When Stefan Ernest escaped the ghetto to hide on the other side, he wrote, "On 29 January 1943, at 5:15 A.M., I leave that cursed city of insult and humiliation, of misery, pestilence, hunger, blood, and death, that devilish home to every conceivable torture and suffering that can be devised by human beings: *the beast*."[13] After the Warsaw ghetto uprising, the ghetto was systematically demolished, and the site used for executions.

Cut off by a barbed-wire fence and guards, the Lodz ghetto was completely isolated, almost entirely separate from its surroundings. Critically, this curtailed the adjacent black-market activities and smuggling that sustained life in other ghettos. Residents were almost entirely dependent on German allocations of food and clothing. This isolation thrust the ghetto into a struggle for self-sufficiency, which in turn fostered a stronger "psychosis of hope" than elsewhere, though, like the other ghettos, Lodz succumbed to an inevitable and horrid decline. The Lodz ghetto was a slave colony where Jews were worked to death. Deliberate and systematic starvation ensured that people were so weakened that they offered no resistance when herded aboard trains. Dawid Sierakowiak's diary writing begins just before his fifteenth birthday in June 1939 and ends in April 1943, four months before he died of tuberculosis. It is a grim record of the ghetto's descent. Sierakowiak detailed a world where everyone was being killed spiritually by hunger and where "everything is vanishing before our eyes." Sixty thousand died in the Lodz ghetto, and 130,000 were deported to the death camps of Chelmno or Auschwitz.[14]

Diaries and memoirs describe the gradual deterioration of the actual landscape of the ghettos, and of the bodies, hopes, and lives of the residents as time went on. Irena Liebman, who survived Auschwitz, described the ghetto inhabitants and their surroundings: "People without faces, their backs curved, their head hanging low. A caravan of poverty. Grey, weary, miserable. The ghetto. Tiny, narrow streets. Little houses without conveniences. A well in the backyard. A refuse dump infested with rats. A stinking toilet full of melting snow, impossible to use. A leaking roof, dilapidated walls. One little room and a small kitchen for seven people." Diarist Leon Hurwitz, who perished in Auschwitz, wrote that a serious shortage of fuel during the harsh winter drove people to steal wood to burn: "in the dark of night, people began stripping wood from fences, sheds, outhouses, wherever they could. The colder it got, the more widespread the vandalism became. . . . The courtyards which took on a barren look without fences, were covered with refuse and human excrement." In "The Face of the Ghetto," Oskar Rosenfeld described "mucky paths, half-covered with snow, [that] led between individual houses set here and there, grim and meaningless. . . . We are lepers, outcasts, common thieves, people without music, without earth, without beds, without a world. There is no other city like this in the world. Come here, people from the outside, from over there where there are normal days and holidays, where there are dreams and desire and resistance." By

Passover 1942, Rosenfeld would say, "Every living thing breathes, blooms, creates, wants to grow. The ghetto is the exception. People locked in decaying houses with just enough air to vegetate. They do not grow corn, do not have cattle, poultry, vegetables, fish, milk, fat or bread that they make themselves. There is no fabric, no leather, no metal, you cannot produce. . . . Everything falls apart."[15]

The Nazis conspired not only to make Europe *Judenrein* but to constrict Jews into a world artificially free of nature, as well. With only fragments of the natural world remaining in the ghetto — taunting glimpses over walls or through barbed wire, scarce trees, and the few gardens and fields — ghetto residents savored their recollections of earlier forays into a green world. For city dwellers the open spaces of the city were an essential aspect of social and cultural life. For inhabitants of shtetls, like villagers throughout Europe, a domestic garden was part of life. And although farming was not the predominant Jewish occupation in Eastern Europe, there were Jewish farmers and agricultural experts. There were plenty of memories to access.

Gerda Klein was fifteen when the Nazis invaded Poland. In her town of Bielsko (Bielitz in German) on the border of Czechoslovakia and Poland, she was anchored by her family, but also by her house and garden. In her last night in her family home, where they were confined after the German occupation to the cellar, she felt compelled to make a final visit to her garden: "I had to see my beloved garden again. It had rained during the night and the young fresh grass was wet. I looked at the rich moist soil under my feet. Everywhere memories surrounded me. . . . On the old pear tree there was a mark made by a scout knife driven into it years ago by Arthur [her brother]. . . . There were the narrow, now overgrown paths where I rode my tricycle and wheeled my dolls. There was the little garden house, now badly in need of paint; we had used to paint it every spring." A hanging Japanese lantern remained from her fifteenth birthday celebration. Collecting some violets from alongside the brook, she "held them tight and then sat down on the moist ground and started to cry, thinking of the velvet lawn, of the yellow dandelions that soon would be blooming in abundance, thinking of the birds that sang in the trees at night." Overwhelmed by memories of the garden in various stages of bloom and fertility and in each of the seasons, she realized too that "all this we were not to see any more. There by the brook, thinking and crying softly, I bade farewell to my childhood."[16]

Sara Zyskind was twelve when she was imprisoned in the Lodz ghetto, where she worked in the orphanage. In her memoir, *Stolen Years,* she recounts the story of one of her favorite charges, five-year-old Rishia, who asked incessant questions about the world outside. Having discovered that Rishia had never seen a flower and had no understanding of the natural world, Zyskind "talked to her about the countryside, about forests, rivers, fields, and animals, and made drawings for her of apples, pears, flowers, hens and cats." Rishia and her age peers knew only a world that was "barren and desolate, a mixture of squalor, filth, hunger, and grinding poverty." Zyskind promises to bring Rishia a flower when the war is over, but the child does not survive.

Elsewhere in her memoir, after describing a sequence of deaths and deportations, Zyskind turned her thoughts to happy memories of walking home from school through a park in Lodz with her friends Heltzia and Irka. "Our way led through Sienkiewicz Park, enchanting in its beauty no matter what the season. In the fall, when the new school year began, the park was steeped in gold, yellow, and purple, and we waded through thick layers of golden leaves that covered the ground. . . . Every day we'd be late coming home, and every day we'd be reprimanded, but to no effect. The beauty of the park was too fascinating — it confounded our sense of time."[17]

The first of Dawid Sierakowiak's surviving diaries begins with an entry describing a hiking trip into the mountains before returning to Lodz. In his first spring in the ghetto, he finds that "the smell of spring in Marysin makes your heart break with the memory of prewar times. In normal times we would now be three weeks away from the gymnasium [high school] pregraduation exams, and the longed-for vacation. . . . Damn it! You feel like crying when you remember those things." The landscape dreams of others took them farther afield. Lodz native Abraham Biderman daydreamed of a "fantasy land on a distant continent, rich with fruit, flowers and palm trees."[18]

The sky was seen only in slivers and strips. From the courtyard in Warsaw where Janina David lived, she saw "only a small square of sky" significant enough to become the title of her memoir. Ringelblum found not a single tree in the Warsaw ghetto, while in Vilna (now Vil'ne) there was one grand tree around which "the youth of the ghetto took their walks." On Lag b'Omer, the traditional Jewish arbor day when children would go to the countryside, Josef Zelkowiocz asked, "Lag b'Omer: how does it look in the ghetto? Where will you find fresh, free air for them to breathe?"[19]

The feeling of deprivation could be so pronounced that even in a railroad car en route to Auschwitz, Abraham Biderman recalled watching the changing landscape. "It had been five long years since I had seen the countryside, and I had forgotten the look of open fields and trees."[20]

After the harsh Polish winter, spring is always welcome. But in the ghetto the warmth of the sun, the lengthening of days, and the return of spring and its promise of growth could offer only temporary pleasure, for it was severely tempered by the staggering reality of the conditions under which residents lived and died. Spring was also a reminder of the passage of time, offering people a dual message that oscillated between hope and despair. Surviving another season meant that they might be either closer to liberation or closer to death. Historian Barbara Engelking asks, "Was the first whiff of spring — so exciting in normal circumstances — equally pleasant in the ghetto? Or did it rather, by reinforcing the sense of one's own slavery, deepen depression?"[21]

In the Warsaw spring of 1941, Mary Berg noted that

> on the other side of the barbed wire spring holds full sway. From my window I can see young girls with bouquets of lilac walking on the "Aryan" part of the street. I can even smell the tender fragrance of the opened buds. But there is no sign of spring in the ghetto. Here the rays of the sun are swallowed up by the heavy gray pavement. On a few window sills, long, scrawny onion stalks, more yellow than green, are sprouting. Where are my lovely spring days of former years, the gay walks in the park, the narcissus, lilac, and magnolia that used to fill my room?

The following spring, as the vice on the ghetto tightened, Berg's diary notes that "last night sixty more persons were executed." In the very next paragraph she speaks of their garden. "In our garden everything is green. The young onions are shooting up. We have eaten our first radishes. The tomato plants spread proudly in the sun. The weather is magnificent." A sentiment commonly associated with gardens becomes poignantly dramatized by Berg's circumstance: "The greens and the sun remind us of the beauty of nature that we are forbidden to enjoy. A little garden like ours is therefore very dear to us.

The spring this year is extraordinary. A lilac bush under our window is in full bloom."[22]

In an April 1942 diary entry, Dawid Sierakowiak wrote, "Today was the most lovely spring day. On such a day the poverty and hopelessness of the ghetto situation can be seen in all its splendor." A week later the same spring sun gave him hope: "the sun is shining again, and the Jews have regained hope."[23]

Unaware that 1944 would be the Lodz ghetto's final spring, Abraham Biderman recalled, "When nature re-awakened after a long winter sleep, when the sun took off the snow-woven winter coat from the shoulders of mother earth bowed with cold, when bloom and blossom filled the air with sweet fragrances, the Lodz ghetto blossomed with death and decay."[24] In Vilna Herman Kruk thought that while spring brought sun and warmth the feeling was paradoxically autumnal, presaging winter, and that in lieu of hope it brought a loss of courage.

In Simha Bunim Shayevitsh's Lodz poem, "Spring 1942," spring is not a time of rebirth or the end of winter but a harbinger of death. The world was spinning backward, spring leading not to the joys of summer but retreating toward winter and darkness: "The garden blooms, the sun shines / And the slaughterer . . . slaughters."[25]

Private memories of their former lives helped sustain the spirits of ghetto residents, but organizations dedicated to the welfare of every resident sprang up to provide collective assistance. German policy had changed gradually from one of maintenance of the ghetto, even under horrid conditions, to the unmistakably explicit intent of liquidating the population. Organizations and other aspects of prewar Jewish society reconstituted themselves in the ghettos, and a new organizational structure also emerged; both old and new struggled against German rule in an effort to ameliorate conditions in the ghettos and help people survive.

A long Eastern European Jewish tradition of community self-help was already in place, with specific organizations to respond to the most practical and critical necessities of food, clothing, and shelter, as well as desires for education, arts, and culture. Gardens straddled the territory between the practical and the aesthetic. In Warsaw, a city that had more Jews than any city in the world except New York, the tradi-

Vegetable garden of the summer camp in Rozyczka, Goclawek of the
Jewish orphanage run by Janusz Korczak. The photograph was taken
in the summer of 1940, the last year of the camp.

tional Kehilla, the organized Jewish community institution of self-government, was replaced by the Judenrat, a governing agency created by
the Germans. In Lodz the Germans ordered the creation of a council
of elders. In both cases they constituted a political and economic
bureaucracy that functioned as best it could as a municipality.

Among the prewar institutions to continue their responsibilities in
the ghettos were CENTOS (Centrala Opieki nad Sierotami, Federation of Associations for the Care of Orphans in Poland) and YIPS
(Yiddish sessile aleynhilf, Jewish Self-Aid Society) — which became
ZYTOS (Zydowskie Towarzistwo Opieki Spoleczwej, Jewish Society
for Self-Help) after the surrender of Warsaw. In the Warsaw ghetto
these groups operated dozens of charitable institutions, hundreds of
children's shelters, and, perhaps most critically, soup kitchens, where
120,000 free lunches were served daily and meals twice a day to children. Smuggled food sustained these operations, for the German
food ration was about 800 calories per day, but the assistance was not
enough to save everyone from starvation. The basic social organization to care for the inhabitants was the house committees in each of

the 1,500 apartment complexes built around courtyards that were the building blocks of Warsaw.

There was also TOZ (Towarzystwo Ochrony Zdrowia Ludnosci Zydowskiej, Society to Protect the Health of the Jewish Population) as well as departments for traditional municipal services: sanitation, postal services, housing, and labor. There were the social services of an old-age home, orphanage, hospital, maternity clinic, and children's playrooms. The Germans running the Warsaw ghetto forbade schools for children, but teaching continued clandestinely, as did yeshivas and classes for adults. There was vocational education and, unbelievably, even an underground medical school. Ringelblum called the Warsaw ghetto paradoxically a "free society of slaves."[26]

Not everything was about physical survival. Attention was given to the continuing survival of culture and social life. YIKOR (Yiddish Cultural Organization) organized scientific and scholarly assemblies as well as literary and artistic events. Tekuma (revival) fostered Hebrew culture in the ghetto. Mobile libraries were formed, and there were numerous coffeehouses, theaters performing in Polish and Yiddish, and a newspaper. One person even insisted on the establishment of a Society for the Protection of Animals. There were also brothels, taverns, restaurants, and nightclubs, and Ringelblum notes sixty-one "night spots in the Warsaw Ghetto."[27]

In Lodz similar institutions were established, including, in the Marysin, a House of Culture that held concerts. In Kovno there was an Organization for Rehabilitation and Training (ORT) trade school that offered a course in horticulture. There the Germans allowed only vocational courses to be taught, but classes in other subjects and university-level courses were held in secret.

All these organizations and their activities were directed toward the survival of the community and in resistance of German policies. In the winter of 1941 Chaim Kaplan wrote: "The Jewish community is on a battlefield, but the battle is not conducted with weapons. It is conducted by means of various schemes, schemes of deception, schemes of smuggling, and so on. We don't want simply to disappear from the earth." Even in this dire period he recognized something positive: "We have been healed by our catastrophe. We have become a social community that realizes its obligations towards its brothers in misfortune." Almost a year later, Siedman, the chief archivist of the Warsaw Kehillah, noted in his diary the low suicide rate. His theory was that, "in the face of such colossal communal calamity[,] personal

problems fade into insignificance. Above all, everyone wants to survive until the end. After that the future will undoubtedly be better,
more secure, more pleasurable."[28] Over time, as the knowledge of
death camps and extermination filtered into the ghetto, thousands
more were deported, and the population was depleted, survival by any
means became the paramount concern. In Warsaw especially it
became a question of choosing how to die.

Another organization that continued its prewar mission and activities
was the Toporol (Towarzystwo Popierania Rolnictwa, Society to
Encourage Agriculture among Jews), which since its 1933 founding
had trained Jewish agricultural workers in Poland. The Toporol struggled to continue and expand its mission to produce food in the ghettos of Warsaw and Lodz. This required the effort and cooperation of
the Jewish community and at least the tolerance of the German
authorities.

He-halutz, the umbrella organization of Zionist youth groups, had
established *hacshara* (training farms) in preparation for their members
making *aliyah* (immigration to Palestine). As part of a collective
known as Dror, they left the ghetto daily under German guard to cultivate fields in the Warsaw suburbs of Grochow and Czerniakow.
Grochow operated until the Germans sealed the ghetto in November
1940, and both farms produced food that was smuggled into the
ghetto to mitigate the starvation there. Grachow also acted as a way
station for underground activities. Czerniakow was a private estate of
a Pole whose owner allowed Jews to work there. It was also the clandestine original base of the ZOB (Jewish Fighting Organization).
When the Germans dismantled the Jewish farming operation in
Czerniakow in November 1942, those who worked there joined
fighters inside the ghetto. During the 1943 uprising, the few who
escaped first headed to Czerniakow.

Inside the Warsaw and Lodz ghettos, Toporol assumed responsibility for garden creation. The Ringelblum archive, in a report on
Jewish social self-help, includes a "Report on the Activities of
Toporol" in the Warsaw ghetto from December 1, 1940, to May 31,
1941. Our limited knowledge of the Toporol and its activities is supplemented and described more personally in diaries and memoirs. It
is important to bear in mind that, however impressive their activities,

In January 1938, members of the He-halutz movement at the pioneering training farm (*hacshara*) in Grochow pose beside a display of their produce.

like virtually all ghetto actions of survival and resistance, the efforts were valiant, the results meager. Perhaps that makes Toporol gardens even more inspiring.

Toporol did everything from acquiring land, seeds, equipment, and funds to mobilizing and training workers. The network created gardens in every imaginable spot of land, even on balconies. They gave away seeds, planted vegetables and trees, and made small parks. The bylaws of CENTOS expressed the part of the group's mission that went beyond alimentary sustenance: "We are to instill in the children an aesthetic appreciation of their surroundings . . . direct their attention to growing plants that might bring them closer to nature and provide them with aesthetic experiences."[29]

The Germans drew the boundaries of the Warsaw ghetto deliberately to exclude parks — the only green area inside the walls was a cemetery. People also had "fantasy gardens." Ghetto residents went to upper floors or onto roofs to look out over the green areas adjacent to the ghetto: Krasinski Park and the Saski Gardens. Both of these borrowed gardens could also be seen from the bridge connecting the two main sections of the ghetto. What did the view mean? It could be gratifying, but perhaps it was also a reminder of their earlier lives — and in the ghetto's early period, even a promise that the residents would survive this horrible experience. In his poem "A Window on That Side," W. Szlengel writes about having a borrowed view of greenery:

I have a window on that side
An impudent Jewish window
Onto lovely Krasinski park
With autumn leaves in the rain . . .
In the evening, the dark violet
Branches make a bow
The Aryan trees look straight into
That Jewish window of mine.[30]

Peretz Hochman, after recounting how thousands died of hunger each day on the street, recalls how the carving of the ghetto so it excluded green areas affected residents. He was one who had previously derived pleasure from simply sitting in the park and listening to the song of birds:

Now even that had been taken from us. It was as though somebody had decided we were subhuman and, as such, we didn't need anything. And who were we, anyway, to ask for anything as glorious as to be able to sit in a park.

Of all the beauties of nature, the only thing left for the Jews was the blue sky. The Germans could not take that away from us. The horizon we saw reminded us that beyond the ghetto walls there were fields, forests, streams, mountains and valleys, but none of these had been created for Jews. The Jews had no right to even think about them. We had to resign ourselves to the fact that no flowers or plants, not even grass grew in the ghetto. The entire ghetto contained not even a single garden.

Diarist Chaim Kaplan recalls that, after the German invasion, "we were forbidden to enter the city park. Inside the parks there was space and breadth. . . . [Inside the ghetto] we have been robbed of every tree and every flower."[31]

With the exception of the cemetery, the few open areas in the Warsaw ghetto were found where buildings had been gutted by the German blitz of 1939. Before such sites could be reclaimed for agriculture, questions of ownership were addressed, and the Judenrat assisted in acquiring or in leasing land at various sites.[32] Once a plot was acquired fairly, substantial labor was brought to bear on it to clear rubble and restore the land to a near-natural state suitable for cultivation.

The garden at the Gesia Street jail.

On Okopowa Street, near the cemetery, workers reconstructed a glass house and glass-sheltered seed beds and planted them with 1,500 square meters of beds, including 10,000 tomato plants as well as flowers — nearly 25,000 begonias, petunias, lobelias, and dahlias.

On Gesia Street, at the site of the bombed-out prison, over a hundred workers cleared thousands of cartloads of rubble. Run by the Jewish police, the Gesia Street jail had 1,300 prisoners, among them 500 children, most of whom were in jail for smuggling or crossing over to the Aryan side. It was "indescribably crowded . . . filthy," and the mortality rate was high. Despite such conditions, Emmanuel Ringelblum reported that the former "prisoners have succeed[ed] in doing wonderful things for the children, who run around about half-naked and tanned in the fresh air all day. The children perform calisthenics, sing Yiddish and Polish songs. Mothers come begging to have their children, who have been freed, put back in jail." Ringelblum noted that prisoner gardeners had transformed the tile-covered plaza at the jail "into a flourishing garden whose fruits will bring in more than 200,000 zlotys."[33] In the 1.2 acres they had wrested from destruction, they planted vegetables.

Working in a cabbage field on the site of Skra, the former sports stadium on Okopowa Street in the Warsaw ghetto in 1940. The view is south from the cemetery. The same field became the site of mass graves.

On the bombed-out Elektornalna Street site of the Hospital of the Holy Spirit, workers dug 1,800 pits into the rubble and filled each with soil for tomatoes. On Zamenhof Street, the former jail site of about 10,000 square meters was cultivated. The site of Skra, the stadium, was converted to cultivation. Given the backbreaking work required elsewhere, it was natural to turn to the cemetery, the largest open area that was still green, and plant portions of it as well.

In addition, Toporol members planted gardens for the Warsaw ghetto's cultural and social service institutions. These included gardens at the main shelter home, the orphanage, at CENTOS, and in the quarantine area. They sowed chamomile for use by the hospital. They also created or maintained ornamental plantings at the synagogue on Tlomackie Street, the Jewish community building, and other public sites and squares. At the Nalewski Stalls and Plac Grzybowski, the vegetables were planted so as to produce attractive shapes and patterns. The "Report on the Activities of Toporol," and Ringelblum, lamented the fact that the public sites were not fenced and that the people trampled the plants there.

Courtyards were at the center of outdoor life for most persons. Working with housing committees, Toporol planted gardens in over

Children playing
in the garden at
29 Leszno Street in
the Warsaw ghetto.

200 courtyards (18,000 square meters in their 1941 report), and people also tended gardens on their own (another 25,000 square meters).
Most courtyards established children's corners as play areas. Halina
Birenbaum, who was ten in 1938, and a survivor of Warsaw and
Auschwitz, recalled: "The yard on Muranowska Street was my world
of games and daydreams. In the ghetto these yards served children as
garden, school, reading room, playing field." In early 1940 Gustawa
Wilner worked with the building committee at her apartment to set
up a children's garden she describes as "without flowers or even a single blade of grass." Ironically, this was on Ogrodowa Street, which
means Garden Street in Polish. Ringelblum lauded Toporol's numerous activities, but noted "we've still a long ways to go before the
Ghetto turns green."[34]

Toporol trained the workers who undertook these tasks. In cooperation with ORT (Organization for Rehabilitation and Training),
Toporol offered three- and nine-month courses in village husbandry
that provided basic theoretical and practical knowledge for farming
and gardening. Toporol also ran an entire two-year agricultural training course, which included practical work in the gardens and the farm
as well as professional lectures. There were courses and lectures on
growing vegetables, hothouses, animal husbandry, and herb and orna-

Working in a plant nursery, Glubokoye ghetto. About sixty of the ghetto's population of six thousand survived the Holocaust.

mental gardening. In addition to hothouses, they even constructed beehives and built an incubator for hatching chickens. In 1941 about sixty farm workers were still allowed to work outside the Warsaw ghetto. Toporol trained them all. They also had a program of training children's agricultural teams to till gardens.

When Warsaw native George Topas was fourteen, he entered agricultural school near Wlodzimierz in preparation for emigrating to Palestine. Three years later he became a Toporol instructor, for which he was paid a loaf of bread a week. He supervised a group of teenage students in clearing a site on Gesia Street and was amazed at the success of their efforts given their state of starvation. Although pleased when the site began to produce, Topas thought that the harvest "was symbolic more than real." At the cemetery, where crops were being raised, he marked the "incredible contrast" of students nurturing tomato plants to "preserve life" and corpses being "dumped into mass graves."[35]

In a taped interview, Topas tells a remarkable tale of a woman who contacted him after seeing his name on a letter to *Time* magazine years after the war. Now a journalist in Warsaw, she recalled that Topas was her Toporol instructor and that when he asked her group to fetch water with buckets, he allowed her to rest because she was

In spring 1940, members of a Zionist Youth Organization sort vegetables at the *hacshara* in the Grochow suburb outside the Warsaw ghetto.

so frail. Like the gardens themselves, such small acts of kindness conveyed the most powerful of emotions. Topas worked in the ghetto until midsummer 1941, when the Germans asked Toporol to assemble a group of Jews, up to three hundred, to help work on estates in the countryside.

Toporol made the most of the skills of the ghetto population and drew people, especially the young, from all social classes and backgrounds. Many were eager to shake off the stereotype of Jews as city people with little interest or knowledge of farming. Helena Szereszewska credited the agronomist Dobrynski with its organization, and other agronomists, for example, Israel Sudowicz, were leaders.

The teenaged diarist Mary Berg had a particular interest in the activities of the Toporol, as revealed in the number of diary entries about the organization. Berg, the daughter of a U.S. citizen, lived in the ghetto until her liberation less than a year before its final destruction in spring of 1943. She survived the war. Her book, *Warsaw Ghetto: A Diary,* includes commentary about the impact of gardens under Nazi occupation and the garden's message of regeneration and life.

In a May 1941 entry, a seventeen-year-old Berg describes how the Toporol extended the living space of the ghetto through its transformation of land. "Hundreds of young boys and girls are working the plots on which bombed buildings stood, both in the courtyards and on the streets." Despite Toporol's efforts, the results were meager and the contrast with the "other side" constant.

But Berg remained aware of even the smallest possibilities. The following spring, she reported on progress to introduce green in the ghetto: "Since our courtyard is not covered with asphalt my parents dug it up for a little garden. The seeds we bought at the Toporol have already been planted." She lists the many vegetables her family has planted and refers to a few flowers, as well.

In the quest to capitalize on any available "ground," the Toporol promoted gardens on balconies, for which they distributed soil and seeds. Berg recorded that the ghetto markets sold spring onions that had been "planted in pots and boxes, on roofs and on window sills, in all sorts of odd corners."

The Warsaw ghetto also had other "gardens" associated with entertainment and cultural activities. Berg noted that "in the Little Ghetto on Ogrodowa Street a garden cafe, called 'Bajka' [fairy tale] has been opened. The tables are outside; there is a little grass and two trees. This cafe covers the site of a completely bombed out house. . . . Near by is a 'beach' — a piece of ground on which a few deck chairs have been placed. For two zlotys one can bask in the sun here for an entire day. Bathing suits are obligatory, apparently in order to create the atmosphere of a real beach."[36] In 1940 Helena Szereszewska remembered concerts in a small garden on Nowolipki Street. It had a few trees, benches, and a platform for a pianist. Even dances were held there. On Mylna Street there was an artist's garden and café, complete with a large mural whose appropriate theme was Job.

The extraordinary efforts were punctuated by scarce moments of promise. This was especially true for activities directed toward children. On Grzybowska Street Toporol planted a school garden. Janina David, age ten in 1940, remembered: "A children's playground opened on the bombed site in our street and Mother enrolled me for three afternoons each week . . . the playground was too crowded to allow any running about but there were a few trees and green patches there, and even a few flowers managed to grow for a time. Adults were not allowed in except when visiting a child." In a May 1942 entry, Berg wrote about a park with grass and flowers that Toporol constructed on the site of a bombed-out house: "Today it is green there. Jewish workmen have constructed swings, benches, etc. The pupils of our

The ruins of Swietojerska Street in the Warsaw ghetto after the Nazi reprisal for the uprising of April 1943. The tree to the right is in Krasinski Park, outside the ghetto's walls.

school went to paint a fresco of animal cartoons on one of the walls of the ruined house. All this is done to give the ghetto children a feeling of freedom. The park was inaugurated today. . . . The smiling rosy faces of the children were perhaps the best reward for those who had created this little refuge of freedom for the little prisoners of the ghetto."[37]

Berg's Polish father was sent to an internment camp at Tittmoning, Germany, which he found a "paradise" compared to the ghetto. Transferred to an internment camp at Vittel, in occupied France, along with her mother, Berg asked, "Why is it so beautiful in this part of the world? Here everything smells of sun and flowers, and there [the Warsaw ghetto] — there is only blood, the blood of my own people."[38]

Helena Szereszewska remembered that "in the first days of April 1941, the day before the first Passover meal in the ghetto we were sent a bundle of red radishes wrapped up in paper and some leaves of lettuce so young it hadn't formed heads yet. 'It's from Toporol,' we said happily."[39] The red radishes were grown in Toporol's cemetery gardens. At the Seder they ate hard-boiled eggs and radishes dipped in salt water. The Warsaw ghetto uprising began on Passover two years later.

Despite these valiant efforts, the gardens could only offer a temporary respite from the horrendous conditions. Starvation varied from ghetto to ghetto as the Germans increased restrictions on food and goods entering the ghettos. Sites of promise were easily transformed into places of anguish. On June 30, 1943, after the ghetto resistance had been defeated, the few survivors remained in hiding. From a hiding place crammed with thirty-nine people, Leon Najberg heard the shots executing twenty-four victims in the garden at Zamenhof Street.

Conditions in Lodz ghetto, Europe's second largest, were different. Before the ghetto was established in Baluty, an area of densely populated narrow streets, "in its filth, Baluty had no competition. It held the all-time record," according to Leon Hurwitz.[40] The Marysin area of the ghetto was semirural and would be the site of most garden creation in Lodz. The Nazis simultaneously used the ghetto as part of their extermination program and as a vast labor camp. It is possible to reconstruct the creation and life of gardens in the Lodz ghetto from documents in the Zonabend Collection at YIVO in New York.

Before the war Chaim Rumkowski, the controversial head of the council of Jewish elders, which governed the ghetto, had established an orphanage. Children received instruction on agriculture at the farm run by the orphanage. On May 10, 1940, Rumkowski took over as head of the Department of Garden and Land Cultivation. The group soon offered plots of land to residents and also assumed care of the Jewish cemetery — and by the end of 1940 there were 950 ghetto gardens, likely small ones. Some Jews continued working land outside of the ghetto, but after Germans stopped this practice, workers began "to clean up the ghetto fields and plots . . . in places where, as long as could be remembered, garbage and refuse had covered the ground and foul area had polluted neighboring streets, patches of green grass sprang up."[41] For the first six months of the ghetto, about a thousand persons lived in collectives in Marysin, working the land and organizing cultural events. The Germans dissolved the farms in January 1941, although they allowed some agriculture to continue until the ghetto's final liquidation in August 1944.

In April 1941 the ghetto's department of schools announced: "Children! In order to give the tired and weak ghetto dwellers some rest

Clearing rubble for a garden in the Lodz ghetto.

and fresh air, and in order to make the ghetto beautiful, public lawns and parks with benches are planned. We must protect these places and keep them beautiful — not damage the benches, walk on the grass, pluck at the plants, break off tree branches." At the same time the Bureau of Public Gardens was established in the Marysin to control garden cultivation in that area, about 156 acres enclosed by barbed wire. Dawid Sierakowiak was optimistic: "Most agricultural work in Marysin and on all garden plots has come to a standstill. Nearly all the fields in the ghetto are already plowed, planted, or parceled out by the administration. Quite a wise idea. The grounds around our school are supposed to be cultivated by the students. We have to work for our education. . . . I don't mind the work, though, because I'll get to know the soil a little better. Everything may yet prove useful."[42]

In Lodz it proved difficult to regulate garden use and to secure the gardens, which were, after all, sources of food for tens of thousands of hungry people. The authorities often posted notices attempting to regulate garden practice. There were also instructions on how to protect cultivated areas from damage and theft. In July 1941 there was a notice that if vegetables from the outside did not arrive in the ghetto by August 1, all large garden plots would be subject to expropriation by the community. They had already requisitioned all spring onions and recorded the location of potato plants to discourage owners of garden plots from digging them up prematurely. Sierakowiak wrote, "The only consolation is that the fields are blooming and the crops are supposed to be excellent this year." But soon he added, "All kinds of leaves that seemed inedible before the war (like beet greens, outer cabbage leaves, pigweeds, and a number of others) have become very popular food in the ghetto. All this grass and leaves, however, cannot even minimally satisfy our hunger."

Extremely difficult in an urban setting, garden creation also competed with other needs for land and fuel, such as wood for fences. In March 1941 the Jewish authorities arranged for families without stable incomes to lease plots of twenty square meters, which was seen as sufficient to maintain a family. The department also sold seeds and offered garden instruction. Garden activity continued through 1942. Plots were supposed to be distributed equally, but Jakub Poznanski, an agricultural engineer who worked in the Department of Garden Cultivation, lamented the inequitable distribution of parcels. Members of the ghetto council were privileged with more than their fair share, and this offended his sense of equity.

A gardening consulting service was established along with a lecture series that dealt with the practicalities of scarifying the soil, weeding, hoeing, and dealing with edible weeds. For ten pfennig, one could purchase mimeographed notes of the lectures, along with instructions for growing vegetables. Like any good garden manual, the document offered long catalogs of how much of each species to plant per square meter, what germination and planting methods to use, and other details necessary for optimal cultivation. The service also published a monthly garden calendar titled *Information for Small Gardeners*. The "Garden Calendar for July," dated July 2, 1943, advises that "during July we will reach the peak of our work. Our plants are developing at a top rate." It urges proper watering and tilling and the need to eliminate weeds, "our enemy." It expresses the need to plant only fast-growing vegetables that will ripen before winter: beans, radishes, carrots, and string beans.[43]

Efforts to create gardens and to grow plants did not go unnoticed or unappreciated by other Jews. A surprising number of Oskar Rosenfeld's entries in "Sketches of Ghetto Life" deal with the gardens, their look, creation, and even disputes over territory. Walking through the ghetto, Rosenfeld noticed "a vegetable plot in which some radishes, lettuce, and other things grow, even right next to the open latrine; an appealing little garden," and then added that it was "cared for by hands that until now never touched a thing in nature." He also reported the sensation caused by his neighbor's cucumbers.[44]

Oskar Singer found that "every inch of soil has been planted with vegetables." The ghetto vegetable gardens gave "it a thoroughly neat and rural impression." He also describes the famous "ghetto salad," a vegetable mixture made from any scraps that were not rotten and filled with any available spices to make it palatable. They made 1,500 kilos of *salatka* a day. Dawid Sierakowiak informs us that both his parents worked in the gardens. "I went to see Mom on the garden where she now works. She sits crouched on an upturned pot, and prepares clean soil under beet seedlings. If I were in her place, I would gorge myself."[45]

Roman Kent was born in 1929 in Lodz. His family had a villa outside of the city with a caretaker who lived there year-round. Realizing that a garden could help feed the family, Kent's father acquired several plots in the ghetto. His memoir recounts the stages and obstacles of garden making in Lodz. After plots were allotted and boundaries were drawn, the family removed the stones from the rocky soil by hand—it was backbreaking work. With just a spade and rake they tilled the soil and planted vegetables, doing all the watering with buckets. In the first year the harvest was modest with the produce stored in a crawl space. The second year he says they were "professionals." They germinated seeds in their apartment, and they planted lettuce amid the potatoes. Finding time to garden was challenging, for he and his brother, the prime laborers, worked all day in the factory, sewing knapsacks for the army. By sneaking away from the factory to work in the garden, they risked being caught.[46]

Kent and his brother were more successful than most. Oskar Singer recorded the problems facing gardeners in "Something About Horticulture in the Ghetto." He found "that only in the rarest of cases is the ground thoroughly prepared" for cultivation. People who were "reduced to skin and bones" did not have the energy to water, there were no tools, and a watering can was "almost a luxury item." He asserts that "the person outside the ghetto will never understand that the kinds of things that a gardener takes for granted, which otherwise have hardly anything to do with money, were almost insoluble in the ghetto."[47]

Polish winters are harsh, with temperatures far below freezing, and summers can be oppressive. In the summer of 1942 the temperature rose to 104 degrees Fahrenheit. The heat and caterpillars

Hauling water for
vegetable gardens
in the Lodz ghetto.

destroyed many crops, especially cabbage. Workers "had thought
that by Sisyphean labor they would be able to set a little something
aside for the hard winter months to come, they believed in some better tomorrow, assured them by the labor done in the hours free from
the demands of the ghetto, and now, suddenly, disillusionment and
despair!"[48]

In the midst of a crop loss that meant more death from starvation,
the ideal of the garden was still a hopeful dream. In January 1942 and
again in September 1942 there were brutal *Aktions,* mass deportations
from Lodz of Jews (70,000) and Roma (5,000), to the death camp at
Chelmno. Deportations of this scale ceased until May 1944. Then the
Nazis unleashed direct violence, slaughtering hospital patients and
doctors. Despite the closure of schools and all cultural institutions,
the remaining ghetto residents persisted with acts of spiritual resistance until the ghetto's demise.

In the summer of 1942, a report on agriculture notes an ample
spring harvest and an indication of the character of ghetto gardens:
"The ghetto has many unique features, but the fencing around the
small garden plots in the city is unforgettable. Anything that can protect a scrap of ground from being trampled or pilfered is put into service." Being too precious as a fuel, wood wasn't used as fencing material, but ghetto residents were ingenious in scavenging for iron or
metal to use to construct garden fences. Such protections, however,

"only constitute[d] a sort of moral barrier." In *Children and Play in the Holocaust,* George Eisen offers the insight that play served as a "protective cloak—a spiritual shelter from which the wounds of the ghetto would not seem as appalling."[49]

The report notes that, by 1942, the population of the ghetto was down to about 85,000, or just over half of what it had been when the Nazis sealed the ghetto three years earlier. With food scarce and many people starving, "every square inch of ground is, of course, used to grow vegetables." But there was precious little soil in the urban sections of the city. Flowers had virtually disappeared from the city, not only because there was no way to acquire seeds or bulbs, but also because, as soon as something flowered, it was "quickly stripped of [its] blossoms," stolen either to horde its beauty or to be eaten.[50]

With so little green available in the city to relieve the eye and calm the spirit, after working all day in the city residents walked daily to the fields of the Marysin, where they could see something living and put their hands into the dirt. Some constructed little huts — crude echoes of cottages on allotment gardens — where they spent their time. On hot nights people slept out-of-doors in courtyards and gardens. And fruit trees had to be guarded day and night against pilferage.

In the fall after the 1943 harvest, each *dzialka* (parcel) was carefully gleaned. By Nazi design, little produce was now entering the ghetto, so the Jewish authorities halved the rations. According to Rosenfeld: "In these difficult days, one can observe people equipped with bags and knapsacks, who suddenly appear in the dzialkas. They are looking for something to eat, for anything that the owner forgot to harvest or did not consider worth harvesting; unappealing leek stalks or unsuccessful onions, small, stunted cabbage or shriveled kohlrabi. . . . The hungry stomach is not fastidious, it wants to be filled. . . . Even a few beet leaves can keep one alive for an hour or two."

The following spring (1944) was the ghetto's last. Any available ground was commandeered by the Jewish authorities for the general good. "Where a wooden house was standing just a few days ago, then the Coal Department tore it down for firewood, the broken bricks, stones, and rubbish are now being cleared away and the optimistic owner of this dzialka has begun to till the soil with spade and crowbar." The ground would not yield, however: "not even paltry buraki [beets] — not to mention the nobler vegetables — will grow on rubble and ashes. One hardly knows whether to laugh or cry at the sight of an emaciated Jew desperately striking his crowbar against the merciless, intractable ground."

Times were desperate, and the ghetto chroniclers observed the extremes of garden behavior. Rosenfeld writes of coming upon two neighbors arguing vehemently over which of them owned a strip of soil 16½ feet long by only 2½ inches wide. Rosenfeld wondered, "what's going to grow in that little strip anyway? If farmed right, three heads of cabbage."[51]

In the summer of 1944, weeks before the Nazis would liquidate the ghetto, starvation was rampant in Lodz and mobs from the city descended on the Marysin gardens. Roman Kent and his fellow gardeners gathered together to protect their crops, but to no avail: "During the rampage, there were hundreds of people, and whatever they saw growing was hurriedly pulled out of the ground. Within two hours, it was all over. There was no evidence remaining that anything had even been planted." Kent stood sobbing in the denuded field he had worked so arduously. But, ever resourceful, he and his brother returned the next day to harvest the potatoes buried in earth.

Kent says simply that the gardens were a "lifeline to life" essential to his family's survival.[52]

There is a common fascination with gardens that are created in unexpected places, where the location is unconventional or imaginative. It is rare that a garden can be the source of levity, but there is a report on what some called the Eighth Wonder of the World, the mobile garden: "A worker in the tailoring plant who had a small garden last year but lost it because of the new 'agriculture policy' quickly resolved to fill an old baby carriage with soil and plant a few onion bulbs. He now pushes his garden to the workshop every day and parks it in a sunny spot in the courtyard; from the window he can easily guard his 'garden plot.' The mobile dzialka is quite a conversation piece, and the shrewd farmer has people laughing with him, not at him."[53]

Oskar Singer was struck by the appearance of onions everywhere after a shipment of bulbs arrived. "The onion is the flower of the ghetto. Last year, we recall, there were beets in every window, with an occasional head of lettuce; now onions, onions everywhere. In apartments that were once stores, the tenants now use the display windows as onion plantations. No containers are required. They have simply covered the bottoms of the display windows with soil and planted onions. . . . for anyone who was not assigned a garden this time around, well, he has his onion dzialka on the windowsill."[54]

In June 1944 Rosenfeld recorded a world where the persistence of the ordinary was extraordinary, where the forces of life and death were palpable.

> People go their own way. Some pass by holding flowers, hedge blossoms and peonies, jasmine and other June flowers. People chat, stroll. The dzialkas are full of ghetto dwellers at work. And yet there is a pall over the ghetto. Twenty-five transports have been announced. . . . Everyone is losing a relative, a friend, a roommate, a colleague. And yet — Jewish faith in a justice that will ultimately triumph does not permit extreme pessimism. People try to console themselves, deceive themselves in some way. But nearly everyone says to himself and others: God only knows who will be better off; the person who stays here or the person who leaves![55]

The final liquidation of the ghetto was six weeks later in August. On January 15, 1945, the Russians liberated what were the ruins of the Lodz ghetto. About 204,000 Jews had lived there: 77,000 of them were murdered at Chelmno, 65,000 murdered at Auschwitz, 43,500 died of starvation and disease in the ghetto, and 11,000 were deported to labor camps. Only about 10,000 Lodz ghetto inhabitants survived.

Stories from the Kovno ghetto illustrate the garden's promise to nurture the spirit as well as the body. On December 8, 2003, in the YIVO library in New York, I sat listening to Esther Mishkin, a short women with a brilliant smile. She vividly recalled events of sixty years earlier. Her father, Reuben Yitchak, planted a garden on 16 Parvenu Street in the Kovno ghetto. A rabbi and *shochet,* her father asked his cousin, a pediatrician, if he would make a garden in their yard. Yitchak planted cucumbers, tomatoes, and potatoes. His daughter could not recall where he got seeds for the garden. "Did you work in the garden?" I asked. "Sometimes," she said, but added that her father "adopted the whole thing." She recalls observing her father watching the garden grow. She remembers "him sitting in the garden, his vegetables, it became part of him." The output was not substantial — he grew only food for their table, but it meant much more. She said it was important that "something was growing there." About her father she said that watching the garden grow "gives him a feeling that something is

Cultivating a tomato patch in the Kovno ghetto.

growing, that we can survive somehow."[56] His wish was fulfilled only for his daughter: the remainder of her family died in the Holocaust.

Mishkin was eighteen when she escaped in the last few days before the ghetto's demise in 1944. She made it to Israel in the mass illegal immigration before Israel was established in 1948, emigrating to the United States eight years later. A retired social worker, she now is a volunteer at YIVO. In 1997 she returned to Kovno for the first time and visited the site of the garden. It was much smaller than she remembered, but she thought it looked worse, for the land was no longer maintained as it had been in the ghetto. She noted with some pride that the Jews had kept the ghetto in Kovno very clean.

Vilna native Nina Holzman had been a young teenager in the Kovno ghetto. Her father made a garden and sold the extra produce. She recalls, "Whoever wanted some greens in Kovno, in the ghetto, would come to us and we grew carrots, and beets, and tomatoes, and cucumbers. . . . It was a large lot completely unused piece of land. He [her father] dug it all up." He fertilized it while the family weeded and cared for it. She proudly remembers that "we had tomatoes until December."[57]

Another Kovno story illustrates an inherent conflict between the

With a yoke across his shoulders, a man carries water to his plot in the Kovno ghetto.

patience and time required to wait for a garden to mature to realize its full potential and life-sustaining produce, and the bodily imperative to eat whatever is available to alleviate — momentarily — hunger and the prospect of starvation.

Memoirist William Mishell had been a university student and in 1940 worked part-time as a contractor. In *Kaddish for Kovno* he recalled an event in the second week of October 1941 when the ghetto's vegetable gardens were raided by starving Jews, much like the events Roman Kent reported in Lodz in 1944. A week earlier, two thousand Jews were massacred at the Ninth Fort in what became known as the Small Ghetto Aktion, and on October 28 ten thousand more were exterminated in the Big Aktion. Hunger had driven people to steal still-immature vegetables from those living in "peasant homes [that] had little vegetable gardens." To stop the pilfering, the Jewish authorities announced that "all vegetable gardens were ghetto property and nobody was to touch them. The administration was planning to gather the vegetables from all gardens and distribute them to the entire population. . . .

"The fact that the committee intended to appropriate all the vegetable gardens had now become public knowledge. Nobody, however, was willing to entrust the committee with this task. Everybody figured that most of the vegetables would end up with the people having a hand in the pot and the population at large would remain with nothing." The very next day, the desperate people invaded the gardens and clawed out of the soil every bit of green. "It looked like a locust plague had descended on green fields. At first the Jewish police tried to stop the mob, but it was hopeless. Driven by hunger, people not only attacked the police, but also fought with each other for as little as one potato. When people living in houses which had no garden saw what was going on, they, too, entered the melee. There were now people heaped on top of each other until every green spot was covered with humanity, fighting for a share of the crop. Within a couple hours . . . not a single green leaf was left in the ground. When there was nothing else to dig up the mob dispersed." Mishell lamented the "tremendous loss of food to the ghetto as a whole" and seemed unable to grasp the desperation that drove the mob: "Had the population waited for several weeks the vegetables would have been twice their size, but nobody was willing to wait."[58]

With rations from Germans providing only one-third the minimum calories for survival, growing vegetables was essential, but it wasn't enough — smuggling was also negotiated with Lithuanians outside the ghetto. Conflicts with the German authorities increased as the Germans made it more and more difficult for the ghetto to secure ample seeds and tools. Their lack of cooperation was vindictive and did little to hide their ultimate motivation. Inside the Kovno ghetto, the Jewish council had about six acres of vegetable gardens in four locations between the ghetto proper and the Vilija River. Shlomo Kelzon had three hundred persons working there, supervised by Misha Mudrich. An agronomist and Zionist activist who had been director of the Jewish People's Bank, Kelzon said proudly, "Even when I was in banking I followed with great interest the literature and the developments in agricultural research; now I can put this knowledge to use for the benefit of the people of the Ghetto."[59]

In an attempt to ensure equitable distribution of the crops, the Jewish Council hired children as special garden guards known as Eshel (Irgun Shmirat LeGanim, the Organization of Garden Guards). Chaim Nachman Shapiro, eldest son of Chief Rabbi Shapiro and head of Culture and Education of the Jewish Council, organized the Eshel to stop theft from the gardens and to provide "clandestine education." The goal of the organization "besides vigilance, includes Hebrew education and study," wrote Shapiro. The young guards began their work in the gardens in June 1942.

Two women collect potatoes in the Kovno ghetto.

Avraham Tory recorded in his diary that hunger that year was indeed diminished, due primarily to the efforts of the gardening authority and to the residents' diligent and careful work in the vegetable gardens. Their success was such that "the German local authorities and the Gestapo have had to acknowledge that the vegetable gardens in the Ghetto are better cultivated than those in the city. The Jewish genius, and the talent displayed by the Jewish people for adapting themselves to any conditions, has been given expression in the form of vegetable plots and fields in the Ghetto."[60] The council even awarded prizes to the gardeners. Having learned from experience, the following year ghetto inhabitants waited for vegetables to ripen.

A few other natural places in the ghetto offered comfort. Eighteen-year-old Ilya Gerber found pleasures at the beach, an area along the banks of the Vilija River. "The best thing about coming to the beach is that you forget the situation in which we find ourselves. You cheer up, you play, you do a bit of sports. If the weather is good, the beach is filled with Jews — you couldn't fit a pin in. . . . I find freedom here. . . . The sounds of the ghetto have no access to the beach."[61]

In E. L. Doctorow's novel *The City of God* a character appears who

A member of Eshel (Irgun Shmirat LeGanim), the garden guards in the Kovno ghetto. *Eshel* is Hebrew for tamarisk, the tree Abraham planted.

may be a fictionalized version of agronomist Shlomo Kelzon. In the novel, his daughter, Sarah Blumenthal, remembers: "Every morning when I arose, I looked out across the street at the vegetable garden that my father had laid out for the community. Even in the cold, harsh weather, with the ground bare but for the dried-up stalks of plant stubble, I could see the furrows that outlined the different sections and imagine his thoughts as he worked out what should be planted and where. In the afternoons I liked to walk there when it was dark enough. Nobody bothered me."[62]

In July 1944 the Germans destroyed the Kovno ghetto. On August 1 when the Soviet Army entered Kovno, a few survivors emerged from their hiding places in bunkers.

As the Nazis took power in Germany, their persecution of Jews pervaded all aspects of life. Even before restricting habitation to ghettos, Jews were forbidden to enter and use public open spaces. Given the horrific conditions of the ghettos of Eastern Europe, a garden or park might be seen as luxury, but the desire for some contact with the nat-

The vegetable garden of the Lodz ghetto hospital at 36 Lagiewnicka Street sported a scarecrow, complete with a yellow star.

ural world and a quest for the restoration of some semblance of normalcy represented in the common landscapes of garden and park was critical. A garden was a minimal form of modest recompense. Its creation was one of many mechanisms directed at individual and community survival.

We have already examined the physical survival provided by ghetto gardens. We turn now to the spiritual resistance put up by Jews in ghettos against the Nazis and to the spiritual sustenance their gardens yielded.

There was a stark contrast between prewar and pre-ghetto life and the current reality, both in the physical landscape and the mental landscape. Memories of places ghetto inhabitants had known before the war provided solace, but they were also potent reminders of the gravity of their situation and of those other places and times.

In an atmosphere of mounting repression and persecution, the Jews carried on vigorous cultural and spiritual activities, clubs, study circles, lectures, drama, holiday celebrations — what Yitskhok Rudashevski defines as "passive resistance," which "symbolizes the Jew's enduring faith in the redemptive power of the spirit."[63]

People sought protection from the forces around them, but they also offered resistance to those forces. Actions directed toward pre-

The staff working in the garden of the Lodz ghetto hospital.

serving one's person, dignity, and humanity took great courage. Garden creation was only one of many such actions. Gardens gave ghetto residents both psychological protection against harmful forces and an outlet for assertive action exactly against those horrors in an attempt to preserve life and dignity. The horror of the Holocaust was caused by humans, but so too are the human responses to it in all their manifestations. People worked individually and in concert with one another in efforts ranging from direct opposition and resistance to passive and spiritual resistance, against what Raoul Hilberg calls the "machinery of destruction."

The Nazis' program was one of deliberate dehumanization and degradation. The slogan of Jewish communal activity in the Warsaw ghetto was "live in dignity and die in dignity!" But how does one sustain or even enhance one's dignity? How does one remain fully human? One way is through cultural continuity, honoring and even reasserting the habits and traditions that have served you well. The communal institutions and spirit of the Jewish community were aids to survival, requiring great collective resolution and courage. Mutual aid, education, cultural activities, and work were all methods of defying the Nazis' evil intention. The range of actions is sometimes surprising and invariably inspiring. Chaim Kaplan found that "there is a lot of frivolity in the ghetto, in order to somewhat lessen its sorrow. In the daytime when the sun is shining, the ghetto groans. But at night everyone is dancing even though the stomach is empty. . . . Every dance is a protest against our oppressors." Stanislaw Adler used a flowering metaphor to find that "in spite of all, the ghetto had produced some remarkable standards of conduct, and the cultural life among the doomed masses has not died, but rather blossomed."[64]

Much like the creative activity of artists, which allowed an imaginative escape from the conditions of the ghetto, so too the garden. In addition to physical sustenance, the garden could offer a form of spiritual nourishment. However, there are important distinctions to be made depending on the type and the spirit of garden work. Forced and slave labor was not resistance, but voluntary activity could be. There could be a fine line, for surely the conditions leading to garden making were forced, while the response was an imaginative and creative one. Perhaps the distinction hearkens back to the labors of Adam in Eden; tending the garden as a steward before the Fall and working the land as a laborer after the expulsion from Eden. It is essential to remember that *garden* is not only a noun but also a verb: the work of the garden affords it own meaning and pleasures, to both the mind and the body and perhaps the soul, as well.

Josef Zelkowicz, one of the chroniclers of life in Lodz, is credited with authoring "Blessings of the Earth." In it he explains that ghetto inhabitants gardened with the zeal of converts, merging into a faceless, undifferentiated group. This communal aspect was exemplified by the sight, after a day in the factories, of the workers already in the fields: "your impression is that [the] population of the ghetto has lost its face and is nothing more than backsides, sticking out from amid green leaves and thick stalks." Whole families are involved in the endeavor to coax produce out of the earth. "All the work is done kneeling, bowed, bent over — one sees no heads, no faces — some sort of wild, passionate service to God, that must be carried out on one's knees. Some sort of desire to emphasize that to farm, no head, no face is needed — only hands! *Nu,* and feet, which even when bowed and bent, can stand on the earth."[65]

British geographer Steve Pile contrasts what he calls spaces of domination with spaces of resistance. These can have external and internal dimensions. While the Germans kept the Jews as prisoners in the ghetto, they could assert an internal space of resistance, a "head

Working with a crude plow in the Kovno ghetto.

life." Garden making can surely be seen as one of many defense mechanisms. While they were not soldiers, ghetto residents were engaged in a battle. Isaiah Trunk offers a potent military image when he describes the ghetto population as creating "an effective armor against degradation of their humanity and Jewishness."[66]

In Lodz Dr. Israel Milejkowski thought that "the Ghetto's chief curse lies in the fact that we cannot be creative here. Creative is what we were before the Ghetto, when we created cultural values for ourselves and all mankind, for we are capable of creativity, but only in more or less free conditions. In the Ghetto this is impossible." While it was almost impossible to exercise, the creative impulse was strong, in the creation of art and culture, but also maintenance of a creative spirit, the critical ability to recognize the beautiful, good and ideal. "*Endurance and survival* must be our current slogan," said Milejkowski. As forms of spiritual resistance, gardens could contribute to both. This was an internal struggle as well, a preservation of an inner freedom and sense of self while in bondage. Oskar Rosenfeld recognized the importance of the psychological dimension, when he came to the realization that "calming our nerves is as important as eating."[67]

Gardens could address both of these concerns. Morale is a term most often used in relationship to soldiers, but ghetto inhabitants were civilian combatants in the war against the Nazis. The garden could help sustain one's spirit and buoy morale.

People overcome danger and fear to take heroic action, which transcends the normal range and confounds our expectations. These were heroic gardens and gardeners. This was a heroism of everyday life that took its own kind of courage. Pushed past the limits of endurance, people nevertheless persisted, aware of their tenuous hold on retaining a sense of basic humanity. The testimonies of those who were there are most telling. Eisen quotes Warsaw ghetto hero Genia Silkes: "To live one more day is resistance. Amidst the dysentery and typhus, the starvation, is resistance. To teach, and learn is resistance." The chroniclers and diarists often lament a failure to live up to the ideals of the community, but given the situation, as Marek Stok wrote while hiding in Warsaw, Jews showed "just how resistant and adaptable they are by nature. Deprived of everything, subjected to constant humiliation, they are bowed but not broken."[68]

Each of us who reads these accounts finds different meaning and lessons, or finds none at all, for it is difficult to draw conclusions or derive meaning from these defining events in human history. Primo Levi thought that one consequence of the Holocaust was that it brought shame on our image of human nature. Yitzhak "Antek" Zuckerman was one of the organizers and leaders of the Warsaw Ghetto uprising. He survived the war and became one of the founders of the Ghetto Fighters Kibbutz (Lohamai Ha-Getaot) in Israel. Antek thought that the most important lessons from the uprising were not military but about the human spirit.

At their best, people acted in accord with their principles and ideals. Stanislaw Adler found that the Jewish population in Warsaw, though "robbed and many times resettled, had not retreated to selfish egotism. Almost everyone shared in his fellows the remnants he succeeded in rescuing. The more suffering one experienced, the more ready one was to help others."[69] Peah, a section of the *Talmud*, prescribes that a corner of the field is to be left unharvested for the poor to harvest, for with ownership of property comes a social and ethical responsibility to the community. Understanding that those who have little are under even greater hardship, it also proclaims that in times of hardship the proportion of the field to be left for the poor must be larger. This precept was lived out in the ghettos: in the creation of and energy put into Toporol and other Jewish organizations; in the usurpation of vegetable gardens by the Jewish authorities in Kovno when starvation threatened the population; and in many other episodes of compassion and charity.

These actions were also translated into a religious precept, Kiddush Hahayyim. In 1940 in Warsaw Rabbi Isaac Nissenbaum said, "It is time for Kiddush Hahayyim, the sanctification of life, and not Kiddush Hashem, the holiness of martyrdom. In the past the enemies of the Jews sought the soul of the Jew, and so it was proper for the Jew to sanctify the name of God by sacrificing his body in martyrdom, in that manner preserving what the enemy sought to take from him. But now it is the body of the Jew that the oppressor demands. For this reason it is up to the Jew to defend his body, to preserve his life."[70] Any acts of spiritual resistance and spiritual shelter, including garden making, were contributions to Kiddush Hahayyim, the sanctification of life.

Any expression of hope or faith in the future was in opposition to fear and despair. Jews needed hope to cope with their situation, but the Germans also manipulated the situation, knowing ghetto residents needed a modicum of hope in order to sustain their labor, while keeping them unaware of their inevitable fate. Jews had a history of surviving oppression. They did not know that what they were experiencing this time was different; it was genocidal anti-Semitism, where historical experience and a tradition of accommodation and coping would not succeed. Engelking suggests that hope needed to be calibrated, that a certain level aided survival, but that too little or too much could prove fatal. There was what Alan Adelson calls the "instinctual struggle to hold on to human experience: family, art, education, sex, religion, hope. But also of the progressive loss of those values to grief, exhaustion, and starvation."[71]

Fear was pervasive. There was little a garden could do to combat this except temporarily assuage the relentless stress. There is a distinction between the garden as a refuge and as a respite. The garden as refuge suggests that it can function as a sanctuary, a place protected from outside forces. A respite is only a temporary material or psychological sanctuary, for one will soon be at the mercy of external conditions that lay siege to one's shelter. The ghetto gardens offered places of sensory difference, of quiet, shelter, and elements of the natural world. It offered opportunities for calm, a change of mood, even

Stafania Ross, wife of the photographer Henryk Ross, in a garden in the Lodz ghetto.

a temporary forgetfulness about one's conditions. In the ghetto, gardens were only brief respites, but that does not lessen their significance for those moments.

In an interview with a survivor, Irena, Engelking describes how "we lived relatively normally, we ate, we slept, we made love, were unfaithful to one another, we experienced completely civilian tragedies. . . . It's deep down in human beings, it wasn't really conscious, it's a defense mechanism."[72] Normal behavior in abnormal conditions took courage. The ordinary became extraordinary. The expected unexpected. Who imagined gardens in the ghetto? The garden was also a small but potent reminder of a life free from deprivation and humiliation. Gardens conformed to the expected cycle of seasons and growth and life; a garden was a demonstration of life in order, not a world turned upside down.

Each ghetto was different, but until the summer of 1942 in Warsaw most persons there believed they would survive the war. By the fall rumors of the death camps had slowly penetrated the ghetto. Yet hope, ever resilient, persisted. Only forty thousand Jews were left in the ghetto when Stanislaw Sznapman wrote about hopeful news from the Russian front: "We want to live to see light triumph over darkness, justice over tyranny and freedom over oppression and terror. We yearn to build a better world. But will we make it? Is it not too late?"[73]

Simha Bunim Shayevitsh's poem "Lekh Lekho," written in the Lodz ghetto, moves from telling of the extreme burden on the Jews to recognizing life's beauty to, finally, rousing those around him to strength and resolve:

> So let us not weep, let us not
> Moan, and to spite our enemies
> Let us smile, only smile, that they
> May be amazed at what Jews are capable of.[74]

Shayevitsh's exhortations encouraged spiritual resistance.

In the Vilna spring of 1943, Herman Kruk noted that like the previous year gardens were being planted in almost all the ghetto's courtyards. "Instead of flowers over us, we will make our courtyards bloom for the time being," he wrote, perhaps with some awareness of his fate, but also in a spirit of resistance.[75]

FOUR ❧ Barbed-Wire Gardens

*Allied Prisoners of War and Civilian Internees
in Europe and Asia in the World Wars*

> The joys of summer were made a little real by the pretty flower-beds
> that we planted around and opposite our barracks, and by the biscuit
> tins filled with pansies, violets, and bluebells that were suspended
> along the side of the wooden staircase. The cost of these floral deco-
> rations was borne by inmates of each barrack, whilst the gardening
> was done voluntarily by experts and amateurs. These flower-beds
> provided cheerful surroundings on a summer's afternoon for a siesta
> in a deckchair.
>
> ISRAEL COHEN, writing from Ruhleben

ALONGSIDE WAGING WAR, armies take prisoners, capturing innocent civilians as well as enemy combatants. Historically, the fate of the
prisoners was brutal and tragic: most were slaughtered on the battlefield, while others were sold into slavery or held for ransom. As war
became more "civilized," these practices were seen as barbaric. Prisoner exchanges and paroles were more common in the nineteenth
century than previously, but armies were still reluctant to return
potential combatants to their adversaries. The horrors of the Crimean
War led the Red Cross to administer aid to the wounded and to the
first Geneva Convention in 1864. This mission was extended to prisoners of war during the Franco-Prussian War in 1870. The era also
brought attempts to codify the behavior of combatants. The Hague
Conference of 1899 led to the Regulations Respecting the Laws and
Customs of War, leading to a second conference in 1907 stating that
POWs were to be treated humanely. After the Great War, the 1929
Prisoner of War Code of the Geneva Convention spelled out the
rights of prisoners in great detail. The conventions prescribed standards for humane treatment, housing, food, medical care, mail, religious freedom, and ultimately repatriation, and proscribed certain
treatment. Like many documents of international law, however, the
standard detailed in the Hague and Geneva Conventions has rarely

been honored. Yet the law, and its 1949 revision, remains the criteria by which to measure the behavior of captors and the conditions under which prisoners are kept.

The experience of being a prisoner of war or an interned civilian is inevitably traumatic. However, the experience of individual prisoners varies depending on location and the principals — not just prisoners but captors, guards, and commandants — directly involved: some prisoners might receive relatively humane treatment and even modest comfort (although this is rare), whereas other prisoners might be subjected to extreme deprivation and sadistic brutality.

The prisoner-of-war camp is a product of modern warfare. There have been POW camps in other than the twentieth-century world wars, and there are thousands still imprisoned as of this writing, many in what are euphemistically called "detention facilities." Conditions are often miserable, with internees ill-clothed, housed in overcrowded conditions, worked to exhaustion, and suffering physical privation from hunger and disease. Prisoners suffer the psychological trauma of imprisonment, boredom, depression, and loss of contact with the world outside. Under the best conditions, they are incarcerated, their movements are constrained, and they must await the termination of hostilities to be repatriated. Prisoners of victors have often fared better than those captured by the defeated forces, but they have also been the victims of revenge.

This chapter focuses primarily on the Allies who were in the POW camps and civilian internment camps of World Wars I and II. These camps share some of the qualities of other types of involuntary incarceration: concentration camps, refugee camps, World War II ghettos, and slave labor camps.

In the total world wars of the twentieth century, millions of persons were taken prisoner. For some imprisonment was short-lived; for others, especially those captured at the beginning of the war, it lasted years.

The belligerents were not prepared for the scale and scope of prisoners taken in World War I, nor were the agencies that attempted to monitor their welfare and provide assistance. The statistics are approximate but staggering: Germany held 2.8 million Allied prisoners — then equivalent to the population of Chicago — of twenty-nine nationalities in 150 camps. The Germans also put prisoners to work in over two thousand detachments throughout Germany. Captain Horace Gilliland, who was captured at Ypres in 1914 and later escaped, reported that prisoners were "leased out like slaves to the owners of factories, farms, and mines."[1] Austria-Hungary held 1.75 million prisoners, largely poor and illiterate soldiers from Russia, Italy, Serbia, and Romania. There were a half million German and Austrian prisoners in almost nine hundred Russian and Siberian camps. At war's end France had over 400,000 POWs in ninety permanent camps. About 145,000 were in camps in Britain, including 30,000 German civilians interned on the Isle of Man.

Before the creation of the League of Nations or the United Nations, the Red Cross and the YMCA acted as observers and as international relief agencies providing assistance. A Red Cross division dealt specifically with parcels, mail, and money, and many nations had prisoners' welfare organizations, such as the British Prisoners Fund and regimental associations. Conrad Hoffman, secretary of the International Committee of the YMCAs in charge of work with POWs in Germany, in his report of German camps noted that British, French, and Italian prisoners were well off since their governments sent food to their captured military, unlike the Russian, Serb, and Romanian governments. Hoffman also reported that the Germans initially housed French, British, and Russian prisoners together, but there was so much friction between the troops that the nationalities were separated. As the war progressed and conditions deteriorated in Germany for civilians, they did so for prisoners, as well; the standard of living for POWs is generally similar to that experienced by the poorest civilians in the area. In general, conditions in Germany deteriorated the farther east one went. In East Prussia prisoners lived mostly in dugouts rather than barracks, and malnutrition was common.

Carl Dennett was the American Red Cross deputy commissioner to Switzerland in charge of finding, feeding, clothing, and otherwise caring for U.S. prisoners in German prison camps. He helped establish Camp Help Committees, to which prisoners elected members (the YMCA set up similar committees). Relief aid was funneled through these groups, which organized and distributed supplies and initiated assistance projects in the camps. Dennett found Germans' treatment of prisoners wanting: "Germany . . . notoriously failed to even provide them with the necessities of life, and it is a fact beyond dispute that the ravages of disease, including tuberculosis, due to malnutrition, and even starvation, have killed tens of thousands of prisoners in the hands of the German military forces."[2]

The onset of World War I saw thousands of individuals suddenly classified as enemy aliens. In England, 26,000 Germans found themselves prisoners. The Germans interned 4,000 British subjects, some longtime residents of Germany, but also visiting businessmen, seamen, and students, at Ruhleben, a racetrack just outside of Berlin. Negotiations for an exchange of these civilian internees sputtered throughout the war, with little accomplished.

By World War II the parameters of total war, which make little distinction between combatants and civilians, were well established. The millions of captives, both military and civilian, and the high numbers of internment sites were unprecedented, according to journalist Ronald Bailey. By war's end an estimated 35 million prisoners had been taken, 11 million of them German. But most of these did not become inmates of POW camps. All combatants created POW camps both near the areas of combat and in their homelands. By the end of the war, Germany had 248 camps and 2.39 million prisoners, including 225,996 U.S. and British. The United States and Great Britain had 193,637 Germans in hundreds of camps. The Japanese imprisoned 132,000 British and U.S. soldiers as well as 75,000 British, U.S., Dutch, and other allied civilians.

Although the Geneva Convention had been signed in 1929 by all World War II belligerents except Russia, it had little effect on treatment of POWs. Although a signatory, Japan never ratified the convention and ignored it throughout World War II, along with the Germans and Russians. Instead, prisoners' nationality, who their captors were, and where they were taken prisoner were the primary determinants of the fate of POWs. Hitler, Stalin, and Emperor Hirohito exhorted their soldiers to fight until death. Because the Japanese abhorred surrender, which they viewed as gross cowardice, indeed few allowed themselves to be taken prisoner, and their own treatment of prisoners was notorious: 28 percent of Allied prisoners of the Japanese died in captivity (on the Bataan Death March, the percentage spiked to between 40 and 60). The loss of life on the Eastern Front was also horrific. When Germany invaded Russia in June 1941, there was a mass slaughter of prisoners on both sides. Between 65 and 80 percent of the 5 million Russians and 45 to 50 percent of the 2 to 3 million Germans captured on the Eastern Front never returned home, whereas 99 percent of the 5 million Germans in U.S. captivity returned home after the war.[3] Four hundred thousand Germans had been housed in stateside camps that by World War II standards were luxurious rest camps.

In his study of POW narratives, Robert Doyle observes that "in capture, the individual separates from his primary culture and begins the
journey into a world of chaos. The prison landscape is the body of that
chaos; it represents a place of evil, a place so horrible that only the
most graphic terms can describe it."[4]

Prisoners had to be incarcerated and looked after — or neglected,
either willfully or unintentionally — by their mortal enemies. In both
world wars, the convention that required better treatment for officers
meant that some were housed in hotels, libraries, or even châteaus.
However, most POW camps were created from the ground up, sometimes by prisoner labor. Daniel McCarthy, a U.S. doctor, reported on
the conditions for British and Serbian POWs in Germany before the
United States entered World War I. The typical camp, built to house
between 10,000 and 12,000, was up to two miles long. Low wooden
barracks were organized into units: blocks or battalions of 2,000 men
each, and 10 barracks, each housing a company of 200 men. For each
division of 1,500 men there were latrines and wash houses and one
kitchen. McCarthy found that "even in well kept camps they appear
sordid and unkempt." Surrounding each camp were watchtowers and
two rows of barbed wire twenty feet apart.

At a camp named Minden, he noted that prisoners were confined
to their block area, where their view was restricted entirely to the
confines of the camp and the sky overhead. He saw no evidence of cultivation in the block where noncommissioned officers were confined:
"the surface area is of hard yellow clay without any grass or other evidence of vegetation." In the area housing enlisted men, however, was
evidence of care and morale in the form of a "few flowers . . . grown
in the window tops of the barracks."[5] At the camp where Horace
Gilliland was interned, a muddy exercise yard was surrounded by
wire, and the noxious smells from the latrine and the rubbish heap in
their midst saturated everything.

One change since World War I was that large numbers of prisoners were anticipated in World War II. The Germans established a
hierarchy of camps with a specific terminology: *Lager* is German for
camp; *Stalag* was the shortened term for *Stammlager,* the prison camp
for noncommissioned officers and enlisted men; *Oflag* (*Offizieren-
lager*), a camp for commissioned officers; and *Luftlager* (*Luftwaffelager*)
or *Stalag Luft* was an airman's camp. A prisoner of war was a *Kriegs-*

gefangenen, shortened by the British to "Kriegies," their proud slang for a POW.

As in World War I, castles, forts, and schools were pressed into service in Germany to house prisoners, though in World War II the POW camp was most common. Stalag Luft 3 at Sagan, 90 miles southeast of Berlin, was typical. Originally a prison for British and Canadian soldiers, at the end of the war it held a majority of American soldiers (about 95,000 U.S. soldiers were German POWs). It grew into a large, overcrowded complex of six compounds with 10,000 prisoners. The perimeter was lined with two lines of nine-foot-high barbed-wire fences, with additional barbed wire tangled between the fences. Thirty feet from the fence, a warning wire marked no-man's-land — you were shot if you crossed this boundary. Odell Meyers spent over two and half years at Stalag Luft, which he described as looking like a "temporary scab," from which the prisoners could see the world only through barbed wire.[6]

In Asia conditions were generally worse. The Japanese had made no provisions to take prisoners; they ran out of barbed wire to encircle the camps and had provided no training for those running the camps. The Japanese had 227 POW camps scattered across the western Pacific on Japanese islands and on captured territories in Indonesia, the Philippines, Singapore, and Hong Kong. As had happened in Europe, existing institutions were taken over for use as prison camps, including Stanley Prison and portions of St. Steven's College in Hong Kong. In Singapore, a large portion of Changi Island became a POW camp and was also a transit point for prisoners as well as some civilian internees. Changi's prisoner population vacillated between 5,000 and 45,000 as the Japanese used more prisoners for work parties as the war progressed.

The contrast between setting and circumstance could be striking. In Sergeant-Major P. H. Romney's letter diary, he wrote: "It was not always easy to realize that we are prisoners, for this is one of the most delightful parts of the island, the area is very large, and although there is a wire fencing it is so far away from sight [the fence would later be moved] that there is not a continual reminder of our lack of freedom. . . . There is a large sea frontage extending as far as the eye can see. . . . Within the area [was] a wealth of bougainvillea, delicately-tinted temple flowers, and bright yellow cassia, and some of the loveliest trees on the island."[7]

Even in camps that were in idyllic settings, the fact of imprisonment was paramount. The island of Haruku in Indonesia had abundant food from fish and gardens. The locals grew sweet potatoes, tapioca, tomatoes, bananas, chiles, coconuts, and papayas, but Richard Philps, a British doctor who was interned on Haruku, reported that the Japanese harvested everything before the prisoners could eat it. At the Berhala Island internment camp off the coast of Borneo (Malaysia), two sides were enclosed by barbed wire, and the other two sides were a thirty-foot-high wooden fence. Agnes Newton Keith found that it "shut off all view save what we saw through the crack. This high, impenetrable barrier standing close to our living quarters, the first and last thing we saw every morning and night, nearly drove us mad." Once when a gale wind shook the fence, the internees pushed on it in an effort to topple it, screaming "with the wind and the joy" before they were stopped by guards.[8]

Prisoners had endured the trauma of surrender, capture, and interrogation. Following that was often a difficult journey to camp, usually involving long marches or being packed into trucks. During the trek prisoners were typically poorly fed or not fed at all. When they finally arrived at camp, most prisoners almost welcomed being there. They knew that combat was over for them. They soon learned, however, that now they would be forced to fight against "disease, hunger, brutality, boredom, and despair, . . . [in a] battle for survival," one that took equal courage.[9]

Prisoners were at the mercy of their captors for the essentials of life. Competing with the scarce resources of a country at war, they were people to house, mouths to feed, and bodies to clothe, and they had to be guarded.

In 1918 a German prisoner's rations were 200 grams per day of bad bread, watery soup, coffee made of toasted acorns or chestnuts, and the rare treat of vegetables or meat. On this starvation diet, those who did not receive food parcels from home were dying, according to Red Cross official Carl Dennett. British prisoners received parcels from home, the French less, and the Russians not at all. In the course of examining prisoner packages, captors were free to loot the contents. To those who actually received them, their packages meant the difference between survival and death.

Food was consequently the prisoner's obsession. Rarely was the

amount or quality satisfactory. American pilot Odell Myers was imprisoned for almost three years. In World War II, always hungry and
obsessed by food, he wrote in his memoir, "etched in my memory are
man-shaped skin from which all juice has been drained" — as if the
men themselves had turned into images of food.[10] Prisoners of Britain
or the United States ate better than they would have at home, those
of the Italians or Germans got 1,500 calories per day, and those of the
Russians and the Japanese slowly starved on 500 to 600 calories per
day. Supplements from the Red Cross were literately life saving, but
the Soviet Union refused to participate with the Red Cross, as did the
Japanese, dooming many who were held in their hands. When necessary, prisoners became omnivorous and violated both their accustomed taste and cultural norms in order to survive. They ate any animal, including dogs, cats, rats, snakes, and insects, rarely discarding
any body parts. They ate all known edible plants, but also grass and
even ornamental shrubs known to be poisonous. Prisoners demonstrated remarkable ingenuity in brewing and cooking to both stretch
their food supplies and make their meals more palatable.

The Red Cross supplied 19 million food parcels during World
War II. The standard 1943 package contained "one pound of raisins
or prunes, 6 ounces of liver pate, 4 ounces of soluble coffee, 12 ounces
of corned beef, 8 oz. of sugar, 1 lb. powdered milk, 1 lb. of oleomar-
garine, 8 oz. of crackers, 4 oz. of orange concentrate, 8 oz. of cheese,
8 oz. of salmon, chocolate bars, cigarettes, bars of soap." A Christmas
package had turkey, sausages, jam, candy, ham, a washcloth, and pictures of American scenes. Guards often pilfered articles from the Red
Cross packages.

The theater of war was critical in determining whether outside
help actually made it into the camp: although the Red Cross shipped
deliveries every four months, camps in the Pacific received only an
average of 1 to 1.5 deliveries per camp in four years. The aid provided
by the packages when they finally reached the hands of prisoners was
more than physical. A Canadian doctor in a camp in Hong Kong said
in response to one rare Red Cross package that his Japanese captors
allowed through: "God Bless the Red Cross! They helped in a small
way, to nourish starving men but they represented something as
important as food: hope. They came from home — we were not
entirely cut off, but had friends who cared and could help us. The out-
look never seemed quite as black again."[11]

Food was just the first concern facing POWs and civilian internees, however. Englishman Horace Gilliland summed up his experience as an officer POW in World War I: "The pestilential unsanitary filth and the nauseating stench of camps without any sort of drainage; the biting cold of the long winter without adequate warmth; the daily slaving of cooking tinned food and washing up greasy plates in freezing water afterwards . . . the mental torment of being without any authentic information of the fortunes of war or the fate of those dear to us."[12]

André Warnod saw his fellow World War I prisoners at Merseberg, Germany, dying of hunger and sleeping on verminous mattresses — these were men "who have not been warm for a moment all the winter." He found that "it takes courage to accustom oneself to live in these little pens, like those of an animal in a zoological garden." Under conditions like these, Able Seaman James Farrant, imprisoned near the Russian front and put to work building a railroad in frigid temperatures, found that after a period of time, "the veneer of civilization was wearing off rapidly."[13]

The conditions of civilian internment camps in World War I were not as harsh as POW camps. Ruhleben (German for "quiet life") was a racetrack in suburban Berlin that had stables, grandstands, and a few large houses. Conditions there were poor at first but improved gradually as a highly heterogeneous group from all parts of Britain and the empire organized itself as a community. Almost five thousand were housed in the stables, where they converted the horse boxes into homes for four years. The camp was still a mud-filled swamp when it rained, cold, with poor latrines and wretched food. At Ruhleben, too, assistance from home was essential.

Canadian J. Davidson Ketchum had been studying music in Germany but ended up being interned. He described Ruhleben as being "settled" by the British, as they parceled out land and life took on a routine. With the tacit acceptance of the Germans, who had learned that the men behaved better if left alone, Ruhleben took on the vague appearance of an English village, populated with tradesmen such as carpenters, shoemakers, and a barber. In the heat of the summer and with persistent vermin, people spent as much time as possible outside. As soldiers had done with the trenches, the internees named areas of the camp after London streets. Trafalgar Square, the administrative center, was lit at night; Bond Street was where the canteens were found; and Fleet Street was the office of the *Ruhleben Daily News*. But they named the latrines after local German places: Spandau and Charlottenburg. A popular activity was walking up and down in front of the grandstand known as the Promenade des Anglais, which

Trafalgar Square at Ruhleben, October 1918.

the camp newspaper referred to as a "cosmopolitan causeway." From here the view was of the chimneys of the munitions plant at Spandau, in west Berlin. According to Ketchum, that view was the only "relief from drabness — a ridge and a patch of woodland, always alluring to those who could gaze but not enter."[14]

A committee headed by William Howard Taft reported on the war work of the YMCA during World War I. It saw the POW as a "strangely pathetic figure — a youth, conscious of no crime, yet deprived, in the full vigor of his manhood, of nearly all outlets of human activity . . . living in an atmosphere of constant hostility, owing his very life to the sufferance of his captors; a man without rights."[15]

Conditions in camps changed over time, and as their captors suffered military losses and difficulty in feeding their own populations, the prisoner's lot deteriorated. At places such as Changi, a former British fort in Singapore largely populated by British and Australian POWs, they even had a degree of autonomy.

Apart from the unavoidable distresses of living as a POW, some POWs were put to hard labor. Japanese treatment of prisoners on work parties building railroads and death marches was brutal; prisoners were beaten, starved, and worked to death.

The fence that surrounded the prisoners sometimes also connected them to the outside world. Ultimately, in all camps, the fence was the constant reminder of prisoners' condition. They could often see through the wire, but its strands and spikes defined the boundaries, physical and psychological, of their existence. The question then became how to cope with confinement and remain active and engaged.

In World War I, the German doctor A. L. Vischer coined the phrase "barbed-wire disease" to describe the psychological condition that afflicted most POWs. The name evolved to "barbed-wire attitude" or "psychosis" in World War II, but it was also known by more colorful expressions: barbed-wire-itis, stalag syndrome, going round the bend, brain-fag (short for brain fatigue), cafard (the French term), stir crazy, wire happy, or just nerves.[16] Everyone suffered—the only difference was one of degree.

The causes of the condition were clear: the complete lack of privacy and the ability to be alone caused by overcrowding, life in a timeless present where the duration of imprisonment was unknown, the lack of communication with home or contact with the outside world, and the dreary, monotonous existence. In addition to the privations of imprisonment, captives endured a combination of poor food or hunger, powerlessness in the face of captivity, loss of intimacy, a sense of uselessness, and at the extreme end, humiliation, punishment, maltreatment, and death. Some of these factors are common to all prison experiences, but others are distinctive to the POW condition. The accumulation of these stresses led to depression. Prisoners and internees suffered from lethargy, acute irritability, melancholy, and "neurasthenia." Their emotions oscillated between hope and despair, with an underlying sense of futility. Even Ruhleben, known for its self-organization, was called "the City of Futility."[17]

Barbed-wire disease had identifiable stages. People had been plunged into a place and circumstances that were strange and fear-inducing, and where the future was insecure. At first prisoners were relieved to be in a camp after the tension of battle and were curious about the camp. Invariably the initial adjustment period was followed by acute stress. Most ultimately adapted to conditions, but Vischer found that after two or three years almost all POWs "sank into a settled melancholy."[18]

The frontispiece from
A. L. Vischer's *Barbed
Wire Disease* (1919) was
evocative of barbed
wire's perverted
similarity to vines
and thorns.

The disease was aptly named. Barbed wire is the iron strand that
mocks and perverts the natural vines and thorns on which it is modeled. André Warnod saw the endless lines of barbed wire as the "only
vegetation of this desolate place, climbing from stake to stake round
the camp like strange and cruel and cunning creepers, forming a fence
six feet high . . . unwearied creepers strengthening and consolidating
the cage on every side. We soon got to feel that we were cut off from
everything here, and the rest of the world would be spent on the
wrong side of these iron strands. . . . Like captive and domestic animals, prisoners see things from a great distance." A. L. Vischer wrote
that, "more than anything else, the barbed wire winds like a red thread
through the mental processes of the prisoner." The *Lager Echo,* the
prison camp newspaper at Knockaloe on the Isle of Man, noted that,
"physically, the prisoner is powerless. But in spirit he gnaws unceas-

ingly at the roots of the thorny hedge." Alluding to the sufferings of Christ, one prisoner said, "We live in a kingdom of thorns . . . and the pins that prick us on all sides are like a nightmare."[19]

Large numbers of individuals, often strangers to one another, were crowded together in conditions that precluded privacy and solitude. It was an oppressive, claustrophobic experience. U.S. pilot David Westheimer was shot down and imprisoned in Italian and then German POW camps. In his memoir he recalled, "We missed simple privacy. We were never alone." Once when he had the flu, he was allowed to stay in the room alone at morning appel (roll call) and he recalled that the "minutes of solitude I had in the room were almost as good as freedom." At Santo Tomas in Manila, Alice Franklin Bryant found the "complete lack of privacy, of a moment's solitude" to be equally hard as hunger. She suffered from what she called "mob-ophobia."[20]

The barbed wire both shut out the world outside and contained prisoners in a "herded existence." The world beyond the barbed wire could torment the prisoner within the enclosure: "Through it he gained tantalizing glimpses of the great free world beyond; by it he was forever hurled back into his own drab and hated camp." An amenable landscape may have offered solace for some, but Vischer found that "even a beautifully situated camp is no preventive. I recollect a most charming one, situated among trees and looking on to hilly country; yet just here I met with several very bad cases."[21]

Confined in space, prisoners were also "locked in our timeless space" living a "purgatorial existence" where the duration of their imprisonment was unknown. In many ways the calendar stopped, as the normal flow of time was interrupted. The future, which is always uncertain, became even more so. "The worst shock" about the internment experience, said Ketchum, "was [the] wiping out of the future." Odell Meyers felt that the "futureless present" was "like a daily dose of a progressive poison, almost undetectable in its early stages" and a "very sophisticated and insidious torture" to which "no one was immune but some had more resistance or resilience than others."[22]

With no end in sight, prisoners just marked time. The dreary monotony of the camp was one of its most oppressive aspects. Conrad Hoffman found that the "lack of privacy and monotony of the camp . . . were the features hardest to bear." From a German POW camp in Poland, Giovanni Guareschi wrote, "this endless boredom is like an unrelenting noose around the neck." He suffered from "despair, that is to say, the oppressive, unbearable feeling of total impotence." Israel Cohen was at Ruhleben for nineteen months, and his account of the camp was published in 1917, when thousands were still imprisoned. He too wrote about the monotony and limitations: "the mere loss of physical liberty is the least of the evils that have to be endured: much graver and more injurious are the isolation from the outside world, the restriction and censorship of private correspondence, the constants brooding upon the uncertain future, and the oppressive monotony of daily life. . . . You are familiar with every barrack and canteen, with every shed and store, with every road and mud-puddle, with every stone, and hollow, and declivity, and drain-pipe, with every shallow outline throughout the area of less than half a square mile."[23]

The maddening familiarity of every detail of the crowded camp was a stark contrast to being cut off from the world they were most familiar with: the world at home. Powerless, under the absolute control of their captors, and with little contact with the outside world, they often felt abandoned or like pawns in a larger game. They were victims of "idiocide," the philosopher Paul Weiss's term for the "killing" of the individual as a unique, integrated human being.[24] They suffered the anxieties of not knowing what was happening at home and whether their families knew of their condition or even survival.

Oflag 4C at Colditz Castle, a Sonderlager or special camp, was designed by the Germans as an escape-proof World War II camp for officers. In his poem "Mood Madness," prisoner Lieutenant Alan Campbell, Royal Artillery, writes, "The lack of Beauty, loss of Freedom / In our deeds and in our hearts / Has the monotone of boredom / Fashioned us as men apart?" He implores, "But spare my thoughts such maudlin brooding / O spare my soul this cancer of despair."[25]

Campbell's depression was barbed-wire disease's most common manifestation. Captain Douglas Lyall Grant was well treated as an officer, but in his diary on June 16, 1916, he wrote: "Today had been one of the hardest, a continual fight against depression. I never knew a heart could be so heavy and I never realized before how nearly mental illness could make one physically sick." Conrad Hoffman found that imprisonment and the monotony of camps was unbearable for many and that insanity and mental derangement were not uncommon. Civilians interned solely because of their nationality suffered most intensely. After over two years' imprisonment at Ruhleben, E. L. Wright wrote home: "This is my 'blue' season and I must relieve my feelings somehow. In the winter one looks forward to the spring 'offensive,' but when summer is nearly over and the situation unchanged, it is rather disheartening to have to look forward to another year of it. It is always 'next year.'" Also at Ruhleben, Israel Cohen thought that many prisoners never overcame their initial depression and "sank deeper into a state of incurable melancholia." He thought, "no visitor . . . however profound his sympathy, however acute his observation, however shrewd and penetrating his sagacity, and however long his visit, can appreciate even a tithe of the cumulative effect of the physical, mental, and moral sufferings of the men who have been interned here."[26]

More privileges were granted in officers' camps, which also had more activities than camps for enlisted men; enlisted men were often subjected to harsher treatment than were officers, and not surprisingly they suffered more depression. Prisoners became despondent, and some succumbed to a constant depression, but many more made efforts to overcome their situation. They drew on their personal resources, found ways to channel their emotions, and contrived individual defense mechanisms. Prisoners depended on their fellow prisoners, and some camps developed into unique communities. Each camp certainly had its own collective identity, and this was especially true for civilian camps. People also drew strength from their cultural expectations. Author David Rolf asserted about the British that "it was [their] sheer, bloody-minded determination to find something positive in the most disappointing and miserable situation that undoubtedly helped many British prisoners to survive when they reached permanent camps in Germany and occupied countries."[27]

At Changi in Singapore, the POWs had some freedom of movement, were able to organize themselves, and, even given the unequal balance of power between captor and captive, asserted a small degree of autonomy in resistance to their Japanese captors. Their actions reinforced their sense of community. At the same time, in Santo Tomas in Manila the interned men, women, and children created a surprisingly resilient community. As the war continued and the Japanese began to lose, conditions on the campus deteriorated, and starvation and loss of hope took its toll. Yet there was still a sustained resistance and demonstration of human resiliency under dehumanizing conditions.

Soldier Horace Gilliland recognized that "fine deeds are done in the heat of action . . . but it takes a braver and more steadfast spirit to pass smiling and cheerful through the endless stunted and hopeless days of a prisoner's life." The maintenance of military discipline was sometimes critical for morale. The saying that "a good soldier is a good prisoner" proved true only when a camp maintained proper internal military organization.[28]

The most natural response to imprisonment is to long for liberation or escape. In fact, however, escape from POW and civilian camps in the world wars was attempted by only a few, and success was rare. While some exchanges did occur for most, liberation would come only with the war's end. In the indeterminate interim there were many responses to imprisonment. For military men, the maintenance of discipline was critical, but especially for civilians the institution of organization and activities of all kinds was essential to making time pass and surviving the experience. Both were possible only with the tacit approval of camp authorities. To combat his depression in the camp, Odell Myers felt "I had to reinvent hope. I had to reinvent a future. . . . Mainly out of memories and whatever intellectual activities were possible. Then, by every conceivable means I had to bolster them with physical activity, even with activity whose only value was narcotic."[29] Keeping busy allowed prisoners to engage their minds and bodies.

We think of work as a way to earn a living and tend to forget about its other functions. The camps, of all kinds, emphasized work's broader meanings. The simple fact of keeping busy was critical. Work gives one a way to keep mind and body occupied, it fosters a sense of dignity and self-respect, and it can produce measurable and helpful results. POWs could be assigned to brutal work camps, but if treatment and conditions were even marginally decent, labor — assigned or voluntary — offered much to the POW. It could alleviate feelings of helplessness and was a way to confront the boredom and help pass the days. Israel Cohen found some individuals who became so occupied that they forgot where they were, but he also found "Jeremiahs, who deprecated all forms of entertainment or amusement as incompatible with their lot. 'Why make a theater in the Camp?' protested the pessimists; 'why print a magazine/why plant flower-beds?' "[30] Some prisoners had the opportunity to engage in their occupations, but more often they developed new skills or discovered hidden or repressed talents.

Leisure-time activities and creative outlets assumed an importance inside the wire they did not have in the free world. In Germany, André Warnod thought that away from his native France and always looking at the "same ugly and tedious view . . . all life seems frozen and checked, and in the end one is stupefied into indifference and disgust at everything." Warnod drew a parallel between fighting the enemy on the battlefield and fighting against the "torpor, the depression" that was as powerful an enemy, though the prisoner had to struggle against a "foe that is secret, patient, unrelenting, and intangible." He understood what many POWs also realized: it was essential for survival to "recover and react against this dangerous torpor, and to do *something*, it does not matter what," as Ronald Bailey put it.[31]

World War I POWs organized schools, theaters, and orchestras. The demand for musical instruments drove prisoners to make their own along with other handicrafts. Camp newspapers included one called the *Barbed Wireless* for U.S. soldiers. Athletic activity was particularly popular, not surprising given the youth of the soldiers. Horace Gilliland was moved to Bischofswerda, Germany, a cavalry barracks with a ninety-by-sixty-yard parade ground and a cavalry school training ground where they played football. The British had even convinced their captors to build two hard tennis courts. They even adapted places to play golf. Contests of all kinds, including garden competitions, were held. Private religious observance can occur individually, but the communal aspect of religious services was essential. André Warnod referred to a hut that had been converted into a chapel as the "gate of paradise."[32]

Perhaps the war's most stunning example of social organization was at Ruhleben. Almost fifty years after his internment, psychology professor J. Davidson Ketchum wrote about the prison camp society at Ruhleben. He thought the population, a cross section of British society, and the "challenging conditions of their internment" made possible the creation of a unique social world, "a world so complete and many-sided that its existence in a prison camp is almost unbelievable." The Germans "penned them up and left them to their own devices." They required no work, nor recreation, and imposed no social structure. Ketchum felt they created a community where they no longer thought or acted as prisoners and where morale was dependent on one's participation in organized activities.[33]

Israel Cohen, chairman of the Ruhleben Literary and Debating Society, was a typical participant in community life. He found that "all the hardships its inhabitants had to endure were due to the enemy con-

The Italian Chapel at Lamb Holm on the Orkney Islands was constructed in a Nissan hut by Italian POWs during World War II. Domenico Chiocchetti painted the interior.

trol; all the comforts — such as they were — that we were able to enjoy were the fruits of our own efforts." They created their own civilian self-government and community organization "with most of the qualities and attributes of a free community, supplemented by its own specific features. We had our own habits and customs, our own fashions and etiquette, our characters and celebrities, our rumors and excitements." Committees essentially took on the responsibilities of a municipal government. Each barracks had a captain, and there were barracks postmen, policemen, and cleaners. There were committees for kitchens, canteens, finance, sanitation, education, entertainment, mail delivery, and sports. Sports played a major role, as they did in all POW situations. Football (soccer) clubs formed the very first week, and in winter the prisoners flooded the fields for skating. Ketchum called sports, along with theater and music, the "salvation" of prisoners.[34]

There were both formal and informal educational networks at Ruhleben. Numerous lectures were held, and the Ruhleben Camp School grew to seventeen departments and 246 teachers with up to

1,500 internees — a third of the camp — taking courses. One course in practical botany equaled a first-year university course. Cohen reported that "all the living material required was obtained from the pond in the centre of the race-course, which contained a good variety of flora and fauna," and other samples were sent by professors from Munich and Cambridge.[35] Many internees even prepared for exams to enter Oxford upon their release. In 1917 E. L. Wright wrote home about life in camp, telling his parents that he kept busy by taking courses and by playing tennis and cricket most days.

With permission from the German authorities, money from the British government, help from the U.S. Embassy, and parcels from home, a variety of clubs and associations sprang up at Ruhleben. There were history, science, orchestra, music, cinema, and drama clubs. There were banking societies and an Irish Literary and Historical Circle. There were associations of various "territorial" societies representing the soldiers' homelands. There was also the Summer-House Club, the Corner House, the Café de la Paix, the Twenty-five Club, and the Phoenix Club, which sheathed its exterior in green trelliswork. There were art studios and various handicrafts groups. The first summer there was even a "medal craze" to design a medal as a token for each new internee to commemorate his or her captivity. Cohen attributed the ark for the Jewish barracks to "our Ruhleben Bezalel" — after the creator of the biblical ark.[36] There was a very active garden club.

Ketchum thought that the prisoners "set to work on it [Ruhleben] with all the fervor of child architects on a clean, tide-washed beach."[37] They took great pride in a city they had largely created themselves. The camp ultimately took on attributes of a bustling English village, what had been the actual home for at least some prisoners. The English ideal came complete with flower beds in front of houses (the barracks), and a central green that functioned as a commons and the site for allotment gardens.

World War II prisoners demonstrated similar organizational resourcefulness. Wherever possible there was music, theater, underground camp newspapers, sports, and hobbies. Prisoners also whiled away the time by doing housekeeping tasks — washing, cooking, and cleaning. Guy Morgan found that the "personal freedom of camp life releases an enormous flood of creative and artistic ability. Many people who would not normally have tried their hands, paint, draw, carve, act, produce, design, or learn to play musical instruments."[38] He found his escape in writing, but he also listed gardening among the normal pursuits of prisoners.

The May 1916 cover of the *Ruhleben Camp Magazine* portrays an idyllic, pastoral scene.

Prisoners capitalized on their knowledge, teaching one another. At the "Barbed-Wire University" of Stalag Luft 6, by 1943 there were thirty-seven weekly classes, a significant antidote to mental stagnation. In the Italian POW camp at Chieti, Odell Myers listened to lectures by fellow prisoners at the "University of Chieti." He also engaged in the camp's most popular exercise, as it was at Ruhleben: walking the perimeter, the same behavior that characterizes zoo animals.

The World War II German military manual said that daily exercise was healthy and desirable for prisoners; consequently, requests for permission to do sports were generally granted, with prisoners maintaining the playing fields.

Sometimes the abundance of activities gave a false impression of the traumas of POW life. At Stalag Luft 3, known for its humane treatment of prisoners, prisoners "made such excellent use of the limited diversions available to them that many people gained erroneous impressions about the camp, impressions that obscured the dismal and unpleasant realities of life in a prisoner of war camp."[39]

At Santo Tomas in the Philippines, Alice Bryant was so impressed with the range of activities in the camp that it reminded her of a "combination of Chatuauqua order and European spa." The photographer Carl Mydans thought "it was remarkable how quickly order was formulated out of chaos. Almost overnight the prison camp swelled into an active community, a little city, in effect, isolated by battle."[40] He attributed this to the abundance of time, know-how, and experts for everything. The experts at Santo Tomas, Ruhleben, and other POW and internment camps invariably included gardeners.

Indeed, gardening proved to be one of many activities that helped people survive psychologically. Gardens were a natural antidepressant and therapy for barbed-wire disease. They offered work and a way to pass the time, and their produce sometimes enabled the prisoners' survival.

In all POW and civilian internee camps, gardens were subject to the whim of captors: whether they would be allowed or not, whether the produce would be considered part of the rations supplied by the captors, and how much space would be allowed. Gardening organizations in the camps sprang up to marshal prisoners with local knowledge and prior gardening experience, which gave prisoners a leg up on where, how, and what to plant. Outside help included international organizations such as the Red Cross and the YMCA, but gardening assistance and supplies from prisoners' home countries also seeped in haltingly — particularly in Asia — augmenting whatever supplies prisoners were able to marshal on their own. In Asia, locals in some cases reached through the fence, so to speak, to sell or give supplies and food to prisoners. Few of the gardens were created without extraordinary effort and labor, from clearing land to digging with homemade tools to hauling water. Their successes were further limited by the usual vagaries of the weather, and in Asia prisoners were hampered by a generally lesser familiarity with native agriculture and climate. POW and civilian internees, like the Jews and others herded into ghettos in Germany and Eastern Europe in World War II, had no idea how long they would be imprisoned, and their garden harvests were often compromised — particularly as the war wore on — by the prisoners' hunger. Finally, especially at POW camps, gardening provided a cover for covert tunneling, another activity that gave prisoners hope and kept them engaged in potentially highly productive work.

In Conrad Hoffman's YMCA survey of POW camps in World War I Germany, he found gardens in a variety of camps. At a well-equipped camp near Darmstadt that held mostly French and Russian prisoners, "attractive garden patches were in evidence everywhere. Some had flowers, but most of them were planted with vegetables, which gave not only a pleasing effect but also helped to furnish fresh vegetables for the prisoners. In one compound vines had been planted along the entire side of the barracks and, with a second row of sunflowers, which incidentally furnished sunflower seed for the Russians who regard it as more or less of a delicacy, presented a really delightful aspect." In the hospital compound, "every inch . . . was utilized for the growing of spinach, regarded so highly by the Germans as a tonic and health food. In the summer there had been flower beds as well." Similarly, at the hospital at Worms, "every inch of ground about them [the barracks] was utilized for growing vegetables, and entering every door into a barrack was a hanging basket with blooming plants." Prisoners were even involved in making cemeteries (*Friedhof,* German for *cemetery,* means literally "yard of peace"), and in several camps they held a design competition for a monument.[41]

Garden making was always at the whim of the commandants, who were well aware of the potential propaganda bonus. In the World War I Taft report they noted, "In many cases there existed among camp officials a keen sense of pride in maintaining everything in the best possible order. Many camps had flower and vegetable gardens, the advantage of which to prisoners is obvious . . . in the propaganda camps everything was made as comfortable as possible." In Daniel McCarthy's report on Friedrichsfeld, one of the best camps with 7,500 British POWs, he saw the camp "tastefully decorated with flower beds in front of each barrack."[42]

The garden fervor of Ruhleben was unparalleled elsewhere in World War I, however. In that former racetrack the interned British civilians established a garden society, held garden contests, and had extensive vegetable and flower gardens. The history of the committee of the Ruhleben Horticultural Society as recorded in the 1917–18 annual reports is a remarkable story and a testament to the role of gardening in British society.

Almost immediately after the internment camp was established, Ruhleben's gardens began — in biscuit tins. From this "primitive effort" developed barracks gardens that, despite the duplication of effort and the low level of organization, were productive enough to promise that a broader, more organized effort would yield even better results. Encouraged by a gift of seeds from the crown princess of Sweden, in the fall of 1916 fifty interested gardeners held a meeting. They called themselves the Committee of the Ruhleben Horticultural Society, drew up a constitution, and on December 18, 1916, they announced that they were affiliated with the Royal Horticultural Society. There were soon 943 dues-paying members.

The society immediately outlined a set of ambitious tasks dutifully recorded in their annual reports. They received permission to build a nursery of about 600 square yards, where they cleared the plot, built drainage trenches, and amended the soil with composted refuse and tea leaves. They constructed cold frames and set out thousands of plants for vegetable gardens, but they also grew perennials and eventually set out 20,000 annuals of many varieties for barracks and public gardens. Proud of their efforts, they noted, "Few can have failed to appreciate the patches of brightness and colour which the Society's efforts have brought into the camp." The following year, when the committee met forty-five times, they expanded the nursery and added a heating plant to the greenhouse they constructed. Flowers could now be supplied year-round.

In letters home to Leicester, E. L. Wright often noted Ruhleben's gardens. On May 23, 1915, he wrote, "One or two of the barracks have laid out minute 'gardens' with a foot or two of straggly grass, and a few pansies and geraniums." Next month he wrote, "The little barracks gardens which I mentioned before have developed greatly, and there are some quite fine displays, particularly of geraniums." A year later Wright was still writing of the society's accomplishments. "There was a little bit of fruit blossom to be seen in the garden adjoining the emigrants station over the lane. I should not forget the one or two chestnut trees and lilac bushes in the camp. The flowerbeds in front of Barrack 8 are looking fine now. They have taken a lot of trouble over them, and have the natural advantage of an open space and a row of lime trees. They have got one or two minute rhododendron in bloom, and have even got a bed of small rose trees."[43]

The unique conditions at Ruhleben allowed some ornamental planting, but vegetable gardens were still paramount. In January 1917 prisoners asked permission to use land inside the racetrack oval as a vegetable garden — it became a substantial undertaking. For example, they set out almost 20,000 lettuce plants, 6,208 cabbage, and 7,259

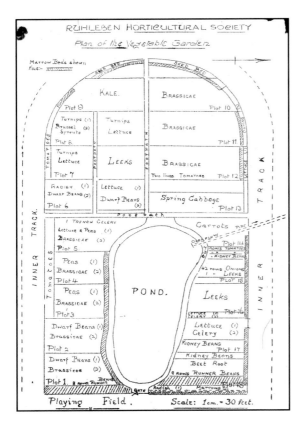

The Ruhleben Horticultural Society's plan for the vegetable garden shows the ingenious creation of a pond in the playing field.

beets. The prisoners received seeds from the Royal Horticultural Society and from well-known British seed firms. The produce from the garden was sold at nominal prices to prisoners. Almost 20 percent of the internees became Ruhleben Horticultural Society members and there was broad appreciation for their efforts. Edward Stibbe, who spent four years at Ruhleben, was pleased that "every man was able occasionally to have fresh vegetables with his tins of meat," and he applauded the society's role in the "planting of small flower beds round the barracks and in various parts of the camp, so that in summer the camp often looked quite attractive."[44]

The society also organized lectures. In one six-month period, the topics were as diverse as melon cultures, microorganisms of the soil, fungoid pests, and how to conduct field experiments. Members also organized flower shows with exhibits by individuals, barracks, and the nursery and vegetable gardeners. The numerous competition categories included barracks garden, public garden, private garden, individual plant, best table decoration, cut flowers, sweet peas, buttonhole, window box, and vegetable. The shows and competitions are a reminder that, like other forms of association, the impact of the garden club may have been as much in the group effort it required as the act of gardening.

E. L. Wright wrote home about the 1917 summer flower show that occupied the entire hall of the camp YMCA. "There were one or two novelties, such as a tiny fig, date and orange trees, grown from stones out of parcel fruit. Another interesting item was a model rock garden, and there was a very fine show of sweet peas. . . . The hall was very nicely arranged and would not have disgraced a country flower show at home."[45]

The Ruhleben camp newspaper and magazine regularly had a garden column. One article written by the pseudonymous Forget-Me-Not took pleasure in even the most modest accomplishments, such as one barracks that tentatively began its garden endeavors in a window box.

Camp commandants granted or denied permission for garden making for reasons ranging from humanitarian to a desire to have a well-ordered and beautiful camp to a need to provide food for prisoners. There was, of course, also a certain propaganda value, not to mention orders from above. The high command of the German armed forces (OKW) granted permission in May 1940 for prisoners to grow their own gardens, with the cost of supplies taken out of the camp budget. In July 1941 permission was even granted to plant flowers in front of barracks, but by November shortages caused the Germans to deny any further beautification requests, though gardens were still at the commandant's discretion.

The Commandant of Oflag 8B singled out vegetable gardens in his camp standing orders:

> For the improvement of the meals and the health of *all* Ps.o.W. [prisoners of war] through extra vitamins, gardens inside the camp are placed at the disposal of Ps.o.W. and will be managed by them. Work in the garden will be carried out by Ps.o.W. officers and orderlies under the discretion of an officer detailed by the S.B.O. [senior British officer] as *Ps.o.W. garden officer*. Individual gathering of vegetables will be punished as theft.
>
> The Camp Commandant intends to increase substantially the gardening area. Since not all vegetable seeds or plants can be put at the disposal of Ps.o.W., they are advised to have what vegetable seeds they especially want sent *now* from home.

The YMCA public gardens were entered in the Ruhleben Horticultural Society contest, August 1917.

Captain A. D. M. Hilton at Oflag 8B Germany wrote home to request some books — they were all about gardening, on topics ranging from soil conditioning to plant genetics.

It was largely at the more privileged officers' camps that commandants permitted gardening. At Oflag 64 in Alturgund, Poland, David Foy reported that "inmates constructed a greenhouse and planted a remarkable camp garden (with seeds from the Red Cross) filled with tomatoes, onions, leaf lettuce, cabbage, and black currants." Fry also noted that prisoners beautified the hospital grounds with flower plantings. In the summer of 1944, Odell Meyers and his fellow prisoners "planted gardens in the hard clay between the barracks. The Red Cross or YMCA supplied the seeds, which we hoped would add a few fresh vegetables to our larder. We tended the struggling plants, watered them from sprinklers made from powdered-milk cans. Weeding was unnecessary, because the soil was too poor to sustain them. The harvest — an inappropriate name — consisted of a few woody radishes for their development. When our gardens were producing their meager bounty and German rations were more plentiful, we (especially I) adopted a cat."[46] When food became scarce, Odell and his mates killed and ate the cat.

Stalag Luft 3 became perhaps the most famous POW camp of the war, for it was here that "the Great Escape" of Hollywood fame was attempted. RAF Squadron leader C. I. Rolfe was shot down in 1940 and spent the rest of the war at Stalag Luft 3. In his "Wartime Log for British Prisoners," a gift from the War Prisoners Aid of the YMCA, Geneva, he kept a garden journal. His long entry, "The Garden of 63/3 in 1944," summarizes the garden's development and includes a garden plan and partial dimensions. The garden "consisted of small strips of 'home made' soil dug in and amongst the typical pine needle strewn sand on which the camp was built. In 1942 Polish officers occupied this room, and they it appears dug into the sand every available scrap of refuse. In 1943 this decayed matter enabled the room to reap quite a good crop of onions, tomatoes, marrows, radishes etc." Rolfe also notes that the spacing of perimeter plantings was "primarily . . . to keep out golf balls and secondly for ornamental purposes."[47]

American David Westheimer was moved from the Italian POW camp at Chieti to Stalag Luft 3. Carved out of a pine forest, the camp was studded with stumps. He watched as a Polish prisoner hauled waste and honey wagons in the camp. There was competition among gardeners for the prized manure. Westheimer soon joined the camp gardeners who received seeds from the Red Cross, YMCA, and home. Gardeners competed for the prized manure, following "the horses everywhere with Red Cross boxes, hoping to get lucky." In the spring of 1944 they planted "onions, radishes, tomatoes, lettuce. Though we cultivated ours meticulously, plucking out every weed and pebble, pulverizing every clod by hand, and watering abundantly, the soil was acidic and we got little for our efforts. Only the radishes flourished." Other vegetables yielded disappointingly little, in part due to foraging hares. "We tried a little fence made of twigs and roots to no avail and then a trap, which caught nothing except Padre Macdonald's cat," lamented Westheimer.[48]

Pilot Norman ("Cy") L. Widen was sent to Stalag Luft 3, where he became known for a scoop he crafted from Red Cross boxes. He used his scoop to collect horse droppings to apply to his prized tomatoes. He planted hundreds, according to author Arthur Durand: "He also had great success with onions, a highly sought after seasoning for the prisoner's notoriously bland diet. It gave Cy great pleasure to be able to share a few of his zwiebel with his buddies. He was also pleased that nobody ever stole any of his carefully nurtured produce."[49] Widen also grew flowers near a playing field, where other prisoners could also enjoy their color and beauty.

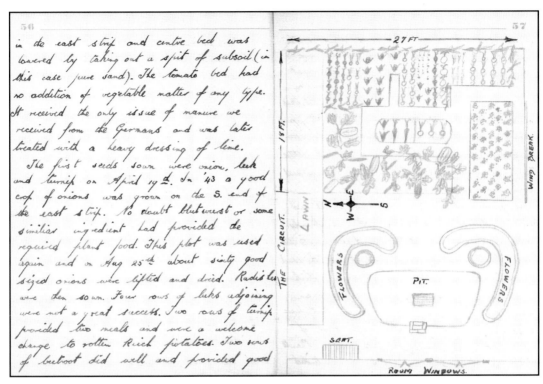

The garden of barracks 63/3 in 1944, Stalag Luft 3, Germany, where C. I. Rolfe was imprisoned from 1940 to 1945. Note the deliberate placement of flowers near the windows.

Not all prisoners found comfort in the efforts of camp gardeners, however. Of his POW experience in World War II, British flying officer Brian Filliter recalled, "You write, and you don't want them to worry about you at home, so you say, 'we're busy making a garden.' 'Gardens!' What a farce! Nothing grew, and people walked all over it. But the folks at home are sending you gardening books."[50]

While providing a long-term source of food and activity for prisoners, gardening also ironically cultivated the hope of escape by providing a cover for those intent on tunneling out. Underneath the camp at Stalag Luft 3, the three escape tunnels under construction required an unobtrusive method of disposing of the displaced dirt. Since the dirt from the tunnel was whitish yellow sand, prisoners dropped the sand into the garden and worked it into the soil. To avoid detection by the German guards, the prisoners ingeniously crafted bags that would be "concealed in the carrier's pant legs or under his coat. A string attached to a pin opened the bottom of the bag, and the sand gradually drained out."[51]

The memoir of British naval officer David James, imprisoned at Marlag, an officer's camp near Bremen, tells how prisoners there solved the problem of dispersing the soil tunneled out of the ground: "You can, if you like, empty your bag in the static water pond, or down the main drain, or sprinkle it evenly over the garden paths, but over there midst yonder tomato stands Lieutenant Van Kyrke, R.N., our disposal king. He takes great interest in ullage pits. A base of sand, covered with tea leaves and potato peelings, may not make the finest garden manure, but it does get rid of a lot of embarrassing soil."[52] Both the tunneling and the garden fed the prisoners' need to surmount a problem with ingenuity and to take pride in a defiant accomplishment under their captors' noses.

Similarly, at Chieti, where David Westheimer was first imprisoned, the prisoners cared diligently for the vegetable gardens outside each hut, but escape tunnels were also in progress, with the same surreptitious dispersal of tunneled dirt. Watching the prisoners so intent on their gardening, Westheimer wrote in his memoir, "our *settore* major . . . asked why we were working so hard. We probably wouldn't be there long enough to enjoy the fruits of our labor, he said, confirming our own views about the progress of the war. He, and we, would be proven wrong, of course."[53]

At camps in Asia, Allied prisoners faced an additional hurdle to garden making: they were unfamiliar with the climate and agriculture of that part of the world. Most POWs were in Asia for the first time, and although civilian prisoners who had lived for years in Asia had a broader experiential base than did POWs, many civilians had lived privileged lives that didn't involve subsistence agriculture.

In Japanese POW camps for officers, small vegetable gardens were generally allowed, but this was rare at camps for enlisted men. However, in the large civilian camps that occupied the forts, schools, and prisons at Changi in Singapore, Stanley in Hong Kong, and the University of Santo Tomas in Manila, gardens became important parts of the camp environment.

In Singapore, thousands of Australian and British POWs were imprisoned in a twelve-square-mile area called Changi, the British army's main base in Singapore on the island of Changi. The Japanese provided minimal rations but also little interference, so gardens became essential to survival. At first the Australian forces put eight hundred men to work digging up the "impressive lawns that were found in abundance around the Changi area" to create garden plots. Eventually a larger camp garden scheme engaged all the Changi POWs. Sweet potatoes were the main crop, but they also grew tapioca, Ceylon spinach, amaranth, kangkong, beans, chiles, and eggplant.

At first the garden produce was a relief from the monotonous diet of rice, but garden production was also a sign of the self-sufficiency of the Changi prisoner. Even the Japanese could not ignore the extreme vitamin deficiencies in prisoners, so in 1942 they too established at Changi vegetable gardens with POW labor, initially 400 workers that rose to 1,000. As the war stretched out and conditions worsened, the Japanese included the prisoners' produce in their ration calculation, thereby reducing the already meager rations and effectively returning prisoners to something approximating a starvation diet. Survivors nonetheless attested to the "positive benefits of keeping active in the gardens, mental as well as physical."[54]

As a physician, Richard Philps lamented the fact that the authorities at Haruku prison in Indonesia did not allow prisoners to grow their own vegetables, which he felt would have helped alleviate many of the POWs' health problems. After he was transferred from Haruku to Changi, where the commandant did allow prisoners to garden, he found that their health improved dramatically. Always at the mercy of their captors, prisoners had to acquiesce when the Japanese took the largest share of their crops — "the only reason why the gardens were allowed at all," according to Philps. He reported that a few men tried private gardens at Changi but were too weak to maintain them. However, when the latrines overflowed after a flood, prisoners were delighted to discover that tomato seed from the waste had seeded, ultimately yielding a "very large crop growing wild up the sides of the gully." Later he was moved to Changi Gaol (Singapore's civilian prison, within the old British fort used for POWs), where prisoners "had a garden, frogs [a protein source] and moneylenders." Philps was placed on garden duty himself when sick, something he knew was for those in a "fairly advanced state of emaciation," but he was pleased both that his fellows allowed him to rest

Officers tending the vegetable garden at the POW camp in Changi,
Singapore, September 1942.

and that the workers had the privilege of a large vegetable stew at
lunch.[55]

STANLEY, HONG KONG   The memoirs of Jean Gittins, William
Sewell, and Elizabeth Nance of their time at Hong Kong's Stanley
camp, in the former Stanley Prison, are indicative of the resourcefulness of people when confronted with an unexpected situation. Half
the civilian internees at Stanley were women of the colonial elite who
were accustomed to supervising servants who in turn did the work.
According to authors Bernice Archer and Kent Federowich, however,
these women were remarkably resourceful, often more so than the
men, in improving the situation for themselves and their families
through hard work.

Crowded into the former prison, Jean Gittins and her friends Bill
and Jeanne Faid initially despaired of having a garden. When other
prisoners stole the produce before it matured, she and the Faids created a garden on a roof to which they could control access. On a
sloped roof they built up beds with bricks and carried up leaf mold for

This drawing by Murray Griffin shows men working at firewood stacks, making compost, and tending vegetable gardens inside the POW camp in Changi, Singapore.

soil. Initially they grew mint and shallots. One crop of 128 shallot bulbs "improved the flavor of the rice and made all the difference to our diet."

As the internees at Stanley organized themselves, thievery ceased and garden making became commonplace. By the end of 1943, they were growing tomatoes, lettuce, carrots, peas, turnips, and celery, and the next summer they added string beans, cucumbers, pumpkins, and even peanuts, which were good for the soil and a good source of protein. They carefully collected seeds from their food rations and from their plants and sorted, packaged, and labeled them. Garden tools were unavailable, so internees fashioned their own. Gittins's favorite to break up the soil was a "small piece of wood about six inches long with half a dozen nails driven through it." Noting the spirit that developed among the internees, Gittins reported that "things were not always easy but, with all enterprise and imagination, and assistance from friends, we had all that was needed."

Hauling water was always a problem at Stanley. In the fall of 1944, the Japanese cut the water main, so internees resorted to using old wells and hauling water in buckets. Interned patrician planters and civil servants learned personally of the difficulties facing Chinese peasants daily. One of the internees, Captain Horner Smith, had been watching Gittins haul water when he shyly offered his assistance. She taught him gardening, and he in turn became a partner and worker in the garden, building a shelter and also tackling the nastiest chore: emptying the septic tank. "The slush from the septic tank was the only fertilizer we had in camp and the garden was badly in need." Gittins also made her own contribution to the fertility of the soil: "I had for some time past saved the water from washing the towels used for my menstruation — I was losing blood heavily — knowing that blood and bone was one of the standard mixtures for plant food. By the time Horner came on the scene, saving every drop of water had become a dire necessity but even this was not sufficient for the hungry soil. As well as the vegetables (the sweet potatoes needed no fertilizer), I had a tiny flower garden of nasturtiums, a solitary wild rose and a clump of mauve coloured chrysanthemums, which turned a lovely shade of bronze after the blood treatment."[56]

Elizabeth Nance and her husband Ancil were young American missionaries imprisoned at Stanley with their children. In the rocky areas of the prison grounds, some men managed to put in gardens between the rocks, where Ancil's garden was the "size of a dining room table." This was insufficient for the needs of the Nance family, which eventually totaled four children, but there was great competition among internees for space, so Ancil turned his attention to a concrete turnaround at the base of their building. He gathered dirt from the hillside until it was ten inches deep on the concrete. When warned by the imprisoned chair of the agriculture department of Hong Kong University that gardening required a minimum of eighteen inches of soil, Ancil just countered, "I have farmed on the hard pan of Fresno, California." Elizabeth says that other internees thought her husband had a "mental condition" and were further convinced when he planted vetch, which causes diarrhea if eaten. When it matured, Ancil turned his vetch crop over, enriching the shallow soil. Because water was scarce, he dug through the pavement to intercept the drainage system. Seeds from Chinese friends included those for sweet potatoes, which became their staple, and Elizabeth attributes her children's good health to eating the leaves, which the Chinese feed to pigs.

Despite the size and demands of their own family, the Nances often invited the most needy internees to eat with them.

After U.S. forces bombed Hong Kong in 1945, many people at Stanley dug up their potato crops, believing liberation was at hand. Despite the family's hunger, however, Ancil saved his for spring planting. Elizabeth Nance reports that he recited the final verses of Psalm 126: "They who sow in tears shall reap in joy, He that goeth forth and weepeth, bearing precious seed, shall doubtless come again with rejoicing, bearing his sheaves with him." A farmer cries, she said, in times of famine when his family may have to eat bark and grass so he can save his seed. Within a few weeks, the prisoners had given up hope that the Americans would land soon, so some apologetically asked for cuttings from Ancil's garden. He gave out bouquets of sweet potato leaves like roses. Elizabeth reported that the garden meant the difference between being hungry and starving, but also that it "meant that you had something to share and help other people."[57]

Professor and author of several books about life in China, Stanley prisoner William Sewell was well aware of the transformation taking place as the British internees were forced to engage in their own form of subsistence agriculture. Stanley's prison and school grounds slowly changed from an institutional to an agricultural setting. The prisoners were like the peasants of a great feudal estate, and the site took on the look of rural China. William witnessed the landscape change as all the scrub, small trees, and rocks were removed and in their place "were little gardens, all the waste land had been cultivated. Rocks had been moved, and others covered with soil so that lettuce or spinach could be grown. I kept rubbing my eyes, hardly believing that I was not back on the hills of Chungking." He joined the lines waiting for sludge from the septic tanks, where "even the smell was authentic." He watched his wife, Mary, digging with a Chinese *tsu-deo,* as their Chengtu gardener had done. In a moment of insight he realized that "so many of the things which we had thought of as typically Chinese were merely the normal results of human endeavor in the presence of need and the absence of money and tools."

The Sewells maintained two of the garden plots that filled Stanley. On one they built stone walls, filled cans with soil, and planted grasses against the wind. The prime worker in the family, Mary "spent most of her time in her gardens: it was a refuge from the turmoil of the flat, and although the work was hard, she enjoyed the relief it afforded . . .

it was Mary who bore the main burden. It was to her we owed health and possibly life itself, for on the bare rations we could hardly have lived. Once the gardens were established we had a vegetable stew every day." They sold produce and also shared the food with those who did not have gardens, especially the elderly and infirm.

The gardens started out as individual enterprises at Stanley, but the meager rations forced the prisoners into communal action. The Japanese promised double rations for those who would work a communal garden. Sports playing fields were dug up as more land was needed and energy for sports ebbed. Produce from the garden contributed to the diet, but the Sewells' nine-year-old daughter, Vee, planted flowers and "was happy when her lilies were placed on the altar, or when she could give a bride a chrysanthemum bouquet, and take nosegays to her friends lying in hospital."[58] Their other daughter, Joy, two years younger, grew nasturtiums, pretty but also edible.

SANTO TOMAS, MANILA   The University of Santo Tomas sat on a sixty-five-acre campus in the heart of Manila. Almost immediately after the Japanese bombed Manila on December 8, 1941, many British and American civilians fled to hide in the mountains, though most were ultimately captured or forced to surrender. The university campus was pressed into service as a civilian internment camp by the Japanese as the number of captives grew. With five thousand internees at its maximum, Santo Tomas was the largest civilian internment camp anywhere in World War II. As at Stanley in Hong Kong, the majority of the internees were a privileged elite, who endured conditions they had never before imagined.

Secretly appointed the historian of the camp, A. V. H. Hartendorp wrote and hid over four thousand pages of his account of camp life. Among those interned at Santo Tomas would be Alice Franklin Bryant, Agnes Newton Keith, and Elizabeth Vaughan, whose memoirs richly fill out our picture of the camp.

With civilian men, women, and children housed according to gender in overcrowded classrooms, the desire for privacy was strong at Santo Tomas. Grace Nash found that "there were to be no doors, no privacy ANYPLACE!" As a respite from overcrowding, a lack of privacy, and a desire for space, the prisoners built a shantytown on the grounds. By September 1943 there were 609 shanties housing 2,200 people. A committee in charge of shanties divided the area into ten-by-twelve-foot lots. At first they made makeshift lean-tos, but soon

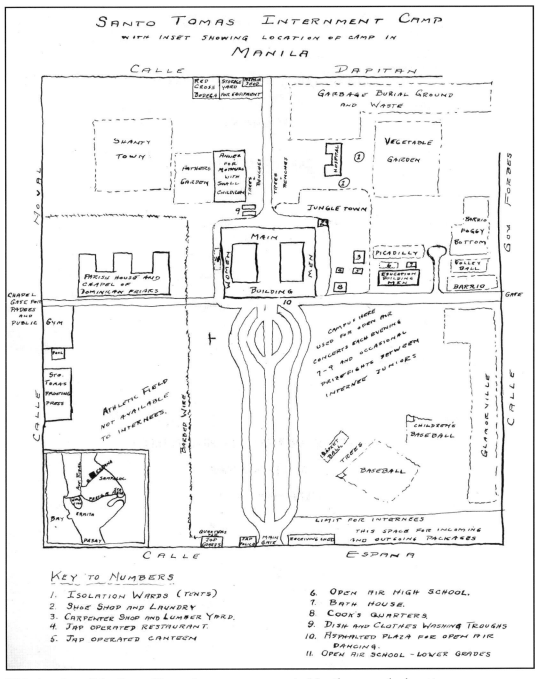

This drawing of the Santo Tomas internment camp in Manila notes the location and relative size of the vegetable garden and other open spaces in the camp.

they exploited local knowledge and tradition, and the shanties evolved into traditional Filipino grass *nipa* huts. Some became even more elaborate and were built on stilts in the traditional style to keep it cooler. The Japanese regulations included an order that they could see into dwellings, so there were no doors, but shutters were allowed when it rained. Bruce Johansen described a small village arising with paths, streets, and areas that the internees named to remind them "of frontier settlements of the American West . . . with a dash of tropical ambiance: Glamourville, Toonerville, Froggy Bottom, Jerkville, Over Yonder, Garden Court (which had the most pretentious homes), Cottage Park, Jungletown, Shantytown, Palm Court."[59]

At first the Santo Tomas civilian internees received or bought food from the local community through the barbed-wire fence surrounding the camp, as their captors provided little. In those early days, people were kept alive, reported camp historian Hartendorp, by the exchange of food and goods at "The Gate, The Fence, The Package Line." The neglectful attitude of the Japanese toward their charges, however, left the prisoners free to internally organize themselves. Food was the primary concern. Gardening, both individual and communal, began quickly, and areas previously used for recreation and livestock were taken over for growing produce. "The rice supply and the garden, it was soon recognized[,] would ultimately determine just how long the internees would be able to carry on," said Vaughan.[60]

G. H. Bissinger headed a garden project committee that had extensive knowledge of local agriculture and conditions; the committee developed a careful plan that would utilize to best advantage the little resources available to produce the highest yield. Once a three-hectare fill area in the northeast corner of the campus was chosen for the initial garden, internees set about clearing it of old cars, cans, bottles, and metal junk. The "material was piled up along the borders of the cultivated area, like the stones on a New England farm," wrote camp historian Hartendorp.[61]

Internees grew the local staples, especially talinum (native spinach) and camotes (yams). Chosen by the committee because it is hardy, not susceptible to insect damage, and fast growing, talinum wasn't popular with many Western internees because it was so unfamiliar. Hunger soon changed their minds. Careful harvesting of talinum and camote leaves allowed continuous production. They also grew pechay, kangkong (a green), concomas, upo, chayotes, mongo beans, and gabi (similar to American-grown elephant's ear), and planted cassava hedges and quick-maturing papaya trees (unripe papayas were boiled as a vegetable). British and American palates had to become accustomed to eating and preparing foodstuffs they were previously unacquainted with. They also grew more familiar crops, such as corn, eggplant, okra, squash, leeks, beans, and ginger.

The first crops were harvested by the beginning of April 1942. The first of the nine basketfuls of talinum went to the camp hospital; the harvest also yielded enough for each person in camp to receive a serving of talinum.

Bruce Johansen describes Santo Tomas as becoming a "small town of involuntary neighbors," and as in all such places the landscape evolved, as well.[62] July was already a landmark month for the garden. Internees had discovered a 1,100-gallon water tank, and sixty workers completed a pipe connection that would allow them to irrigate without hauling water. They harvested 9,500 pounds of talinum that month. The Santo Tomas shantytowns took on the names of foods: Camote Avenue, Talinum Lane, and Duck Egg Drive.

In November 1943 a typhoon and flood put the garden under four feet of water, destroying all the crops. The determined internees rebuilt and improved the drainage system in the garden. In late 1943 and through 1944, however, hunger became serious. Portions of the shanties were removed to create more space for gardens, and 100 internees received private plots to cultivate. Elizabeth Vaughan got one four-by-eleven-meter plot. She wanted to plant peanuts since they grow easily in the Philippines and have a high return, but they require five months to mature. "There are those who say that I will never harvest my crop—that the war will be over before that time Beth and Clay and I have fresh peanut butter. . . . Onions and corn are up between the peanut hills. . . . Fresh, tender corn-on-the-cob with hot butter—what a dream delicacy! The thought spurs me on with gardening."[63]

The Japanese looked on the internees' Santo Tomas gardens with pride and on several occasions brought visiting dignitaries to visit the gardens. In October and November of 1944, even while the Allies were bombing Manila, the commandant ordered that all available space be given over to garden production. The Japanese also made gardens and "hired" prisoners to work on them by paying them with an extra food ration. Work was difficult because prisoners were already slowly starving on about a thousand calories per day, and rations continued to be reduced. The camp garden yielded seventy-four tons of talinum in 1944, but there were thousands of hungry mouths to feed. Internees ate garden weeds; leaves off trees, shrubs, and roots; and even lily bulbs, although these are nearly fatal.

There were private gardens as well as the more ambitious communal enterprises. Alice Franklin Bryant's husband, William Cheney Bryant, was experienced in engineering, irrigation, and all aspects of island life; he had lived in the Philippines since 1902 and had been a provincial governor. The "Gov'nor," as he was known, had also run a coconut plantation. He began gardening immediately and proved to be an energetic and successful gardener. His first garden was lost after the Japanese fenced off that portion of the camp, but his next effort was in a safer location between the wall and barbed-wire fence, where the Japanese allowed access only at certain times. This colonization of marginal spaces was common to many POW gardens.

The Gov'nor's garden was much admired, and Bryant took great pride in her husband's accomplishment: "I was fortunate to have a husband who possessed a great deal of energy and initiative. If I had admired him before the war for being a dirt farmer, my admiration now increased when I saw other men with hungry families sitting around reading novels." His ability and willingness to do the labor of creating and maintaining their garden himself benefited not only the Bryants: he was generous with his labor and with seedlings, readily giving both to help other internees. According to Bryant, "Even after he had became weakened from starvation, he spent afternoons starting a garden for one of his friends."[64]

Elizabeth Vaughan's story begins with the Japanese bombing of Manila on December 8, 1941. Almost immediately, many British and American civilians fled to hide in the mountains. In April 1942 Vaughan and her two children evacuated in a group of nine adults, five children, and twelve servants to a camp in the hills, which they endeavored to make livable. After three weeks, however, life in the hills became untenable, and they were forced to surrender. The group was first imprisoned at the Bacolod internment camp on the grounds of Bacolod North Elementary School. Encircled by an electrified barbed-wire fence, this six-acre camp housed about 150 people. Vaughan and her group were later transferred to the camp at the University of Santo Tomas. In the community where Vaughan lived before the war — known as sugar central, a community built around a sugar mill—the social rank of the household affected everything, including delivery of produce: the Filipino delivery boy worked his way down from the manager through the various engineers and managers, with the lowest-ranking household receiving produce last. In Santo Tomas, however, there was no rank among the internees. But in April 1943, Vaughan would observe middle-aged men in Santo Tomas sweeping leaves and tending flower beds "without regard to previous wealth or position, and all stripped to the waist."[65]

LOS BAÑOS, LUZON, THE PHILIPPINES   To relieve overcrowding in Santo Tomas, that same spring some of the internees were transferred to Los Baños. This experimental farm of the University of the Philippines forty miles southeast of Manila was in a beautiful location, surrounded on three sides by banana and coconut trees and on the fourth side by Laguna de Bay. It was, however, patrolled by guards and fenced in by barbed wire. In the move from Santo Tomas, prisoners tried to salvage what they could from the garden.

Jerry Sams brought one small red-pepper plant to Los Baños, and he and his wife, Margaret, would give people a pepper or two as a kind gesture. Margaret noted in her memoir that the plant lasted until their liberation: "We had one pepper for the day of liberation, and one for the next, and then we would have been finished for there weren't even any new flowers on it. We walked right off and left both of those peppers on that plant!"[66]

In May 1943, Pat Hell, a mining engineer, urged his fellow prisoners to plant a garden, but many laughed at his idea: "What the devil, Pat, our troops will be here before any harvest. Why waste your energy?" Despite the skeptics, he got men to help him and ultimately became the head gardener at Los Baños. Hell had hidden in the mountains and was captured by the Japanese. Fearful and emaciated, according to Grace Nash, Hell "had found new confidence, of a sort, in working hard at our camp garden." By 1945 the gardens had been harvested twice and, despite the fact that the Japanese often took portions of the crop, it still saved many from starvation.[67]

Even with the permission of their captors, gardeners still needed extraordinary stamina to work. Author Agnes Newton Keith was imprisoned on Borneo. Internees at Berhala Island camp were starving by war's end. "Every square foot of the camp was in use for gardens, but the soil was exhausted, and we were exhausted." At the end of the war she inquired about the POW camps near theirs. "It was a barren eroded waste," and she asked why they did not have gardens. They responded that their forced labor outside the camp robbed them of any energy they might have had left to work in the garden. As Keith noted, "A consistent program of starvation, overwork, torture, and beating had made anything beyond mere existence impossible."[68]

Gardens are best understood in context by examining both their physical settings and the mental landscapes that people bring as part of their experience and as a component of their desires. Although the gardens prisoners made were of primary importance to their makers, examining the other landscapes — particularly those that offered a contrast or respite from their plight — helps us understand the full meaning of gardens to the imprisoned.

For civilian internees, especially those in Asia, the contrast between their prewar experience and internment was an inversion of their entire social order from a life of elite privilege, as the Bryants and the Vaughans found. Agnes Newton Keith writes about visiting the home of a British couple at Sandakan in northern Borneo before the war: "Here on the hill was a beautiful garden; the native gardener cut lawns, hacked hedges and trees, but Theresa Mitchell, the British hostess, made the flowers bloom there. Here were spectacular azaleas, orchids, roses, begonia, cosmos. . . . [flowers] that nobody else could grow." Bryant recalled it as a "physical Eden-like framework," but her internment drew her to the realization that "paradise . . . was largely a frame of mind."[69]

The view beyond the borders of a camp could offer solace or frustration, but the fence always loomed. Giovanni Guareschi recorded the "sights of the day" from his Polish prison camp. Beyond the fence he saw that "the barley growing in the field at the east side of the camp has begun to turn golden yellow," but "a clump of red flowers has blossomed between the two rows of fencing." In the camp at Chieti was a walkable perimeter, inside of which was a nine-meter-wide strip bordered by a low wooden rail. Westheimer observed that "when spring came, the only grass in the prisoner's *settori* grew between the guard rail and the wall. It would have been nice to walk on it barefoot but not worth being shot for." There was a wall that "blocked the view of our immediate surroundings except for a few roofs and treetops. The top of an apple tree showed over the wall just behind our bungalow. (When spring came and the nightingales sang in it, it blossomed with rare beauty.)"[70]

At Stanley in Hong Kong, Jean Gittins was refreshed by her contact with nature. "When the closeness of other human beings drove one to distraction, there was escape to be found on the hillside where a moment's contemplation of nature helped restore one's peace of mind. The indestructible beauty of sea and sky, the small green islands set like gems in the blue ocean, the moonlit waters, their mirror-like calm broken only by an occasional ripple of phosphorescent surf — nature soothed and comforted with greater efficacy than any man-made drug could have done." William Sewell found a similar satisfaction. "The sight of the blue sea ever breaking in white waves against the brown rocks, which rise to the green hillsides, was itself a great blessing. However strong our anxieties might be, however much our captors might try to make life difficult for us, nothing could take away the beauty of the sea, the islands, the mountains and the sky." Having first been interned at the crowded Santo Tomas and among those removed to Los Baños, Margaret Sams "could see beyond the fence to the blue mountains in the distance. There was a feeling of space here which we never had in Santo Tomas." Having grown up in the American West, she welcomed the spaciousness. "The green-blue mountains in the distance, the brilliant flowered hibiscus close at hand, and the glistening green groves just over the fence, did a great deal to make the next year bearable."[71]

Forms of deprivation underlie most punishments, and imprisonment — the loss of freedom through captivity — is the most powerful deprivation. Prisoners are deprived, dehumanized, and placed under tremendous stress. Former World War I POW Horace Gilliland thought that the "whole atmosphere was deliberately contrived to break down the spirit, endurance, and health of the prisoners."[72] Even the most well adjusted and humanely treated prisoners (who were very rare) will find it difficult to not "go round the bend" or go "stir crazy" from boredom, fear, and anxiety. But people demonstrate exceptional resourcefulness in finding ways to cope with being placed in horrible predicaments. They are compelled to submit to and comply with their captors, but they also find ways to resist and to defy those captors.

In camps where prisoners were not forced to labor, gardening helped overcome boredom by providing purposeful work. As with the mental escape that gardening afforded soldiers on the front lines of World War I and ghetto residents in World War II, POWs and civilian internees also had a mental respite from their captivity and deprived circumstances.

Gardening's therapeutic value distinguished it from prisoners' other activities. In particular, garden making fostered an adjustment to being placed in these extraordinarily "unnatural habitats."[73] Its produce provided sustenance and variation to diet. The garden helped relieve stress, was an antidote to deprivation, and was a profoundly humanizing activity. As a creative, purposeful activity, gardens engaged all aspects of a person, with an aesthetic as well as practical result.

Gardens and gardening offered prisoners a modicum of control over their situation, one modest way of having authority over their diminished portion of the world and exercising power in an otherwise powerless situation. In February 1943 Colonel Shorland in his Changi dairy summed up succinctly his time in captivity: "assets: work, mentally in office and physically in the garden." For liabilities, he found the "lack of touch with families . . . the worst evil."[74]

Psychologist J. Davidson Ketchum, who was imprisoned at Ruhleben, thought that all the organization and activity, including gardening, meant "that the men could lead a *purposeful* life in internment and thus preserve their mental integrity."[75] Purpose implies a goal, and at a fundamental level a garden has a medium-range goal of the expectation of a plant growing, flowering, and producing. In the simplest, yet also profound sense, caring for a garden could be something to look forward to, both the work in the garden and the hoped-for result.

For the prisoner, the opposite of work is not leisure but boredom — and perhaps that is true of the human condition. Garden activity keeps people busy, but it is not "make-work" in the way smashing rocks or moving something back and forth between two places is. Instead, it is purposeful and productive.

People always become attached to the products of their efforts, but with so little stimulation or opportunity to exercise or demonstrate one's capabilities, the attachment was accentuated. The sense of loss can be one measure of significance. Elizabeth Vaughan found solace

I know a pretty bungalow,
Primly sweet and small,
Where clematis and fuchsia grow
Leaning to the wall.
Where pohutukawa flames
Against Hauraki skies
And red and gold along the eaves
The warm minelia lies.

John Phillips created "Haven," an illustrated poem that appeared in the *Tiki Times,* the hand-printed weekly newspaper of POW Camp E535 in Milowitz, Poland. Most of the prisoners, who worked in a coal mine, were from New Zealand.

in nature, but she worried that "prolonged imprisonment had wrought changes in my mind." When she got permission from the Japanese to expand her peanut patch to include camotes, she went to work digging and planting. Soon, however, a guard claimed her new garden for a foxhole, taking advantage of the well-turned soil. Vaughan protested the usurpation and violation in vain, writing in her diary, "the camotes had a good stand and their wanton and useless destruction by the Japanese has hurt me as deeply as any of the thousands of incidents of the petty wastefulness of this utterly useless and wasteful war."[76]

One of the garden's classic associations is as place of refuge, a sanctuary from environmental conditions, privation, or hardship, a role well suited to the POW or internee. In some situations an existing garden continued and accentuated that function. At the Catholic University of Santo Tomas, the Japanese had left undisturbed a small garden lined with hedges, known as the Father's Garden. Karen Kerns Lewis notes in her memoir the importance of the garden to former and present users: "This beautiful garden and grotto had been a place of prayer and meditation for the university faculty and seminarians before the war. . . . For the internees, too, it became a special place for prayers, solitude, and privacy." She also adds that she suspected "it was also a popular meeting place for midnight trysts," surely another

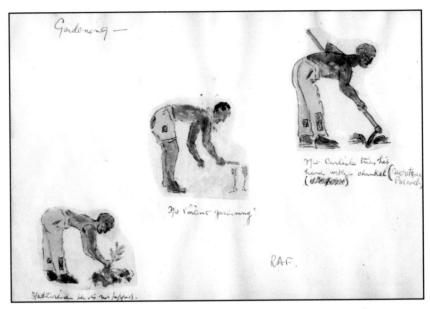

G. D. H. Ross, Group Captain British POW of Japanese in Java from
March 1942 until September 1945, also kept a sketchbook, which included
these two pages depicting gardening.

classic function of garden spaces. Alice Bryant also recalled that,
although originally a "pleasant plot of grass, shrubs and trees, relatively quiet and private," the Father's Garden was transformed by
internees, "crisscrossed with clothes lines, cut up into garden patches,
and disfigured with flimsy shanties."[77]

The mere sight of a garden could provide comfort or a reminder
of emotions that otherwise had no opportunity for expression.
Agnes Newton Keith tells of an outing on which Colonel Suga, commandant of Berhala Island camp, took three of the camp's thirty-four
children into the town of Kuching. The children talked the whole
way and commented on "every green field and flowering canna, every
house and building, every motor and rickshaw, every cow and bul-
lock, dog and cat, every bird in the sky." They were taken to his
house, where he saw that they were fed and let them play with his pet
monkey. When the children were allowed into Suga's garden, Keith
reports that the profusion of flowers and flowering shrubs made
"Rosemary and Anne . . . wild with joy." Moved by the children's

response, the commandant himself "cut an armful for them to carry back to camp."[78]

A. L. Vischer, originator of the term "barbed-wire disease," offered his analysis of what could act as cure for the aftereffects of prisoners afflicted with the disease. He thought it best to return to family and also to one's occupation, but he advised against a return to being a factory worker, which he felt "proceeds so monotonously and joylessly." On the other hand, he proclaimed "cultivation of the land . . . an ideal occupation for the released prisoner. Land cultivation is in itself a noble task; it is of infinite value and it binds man to his native soil. No herded existence with chance acquaintances is involved, no agitation; it is independent of human influence. . . . Migration to the land arouses from no sentimental cry, 'back to nature,' but from the elemental desire for rest, sub-conscious in every individual."[79] Despite his demurral, his prescription seems more romantic than medical, but it does testify to what science has subsequently validated, that gardening can have a profound therapeutic value.

The common in peacetime often took on uncommon meaning in war. Paradoxically, part of the defiant garden's meaning and significance is its ordinary quality, its prosaic characteristics. The ordinary implies consistency and predictability, and in that is found a comfort and security. The regularities and anticipations of life — the expectation of the daily cycle (the sun will rise), of seasonal change (winter will end), of the growth of people (I will grow older), and of continuity in the natural world (the trees will grow taller) — all give stability to life. We expect these things as part of our understanding of existence, and when they are disrupted we find it disturbing, even frightening, and debilitating — we lose our equilibrium, in a sense. Such was the case for prisoners. They were subject not only to the immediacy of the whims of guards, but also to forces far beyond their control and even awareness, such as the progress of the war and the disposition of their fates. Tomorrow was nowhere near assured. In such circumstances, what is common, ordinary, homey, or even subconscious may be transformed. The ordinary can become extraordinary, the common uncommon, and that which is taken for granted can become essential. The delight in what is modestly pleasant can become the object of profound gratification.

In his Polish prison camp, POW Giovanni Guareschi mused, "here everything is seen as if through a magnifying glass: a blade of grass, a hair, a particle of dust. Having lost one world, these prisoners must create another, within the few square feet of sand to which they are confined, and poke it with their everyday discoveries." German Dr. Vischer admired the innumerable methods "adopted by the British [prisoners] at Ruhleben and elsewhere to kill the ennui and to stifle pessimism." He thought that "not enough has been made, I think, of the amusing trifles of camp life and their power to detract materially from the searing and depressing monotony of camp existence — a power out of all proportion to the intrinsic importance of the incidents."[80] Under the right conditions, gardens can assume this exceptional power.

The Ruhleben Horticultural Society committee wrote in its 1917–18 report of the continuous impact the yield from the gardens had on prisoners' daily lives: "A flower show is, with all its beauty and interest, after all an event; the steaming vegetable makes its appeal rather as product of the kitchen than of the garden; but the flower bed with

This drawing by a German POW shows the garden at Stenay, France, at
the prison camp for captured German soldiers, 1944–45.

its colour, and the green creeper with its restful shade, are verily a part
of our daily life, and just as their absence in the early days of the camp
left a void, so now their ever-changing presence satisfies a natural
longing."[81]

Survivors of the prisoner experience often had a newfound appreciation of what had been everyday experience. After nine months of
imprisonment, André Warnod left camp by train. When it stopped
en route, he went out onto the platform, where there were civilians:
"We could see them without a wire fence between us; and at one
stopping place there was grass — grass and wild flowers, where we
could stretch ourselves at length." When Horace Gilliland escaped
and returned to London from the Netherlands, "the long rolling
fields bounded by broad hedges, the picturesque farms nestling in
hollows, with fat cattle grazing over every hilltop, the wonderful
soothing green of the general landscapes, brought a heavy sigh of
content to be back in it all again. Everything seemed as if we had just
left it."[82]

In a May 1945 letter written on his homeward travel after his liberation from a prisoner-of-war camp, Captain A. D. M. Hilton wrote: "We took off at 1900. Oh! Boy what a thrill. En route England, Home, and Beauty."[83] In three words he triangulated what he had been deprived of while a prisoner. He regained three essentials of which he was now surely more aware and appreciative. In a most modest way, a garden could encapsulate and represent them all.

FIVE ❧ Stone Gardens
Japanese American Internment Camps, 1942–45

SHOJI NAGUMO has been called the "father of southern California gardeners."[1] The first week of December 1941, he, Fujitaro Kubota, and Sam Fucuda were working as gardeners and landscapers in Los Angeles, Seattle, and San Francisco. Within two months they would be in assembly camps at the Santa Anita and Tanforan racetracks and Puyallup, Washington (also known as Camp Harmony). Six months later they and thousands of others would be "relocated" to internment camps in remote areas of the American west: Heart Mountain in northern Wyoming, Minidoka in southern Idaho, Manzanar in California's Owens Valley, Tule Lake in northern California, Gila River and Poston in southern Arizona, Granada in southeast Colorado, Topaz in central Utah, and Rohwer and Jerome in Arkansas. Before and after the war they practiced their professions with skill, designing, building, and maintaining gardens and parks throughout the United States. During the war, involuntarily imprisoned by their government along with thousands of other Japanese Americans, they would, under the most difficult of circumstances, create great American gardens.

The Issei are first-generation Japanese immigrants; their American-born children are known as Nisei; their children, third-generation Americans, are Sansei; their children, Yonsei. Kibei were Nisei who were sent to school in Japan and then returned to the United States. In 1940 there were 126,947 "Japanese" on the mainland United States, most living on the West Coast; of these, 37 percent were Issei and 63 percent were Nisei. These people had been in the United States for years, since the U.S. National Origins Act of 1924 limited immigration by Japanese citizens to a mere one hundred persons per year. All of the Nisei were American citizens, and many Issei would probably have become citizens if U.S. government policy didn't prohibit them from becoming naturalized. An additional 150,000 Japanese Americans were living in Hawaii, then a territory.

On February 19, 1942, President Franklin Delano Roosevelt signed Executive Order 9066, which authorized the establishment of military areas "from which any or all persons may be excluded." It was primarily directed at the 120,000 Japanese Americans living in a newly demarcated exclusion zone that included all of Oregon, California, western Washington, and southern Arizona. Given anywhere between six and twenty-one days to put their affairs in order, they were to be removed to undisclosed locations away from their homes and communities. The civilian exclusion order specified that they could take only "that which can be carried by the family of the individual." They sold their businesses, homes, and possessions for a fraction of their worth or they put them in the trust of friends or associates. Little of this would be recovered after the war. The displaced population included 17,000 under the age of ten, 2,000 over the age of sixty-five, and 1,000 handicapped or infirm individuals. By law, being one-sixteenth Japanese by blood was sufficient to be interned.[2]

The stated reasons for the relocation of Japanese Americans were military necessity and the likelihood that these "enemy aliens" would undertake actions subversive to the war effort. This rationale exposed the overt racism of the order, for neither German Americans nor Italian Americans were subject to the order. In a bizarre undermining of the rationale that Japanese Americans posed a subversive, military threat, those in Hawaii and the approximately seven thousand living in other parts of the country were not relocated.

These actions, in gross violation of constitutional protection and civil liberties, were contested by some at the time, but the nation had just entered World War II, and the Japanese American community had few allies. Only in 1982 did the U.S. Commission of Wartime Relocation and Internment of Civilians report, *Personal Justice Denied,* conclude that the underlying causes for internment were "race prejudice, war hysteria and a failure of political leadership." Six years later, the U.S. Civil Liberties Act offered a belated official apology from the government, along with reparations payments of $20,000 to each surviving internee.

In response to Roosevelt's executive order, the federal War Relocation Authority (WRA) was formed. "Evacuees," the term preferred by
the WRA, were to be sent to "relocation centers" or "internment
camps."[3] While these camps were being constructed, a hundred thousand Japanese Americans were rounded up and temporarily housed at
seventeen hastily prepared assembly centers in Washington, Oregon,
California, and Arizona, where they were to be confined and segre-
gated from the general population. A former Civilian Conservation
Corps work camp and two migrant worker camps were put into service, but most persons were sent to nine fairgrounds, two racetracks,
a mill site, and an exposition center.

Most of these had been designed to house animals and had barely
been prepared for human habitation. Stables and stalls were cleansed
and converted to barracks, but the stench of animals remained. The
evacuees scrounged lumber and materials and immediately went
about the task of making the places livable. In the assembly centers
the internees rapidly proved their mettle in transforming an inhospitable place into a habitable environment. Shocked and even bewil-
dered by their incarceration and treatment by their government, the
evacuated population responded in ways that brought to the fore fundamental aspects of cultural identity. An attitude of acceptance and
resignation, of *Shikata ga nai*—"it cannot be helped"—was coupled
with the trait of *Gaman*—"perseverance and fortitude." In each
center they went about the task of self-organizing a community—
complete with newspaper, church, hobby shows, dances, sports—as
well as the physical transformation of the site. They took responsibility for cleaning and landscaping the grounds. They built ornamental gardens as well as victory gardens, the name that had been coined
in World War I for home-front vegetable gardens that contributed to
the war effort. A twenty-two-year-old agricultural student at the
assembly camp in Stockton said that "we set right to work to make
furniture and build a gravel walk. We even planted a victory garden."[4]
The irony of victory gardens for an interned population was dramatic.
In addition, evacuees planted in full knowledge they might not be able
to reap the fruits of their harvest before being uprooted again.

Many Issei had some agricultural experience. In the United States,
racially exclusive laws and their limited knowledge of English
restricted their occupational choices, so many Issei found it easier to

At Tanforan Assembly Center in June 1942, San Bruno, California. The original caption to Dorothea Lange's photograph read: "Mrs. Fujita and her neighbor inspecting the tiny vegetable garden she has planted in front of their barracks."

become employed in agriculture. The native-born and more acculturated Nisei had enjoyed expanded opportunities, but the agricultural tradition was well established. Many immigrant bachelors lived in boarding houses, known as gardeners' colleges, that acted as informal employment agencies and training grounds. The gardeners began to organize, and in 1937 three gardening associations joined forces to create the League of Southern California Japanese Gardeners. They had nine hundred members by 1940 when they began publication of the *Gardener's Monthly* or *Gadena no Tomo*. In 1934, a third of the Los Angeles Japanese American labor force were gardeners (1,500 out of 5,125). Many of these had been farmers, but discriminatory alien land laws drew many to work in the city. Forty-three percent of West Coast Japanese Americans were employed in agriculture and another 26 percent were in agriculture-related activities and business. They were farmers, truck farmers, nursery owners, flower farmers, and orchardists, as well as gardeners maintaining residential properties.

They operated greenhouses and flower shops and ran fruit stands. Before the war, the Japanese dominated the garden business on the West Coast, especially in southern California, the San Francisco Bay area, and Puget Sound. Their skill and industriousness was recognized by all, and there was even some prestige associated in employing a Japanese gardener.

Mine Okubo, a graduate student in fine arts at Berkeley, was interned along with almost eight thousand people for five and a half months at the Tanforan Assembly Center in San Bruno, California, a racetrack and stables. She was subsequently relocated to the Topaz camp in Utah. Okubo became a faculty member of the art school established at Tanforan by the internees and kept a sketchbook and journal in which she recorded her experiences. Okubo drew the victory gardens and noted that "great care and attention were given to them by the owners, who were spurred by competitive pride. The best were those of former truck gardeners and nurserymen." The skill of the camp's horticulturists, designers, and builders was apparent. The caption on one of her drawings reads: "A group of landscape architects decided to build a lake to beautify the camp. Trees and shrubs were dug up from various places and transplanted in the center field. . . . The workmen struggled day after day with limited equipment. For a long time we were kept in wonderment by this activity." She adds significantly, "everyone knew the camp was not a permanent one." Yet a few months later an entry marked the opening of North Lake: "It had been transformed from a mere wet spot in the Tanforan scenery into a miniature aquatic park, complete with bridge, promenade and islands. The lake was a great joy to the residents and presented new material for artists. In the morning sunlight and at sunset it added great beauty to the bleak barracks."[5]

Charles Kikuchi also kept a journal of his Tanforan experience before being sent to the Gila camp in Arizona four months later. His Tanforan journal entry on May 3, 1942, the day after his arrival, notes about the assembly camp's victory garden, "These industrious Japanese! They just don't seem to know how to take it easy — they've worked so hard all their lives that they just can't stand idleness — or waste." A month later he describes the garden the internees have created in the racetrack's infield, adding that he thinks the "whole thing looks like old Japan. Some people just can't divorce themselves from Japan and cling to the old traditions and ways. The garden is an outward indication of this sentiment for Japan. The odds are that the builder of the garden is pro-Japan, although he may have built it for cultural reasons." In his journal Kikuchi, a student at the School of Social Welfare at Berkeley, perceptively ascribes political as well and cultural motives to Tanforan's garden makers. He is well aware of the symbolic messages gardens can convey.

By the end of July, Kikuchi recorded the internees' remarkable conversion in three months of a racetrack and stables into a domesticated space. Internees had transformed a "mud hole" into a level, graveled walk lit by streetlamps, which Kikuchi referred to as Grant Avenue, after the San Francisco street. He noted that "gardens have sprung up all over the place and the vegetables are now ready to eat." The internees had created sports fields and constructed a greenhouse to provide additional ways to keep active and productive. Kikuchi's journal also reveals his awareness of the internees' imprisonment: "Outside I can hear the swish of the cars as they go by down the highway. The barbed wire fence way below reminds us that we are on the inside. On the other side of the highway there is a huge glass hothouse where they raise chrysanthemums and dahlias. The tiny men working hard way in the distance look like ants, but they are free men."[6]

Evacuees would not enjoy their domestication of assembly camps for long, since the WRA was preparing more permanent relocation camps that aspired to be self-sufficient. The WRA's criteria for selecting sites were clear: they were to be far from population centers, a "safe distance" from military installations, but with railroad access and the potential for large-scale agriculture. Ten camps were built, all but two (in rural Arkansas) in the western American desert. (There were also additional Justice Department internment camps known as citizen isolation camps.) The eight desert camps were dusty, windblown sites, devoid of vegetation, unbearably hot in the summer, and frigid in the winter.

Political meaning momentarily put aside, internment camps did have a kinship with other forms of settlements. Each camp was laid out on a military model and at first glance looked like an army camp, but fences and guard towers revealed these as prison camps. As places built with great rapidity, they also fell into the American western tradition of "instant" cities.

Each site had climatic problems and challenges. Manzanar, Poston, and Gila River were in deserts. Minidoka, Heart Mountain, and

Granada had harsh, freezing winters and summer dust storms, as did Topaz, which was covered with greasewood brush. Rohwer and Jerome in Arkansas were in swampland. The internees were coming from the mild climate and environments of the West Coast. In addition to other hardships, they were thrust into alien terrain, as revealed by their first impressions. Jeanne Wakatsuki Houston, who was only seven when she entered Manzanar internment camp, recalled that "some old men left Los Angeles wearing Hawaiian shirts and Panama hats and stepped off the bus at an altitude of 4,000 feet, with nothing available but sagebrush and tarpaper to stop the April winds pouring down off the back side of the Sierras." A commercial artist's first impression of Manzanar "was the bareness of the land. I never saw anything like it. There wasn't a tree in sight, not even a blade of green grass. Coming from the northwest where there were a lot of green fields and forests, the sight staggered most of us. On top of that we had huge dust storms which made life miserable." Transferred from the Santa Anita Assembly Center to Granada (also known as Amache), Lili Sasaki recorded the dismay of the internees upon their arrival: "everybody was shocked because there was nothing but sand and sandstorms and tumbleweeds. Not a thing to see."[7]

The most common observation was of the camp's isolation and barrenness, and in places devoid of almost any vegetation, the omnipresent dust. Toyo Suyemoto recalled that, en route by train to Topaz, the "landscape became dreary, devoid of the greenery familiar on the West Coast. The Issei, who once had gardens or extensive farms, were faced with the sight of vast empty land where the sage grew and tumbleweeds rolled." As buses took them from the train station to Topaz, Yoshiko Uchida observed farmland, which was reassuring. However, the buses crossed into the Sevier Desert, and Uchida's heart sank: "All vegetation stopped. There were no trees or grass or growth of any kind, only clumps of dry skeletal greasewood. . . . The surroundings were now as bleak as a bleached bone." Arrivals at Heart Mountain encountered a similar landscape, and the first experience of some was of a blinding sandstorm. Of Poston, Lawrence Sasano said, "If you went to an area without any trees, totally barren and full of silt knee-high, and if you went into this all by yourself — it would be very discouraging, right? Well, this is the kind of environment they [the WRA] selected. This Poston is Indian reservation, but none of the Indians wanted it! Just barren, worse than desert, it's nothing but silt, knee high."[8] Poston was at an elevation of

4,700 feet, had an annual average of eight inches of rainfall and averaged minus 30 degrees Fahrenheit in winter and over 100 degrees Fahrenheit in summer. At Topaz, Gila, and Poston, internees eventually dug cellars below the barracks to escape the worst heat of the day.

Isolated in sparsely populated areas, these were "semi-permanent new cities" with populations that ranged at their peak from 7,000 to almost 19,000. Poston and Gila became the third- and fourth-largest cities in Arizona, Manzanar the biggest city between Reno and Los Angeles, and Heart Mountain the third-largest city in Wyoming. At the conclusion of the war, the camps were dismantled and their residents dispersed, much as western lumber and mining camps had been. Many buildings were then reerected elsewhere. Ultimately the camps joined the western American legacy of ghost towns. They were to be rediscovered largely through the assertive actions of camp veterans in the Japanese American community. This finally led to their preservation as historic sites; Manzanar, for example, was designated a National Historic Site in 1992.

While each was distinct, the camps had been built by the WRA according to a set of prototypical plans. Guard towers were set along a fenced perimeter (Poston and Gila River were the exceptions), and inside the camp the basic layout was like an army camp. A grid of mostly unpaved roads divided the camp between blocks of wooden barracks separated by firebreaks. Each block had ten to fourteen barracks, with a mess hall, laundry, storage buildings, latrines, and recreation hall. The barracks were 20 by 100 or 120 feet and housed four families of four to six persons each; the families were often strangers to each other. Flimsy partitions merely suggested privacy.

Although residents described the camps as scorching, manmade hells, they nevertheless went to work yet again to transform these new inhospitable environments into something livable — anything to relieve the barrenness and tedium. Internees immediately went about the task of modifying their habitation, building partitions and furniture from whatever scrap lumber could be found. The residents modified the functions of the original WRA structures, converting buildings to fit their needs for worship, meeting rooms, classrooms, libraries, and other community services. By October 1942, half of the blocks at Manzanar had built Japanese *furo* (baths). Over time the internees built additional structures and facilities to meet the desires of the community: schools, churches, judo halls.

Spaces between the buildings were largely unassigned. There were

This photograph by Dorothea Lange shows the victory gardens at
Manzanar in 1942.

large firebreaks between blocks, and some areas were designated as
play areas on plans. Given the cramped and uncomfortable barracks, outdoor spaces were critical. At Manzanar Jeanne Wakatsuki
Houston found that "once the weather warmed up, it was an out-of-
doors life, where you only went 'home' at night, when you finally had
to: 10,000 people on an endless promenade inside the square mile of
barbed wire that was the wall around our city."[9]

Internees transformed the camps at all scales, from the interiors of
barracks to the landscape itself. They planted victory gardens in firebreaks and between barracks and constructed playgrounds and sports
facilities for baseball, basketball, and volleyball. At Heart Mountain
they diverted water from a canal to make a large earthen swimming
pool. They built sidewalks, installed lighting systems, planted trees,

and created parks and gardens. The WRA had provided a raw framework for the energy and ingenuity of the inhabitants, who were domesticating an inhospitable environment. More was at stake, however. According to architectural historian Lynne Horiuchi, "The internees' building programs created community planning and new built environments as a means of defiance, less direct than political organizing, yet significant in transforming the conditions of their internment. By appropriating governance and building processes from the United States government administration, the internees created their own 'town' with their own town architects." The internees participated in a process of building and rebuilding, altering their barracks and camp design. A businessman from California scrounged leftover lumber to build a quintessential American front porch for his family's apartment "so that we could sit out there during the hot evenings." To complete the transformation, he later added a lawn.[10]

These small, instant towns mirrored, as if through a Japanese American prism, the picket-fenced Main Street American life that continued beyond their barbed-wire enclosure. Clubs and organizations were popular. The Boy and Girl Scouts were active, as were the YMCA, YWCA, and sports leagues. A nine-hole golf course of oiled sand was constructed at Manzanar. There were theater groups, dances, classes, and active hobby groups. Cultural continuity was sustained with classes and displays of judo, sumo, kendo, games of go, ikebana classes and competitions, and poetry contests. Buddhism was a spiritual refuge and a "repository of Japanese traditions," and individuals collected materials to rebuild the left-behind family altars (*butsudan*) honoring their ancestors.[11] Japanese language classes, however, were generally forbidden by the authorities.

The abundance of activities and the internees' transformation of spaces to accommodate them helped alleviate the oppressiveness and indignity of the situation. The population was accustomed to hard work, so idleness was a serious morale problem they promptly addressed by keeping busy; taking part in camp life was an important antidote. A male clerk from California working in a recreation program said he "felt happy in a way to find that I was responsible for contributing to something that was constructive."[12]

Many internees were sent to work outside the camps. At Topaz one man recalled the sense of freedom that accompanied getting out of the camp to work on a farm, adding that, on the drive to the farm "I filled my eyes with the sight of green lawns, individual homes, paved streets, and actually water fountains. I never realized how much I missed those things that I had seen so often in San Francisco." For others, the energetic homemaking at the camps had the desired effect of improving spirits. Artist Kango Takamura at first found the mountains around Manzanar beautiful but the heat, wind, and sun oppressive, "but one year after, it's quite a change . . . a year after they built the camp and put water there, the green grows up. And mentally everyone is better. That's one year after."[13]

Arthur Kleinkopf, the superintendent of education at Minidoka, insightfully referred to the internees as "colonists," although one significant distinction between colonists and the internees was that the latter had not volunteered to be relocated. However, like colonists, they were engaged in an encounter with a strange territory, and they adapted their culture to these alien conditions and environments. In that sense the camps had an air of "New" Los Angeles, or "New" Seattle, much like the ethnic enclaves, the "Japantowns" — the *nihon-machi* — they had been uprooted from, but in the camps they were self-contained communities, with the larger culture located well beyond the fence lines.

The standard camp layout imposed by the WRA combined elements of military bases, prisons, and farm workers' housing. The plan had an implicit order, including the potential for an open-space system that went from the scale of a unit, the barracks as a multifamily housing, to the blocks, a collection of barracks, to a variety of community spaces. Like the military layout itself, there was an implied hierarchy of space, ranging from the social relations of the individual or family unit to the inhabitants of a block to the larger community. The internees were given an empty frame that they then modified and filled. This was largely on their own initiative, at times encouraged and even facilitated by the camp authorities.

Working within the static framework of the camp created by the WRA, internees created complete, open systems. They created community parks and gardens for families at the entries to their barracks, gardens and recreational spaces in the open spaces between barracks, community parks, and gardens at mess halls and in firebreaks. There were large communal victory gardens and the agricultural enterprises of orchards and fields. In addition there were the recreational

Children playing by the water channel in the pond and garden complex of Manzanar block 12, an oasis of greenery created in the desert.

spaces of fields, courses, and courts. Baseball was especially popular; Minidoka had nine diamonds, and at Gila River the field, designed by professional baseball player Kenichi Zenimura, had bleachers and dugouts and space for six thousand spectators. At Minidoka there was an ice-skating rink, and at Topaz, following a design by Moto Takahashi, the landscape department built a rink larger than a football field. Canals and irrigation ditches were diverted and excavated to create swimming pools. In some camps, spaces beyond the fences were eventually appropriated as gardens and picnic sites.

The camps had no private yards or fences to obscure activity, so the individual and collective actions of garden making were visible to both internees and the WRA. This garden making was also an open and sure sign of internees exerting control over their situation. Gardens became one of the symbols and signatures of the camps themselves and were pointed to with pride by both the Japanese American internees and the government authorities.

Each garden had a distinct function and appearance. The camps

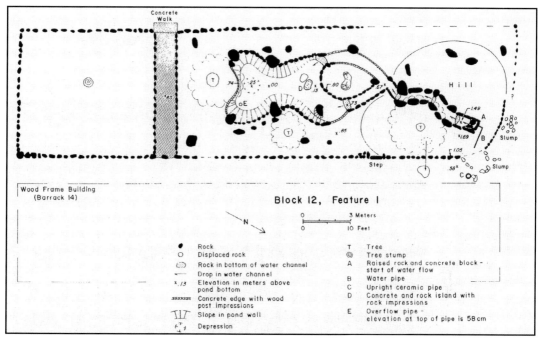

Plan for the garden and pond at Manzanar block 12. The National Park Service has surveyed many of Manzanar's gardens.

were filled with graduates of gardeners' colleges, and their expertise soon came to the fore. Entry gardens were part of the Japanese tradition of dooryard gardens, linking household to community and function as entry and marker, displaying the craft and skill of the resident and embellishing both the barracks and the community space. Barracks gardens displayed great variety, using gathered cacti and rocks, transplanted plants, and plants propagated in the camp nursery. Water features were especially welcome in the arid landscapes. Ponds are essential in traditional Japanese design, but fountains were new elements, part of a still-evolving Japanese American design style. There was an imaginatively wide array of found and scrounged materials, including tin cans, pebbles, bottle caps, and glass. Many persons inscribed their names in cement at the doorstep. Henry Nishi referred to what the internees accomplished as "crude landscaping," but in fact it was often very sophisticated.[14] While people waited daily for the communally served meals at the mess hall, they enjoyed the elaborate displays of great artistry and effort that characterized the mess-hall gardens. Created with rocks and water as well as plants, these gardens were most closely identified with the Japanese American garden tradition. All these gardens brought beauty to the camps and reinforced the internees' sense of cultural identity.

One surviving example of a splendid garden is at block 12 (see illustration on page 167). There, the fifty-foot-long water garden incorporates a roughly hourglass-shaped pond. A small island divides the stream (B, lower right) into two channels, with a cascade on either side as the water enters the pond. The garden is carefully demarcated by a rectangular border of smaller stones.

In these desolate sites, finding and nurturing garden plants took effort. Some people brought plants they had cared for in the assembly camps, and additional seeds and plants were either mail-ordered or gathered locally. Gathering and transforming materials from the immediate and surrounding landscape marked a return to the origins of gardening, even where the natural landscape functioned as a nursery for the gathering of plants. In the WRA report on gardens, Robert Hosokawa observed the activity: "Bit by bit they brought home clumps of grass, mint plants, cattail, reeds and willows. Some found cactus, desert moss and bunchgrass. At first they placed these in bottles and brightened up their rooms. Few had gardens in mind but the materials increased and the idea grew. They carried home unusual formations of lava rock, dug gnarled gray sagebrush to plant as shrubbery along their porches. Children cornered little fish in the shallows of the canal and found rocklike mussels buried in soft silt."[15] As the plant population increased, internees also established camp nurseries to expand seed and plant propagation.

Camp authorities encouraged these activities, as a statement by E. R. Fryer, the regional director of the WRA, reprinted in the *Gila News-Courier,* reveals: "To all of you who live here, I want to give special encouragement in the transplanting of native shrubs and plants around your homes and in the creation of small rock gardens. Many of you brought plants and seeds with you which can also be used. Until irrigation water becomes available, it will be necessary, of course, to plan improvement requiring a small amount of water. I shall watch this program for the improvement of grounds and the beautification of homes with special interest. Later, I hope we can find some way to give special recognition to those whose creations are outstanding."[16]

Eventually, authorities even permitted short, unescorted expeditions outside camp to gather materials, especially stones. Frank

Note the "bonsaied" sagebrush and the Tori gate leading to the park at the northern edge of Minidoka camp.

Kadowaki, an artist who had worked as a farmer at the Irvine Ranch, remembered: "I worked on a Japanese garden for the administration. They gave us a truck and permission to go out and pick up rocks. We'd drive out fifty to seventy-five miles away from camp to bring back rocks — oh, we feel paradise!" These activities merely continued an established prewar garden practice; Arthur Ogami, for example, recalled trips he would make with his father into the hills to find rocks for his garden.[17]

Gathering brought features of the surrounding landscape into the camp and, by removing things from the wild area outside the camp, it also mildly domesticated that landscape. Found stones became the raw materials for compositions complex in structure and symbolism. They were essential in defining garden spaces and demarcating the functional relationships between walkways, barracks, and gardens. Gathering vegetation involved more than simply transplanting: plants were uprooted, replanted, rearranged, and pruned. Sometimes they were left in place but remade. In a powerful image of the cultural transformation of a wild inhospitable place, at the "Wildlife Preserve" in Minidoka Mr. Nitta "bonsaied" the sagebrush in place. His action domesticated the wild plants, made the wild into a garden, and also made it "Japanese."

Agricultural self-sufficiency for each camp was a government objective, and since many internees were in fact skilled and energetic

Chiura Obata's drawing of transplanting trees from the mountains for Topaz, December 1942.

farmers, work toward this goal progressed rapidly. They established seed farms, nurseries, a lath house, and greenhouses, and constructed canals, irrigation ditches, and reservoirs. At Gila River over 1,600 acres were cultivated, and internees redirected effluent from the sewage treatment plant to irrigate a ten-acre farm. At Granada high-school students operated a 500-acre farm. In 1943 Manzanar's farms produced over 42,000 tons of produce. Minidoka's most famous surviving feature is an enormous root cellar.

Despite the commonalities resulting from all the camps being constructed and run by the WRA, the condition and location of each camp was unique. Gila, Manzanar, and Topaz had soils that were amenable to agriculture and gardening. The climate at Heart Mountain was especially harsh, with a growing season of 119 days, but internees nevertheless planted victory gardens and built greenhouses to grow seedlings for the farm. Estelle Ishigo wrote in her memoir that her grandmother ordered seed from a catalog, wanting "to nurse little growing things in her room . . . just once again to see the beauty of young, living plants."[18]

Topaz internees undertook a massive effort to plant over 7,500 trees and 10,000 shrubs in the first year. Uchida described the first Thanksgiving at Topaz:

> The men of our block had spent the entire day planting willow saplings that had been transported into camp from somewhere beyond the desert. The young trees looked too frail to survive in the alkaline soil, but we all felt anything was worth trying. We longed desperately for something green, some trees or shrubs or plants so we might have something to look forward to with the approach of spring. There existed a master plan that called for the planting of one large tree in front of every mess hall and the lining of the two-hundred-foot wide firebreaks between each block with trees as well. It was a nice thought, and efforts to make it a reality got under way in December.

However, most of the 17,500 trees and shrubs succumbed to the desert: "our desert remained a desert, and not even the industrious Japanese Americans could transform it into anything else."[19]

These labors continued, capitalizing on the internees' expertise, and were regularly reported in the camp newspaper, the *Topaz Times*. The city's staff of three landscape architects, including Berkeley graduates Tom Takaki and Don Akamatsu, created and implemented an impressively comprehensive beautification plan under the supervision of Roscoe Bell, chief of the agricultural division. Plans included a mini-park with each housing block, but the plans also specifically gave the residents freedom to participate or individualize these semipublic spaces, noting that "the final appearance of the City will depend largely upon the amount of effort the residents are willing to expend for beautification."[20] It also included plans for athletic fields for baseball, softball, football, tennis courts, and even a nine-hole golf course designed by G. Matsuma, an experienced golf course landscaper. They also addressed plans for walks and paths as well as service areas.

There was also a focus on the civic structure of the camp. Takaki and Nobuo Kawabata, chief foremen of the landscape and gardening section, developed plans for Topaz Plaza, an area between the hospital and administration buildings. A ten-acre nursery under the direction of H. Hayashi and S. Neishi, veteran nurserymen of Oakland, was also established. Mass plantings attempted to ameliorate the dusty and hot conditions as well as beautify the camp.

The original caption of Mine Okubo's drawing read: "In November, Arbor Day was celebrated by the distribution of small shrubs to each block. There was an overnight change in camp scenery. Trees and shrubs appeared in the most unexpected places."

Hundreds of willow and tamarisks, which bloom in late summer, were planted. In the spring of 1943, over two thousand shrubs were shipped from Logan, Utah, for camp landscaping. A picnic area with barbecue pits, tables, and benches was located in a grove of poplar trees.

Mine Okubo's journal recorded these activities. Her sketches of the camp appeared in the *San Francisco Chronicle* along with quotes from Dillon Meyer, the head of the WRA. A rare humorous drawing shows a person tripping over a newly planted tree. She noted the imaginative use of makeshift materials, as windscreens were erected and evening bucket brigades carried water from the laundry to the gardens. In the spring she noted with surprise that, despite the conditions, "green began to appear in the trees and shrubs, especially on those planted near washrooms." The struggle to grow anything at Topaz was constant. Yet despite the setbacks, Uchida observed that the "people of Topaz never gave up in their efforts to improve the camp."[21]

At Granada in eastern Colorado, Atsushi Kikuchi reports that they referred to the place as a sand bowl; when windy, "the whole place filled up with dust. It was almost like a fog." Despite the inhospitable conditions, internees transplanted trees from the nearby riverbank, constructed barracks, and created victory gardens. By the time Kikuchi left, he noted that the camp "was quite green." Wataru Ishisaka remembered "flowers that resembled morning glories. They were a lot bigger than morning glories and really beautiful. The roots

The pond at Poston 1 incorporated bridges and an island populated with
miniature buildings.

were very big, like potatoes. They said that the Indians used to make
wine out of these roots. Digging the roots of the plants became very
popular with the Issei."[22]

George Sogioka thought Poston must be the worst camp, yet he
said with pride that "we built the whole thing. We grew everything —
vegetables and all this and that . . . the Japanese are farmers, they
grow everything in the desert."[23] Gathering was critical at Poston:
Lawrence Sasano transplanted cactus from the desert, including one
fourteen-foot-tall specimen for his garden. Mr. Sato, who met his
future wife at Poston, captured carp from the Colorado River to put
in the fish gardens his family built near their barracks.

Poston's ambitious internees also built three swimming pools along
irrigation ditches that ran through the firebreaks. Men cleared a rare
shaded area full of brush. One resident noted that it began to take on
the appearance of a park with benches and tables. At the request of

Two girls posing in front of their barracks at Tule Lake, northern California.

the camp administration, the sculptor Isamu Noguchi, who was chair of the landscape and park areas, drew plans for parks, recreation areas, and a cemetery, but these were not realized.

Gila River's landscape engineering department employed forty men; it also had a grounds department. Gila residents had already set aside ten acres for community gardens, planted dozens of trees, and beautified barracks when Roy Marubayashi, under the supervision of the landscape engineer Ellsworth Nichols, was asked to develop a general landscape plan for the camp. The departments also landscaped the grounds of the school, the administration buildings, and the hospitals, incorporating citrus trees, palms, and Italian cypress brought from Mesa, Arizona. Marubayashi also drew plans for each residential block, taking into account the efforts already made by individuals. In most issues, the *Gila-News Courier* made a point of praising the individual efforts and "artistic touches" of people like Y. Tomita and Sam Fukuda.

After visiting the Gila River camp in 1943, Eleanor Roosevelt wrote "To Undo a Mistake Is Always Harder than Not to Create One Originally" for *Collier's* magazine. The first lady observed that WRA

Henry Sugimoto's painting *Planting Vegetables* in Rohwer, Arkansas.

contractors had leveled the land completely, removing even scrub growth. She commended the internees for their beautification and domestication efforts: "Around the barracks buildings at Gila, a great effort has been made to ameliorate this condition by using scrap lumber and burlap bags for makeshift porches and awnings. They are now getting screens for protection against the insects. They have made small gardens, some with vegetables and some flowers and shrubs from the surrounding desert, to beautify the barren streets."[24] Ponds, many whimsically shaped, were commonplace at Gila River. Many were constructed partially under the barracks, for cooling, to shelter fish from the sun, or as part of the garden aesthetic.

The natural environment at the Arkansas camps was more amenable to garden creation. At Rohwer, for example, virtually every barracks had a garden, and the camp developed a lushness as tarpaper shacks receded behind the screen of vegetation. Jerome resident Sada Murayama remembered "a trellis with morning glories, forming a tunnel of flowers," and that visitors to the camp were often taken to view a "showplace" block.[25]

Surviving information of garden creation is most abundant for

This photograph of block 5 at Rohwer reveals the differences between the
Arkansas camps and the desert camps.

Minidoka and Manzanar, the two sites that have been the subjects of
extensive research by the National Park Service.

Minidoka Interlude, a yearbook of the camp from September 1942 to
October 1943, includes group photographs of residents posed in
front of their barracks in the camp in Hunt, Idaho. Most pictures
show newly planted trees. Many blocks were individualized with
entry gardens at every doorway, vines trained on the ends of barracks, group vegetable gardens, or stands of sunflowers. The camp's
co-op stores included a flower shop, and several pages from *Minidoka
Interlude* were dedicated to the victory gardens that the children took
care of.

   A 1943 report of the gardens at Minidoka is part of the record for
the camp. "Along the streets of the Minidoka Relocation Center at
random intervals are little gardens, bits of neat landscaping by patient
and artistic Japanese. A few weeks ago the newly-built barracks were
severe and ugly. The dust was deep around each crude porch and it
swirled like smoke when the wind swept through Minidoka." The

author, internee Robert Hosokawa, observed the relationship
between where people came from and the place they encountered:

> The people who moved into these homes were from green hillsides and
> valleys of the coast. They had lived with tree[s] and flowers and broad
> fields of green truck. City people had their lawns and gardens; some lit-
> tle plot to nurse. Even those who lived in yardless downtown hotels
> kept tiny window boxes filled with geraniums and morning glories.
> Minidoka was desiccated, drab and dusty. But life is not worth living
> for these people unless they have something green to cultivate. A few
> brought with them from assembly centers pots of vines or ferns. Most
> of those withered on the train. Tenderly they watered these after reach-
> ing Minidoka to restore their greenness. Some planted radishes and
> onions as soon as they watered down the dust.

The report also details examples of garden creation:

> So it was that Yoshio Hamamoto, resident of Block 2 and an employee
> of the hospital, created a garden. He made a pond of rocks and secured
> enough cement from the dust where a pile of sacks had stood to line
> the bottom and sides. He planted bits of grass and moss to border the
> pond. Then with fish from the canal, pieces of water grass, some mus-
> sels and a frog his garden was complete. It adds much to his home and
> to his leisure moments. Seven bachelors living together at 2-4-E walked
> into the desert every day. It was not long before they had gathered 60
> little sagebrush trees, chosen for their rugged beauty. Patiently they
> trimmed the stunted trees, wired twigs and replanted them in three
> neat rows fronting their barrack. These suggest and often closely re-
> semble the dwarfed pines characteristic in Japanese art.[26]

The WRA superintendent of education at Minidoka, Arthur
Kleinkopf, kept a work diary from 1942 to 1946. His entries are filled
with numerous garden references from their inception and the marshaling of materials through harvests. He observed that "evacuees certainly take great pride in beautifying the homes." Between barracks,
lawns began to appear — the signature element of the American residential garden. Kleinkopf noted that these provided places for children to play and adults to rest. Several hundred acres were given over
to victory gardens. The camp's agriculture club even drew up plans for
the "ideal vegetable garden."[27]

Kleinkopf, an educator, paid careful attention to the school garden
and farm program. In June 1943 he was pleased that "school garden-

ing is certainly being emphasized now. Each grade has a plot to seed
and cultivate." He notes that "many of the pupils and the teachers
have much to learn about gardening. One student teacher asked Mr.
Briggs for the potato plants and was much surprised to learn that one
planted a potato and not a plant. In one row I noticed watermelon and
corn being planted in the same hill." He finds fifth- and sixth-grade
boys carrying water from the laundry room instead of the irrigation
ditch. They said that they were doing that because "they didn't think
that muddy water would be good for the garden."[28] In July Kleinkopf
wrote with pride that the first peas from the gardens were served at
the mess hall. In addition to the smaller school gardens, there was an
experimental farm of fifty acres for the high school as well as a 300-
plus-acre farm to sustain the camp.

Work to beautify the camp also continued unabated. A March 1944
entry in Kleinkopf's diary describes efforts to beautify the area
between blocks 16 and 17, which was to be made into a "natural" picnic area:

> Mr. Nitta, a Japanese gardener, has volunteered his services to do some
> landscaping here. He has landscaped a large area of sagebrush by remov-
> ing all the small scrubby brush, leaving the large ones standing, and has
> planted flowers here and there in the area. He has also constructed
> windbreak walls of lava rock and out of old junk material has made
> camping stoves. One could never imagine a sagebrush area being made
> into a picnic ground, but this one really looks beautiful. Residents and
> particularly the school children are invited to come on picnics. Near this
> sagebrush park there are many gardens of flowers and vegetables. Water
> for this is carried from the nearby irrigation canal. Footbridges with
> banisters and overhead decorations adorn the place. It is one of the
> bright spots of the entire camp.[29]

Over time, internees developed an appreciation and even a sense
of stewardship for the distinctive aspects of the southern Idaho landscape. The *Minidoka Irrigator* reported on the making of an area just
beyond the fence designated "for the preservation of wild plant life"
under the supervision of C. Natsuhara. The article also quoted C.
Misuki's disappointment at the abuse of wild plants by careless residents. "This is not right. We must practice more care in the future or
wild life will disappear altogether," he stated. This concern for conservation echoed the sentiments from Gila, where an editorial titled
"Cactus Cutters Cautioned" in the camp newspaper urged that "when

the days of peace come again and we leave here let us leave these cactus plants as they are today — standing in all their splendor and not dead . . . rotted things on the ground."[30]

A 1943 *Minidoka Irrigator* editorial observed how conditions at the camp fostered an appreciation and awareness of nature. "We hadn't learned to appreciate the good that comes with Nature — until Minidoka. Then the 'beautiful, silvery sage' became a standing joke. Dust and mud became part of the furniture. People learned to wince when they saw a blade of grass uprooted. A struggling green shoot became a dear thing to be coddled and petted. Wistful groups took to gazing longingly at the trees faintly visible beyond the miles on end of sagebrush."[31]

Minidoka education superintendent Kleinkopf was a keen observer of how individuals made use of the environment in which they were thrust. After admiring an artful display of crafts made from the lowly sagebrush, he noted in his diary that, "had Mark Twain been here he might want to re-write his description of the sagebrush. It has been transplanted to many rock gardens around the barracks together with moss, cactus, and desert grass. It adds much to the artistic beauty."[32] Kleinkopf admired the internees' abilities as colonists to see a strange environment with new eyes and to recognize the value and usefulness of the new things they encountered.

Located in California's Owens Valley between the towns of Lone Pine and Independence, Manzanar is familiar to those who know the story of the theft of the valley's water to feed Los Angeles's insatiable thirst. It is an arid landscape, in the rain shadow of the Sierra Nevada, but the snowmelt of the mountains provides an ample water supply. Ansel Adams, who photographed the camp in 1943, found grandeur in the site: "I believe that the arid splendor of the desert, ringed with towering mountains, has strengthened the spirit of the people of Manzanar. I do not say all are conscious of this influence, but I am sure most have responded, one way or another, to the resonances of the environment. From the harsh soil they have extracted fine crops; they have made gardens glow in the firebreaks and between barracks."[33]

Here too open spaces were appropriated and gardens of all sizes created. Home to the largest group of professional gardeners — nearly 60 percent of the internees were farmers or gardeners — largely from southern California, Manzanar displayed the sophisticated skills of this community. According to the National Park Service *Cultural Landscape Report,* the gardens "became poignant expressions of an era in Japanese American history when landscape gardening was at its apex as a profession in the United States."[34] The WRA supported garden and park projects and even paid some landscape professionals.

Gardens and lawns, encouraged by the WRA to help control the omnipresent dust, came almost immediately. By August 1942 the lawns were so successful that the camp newspaper, the *Manzanar Free Press,* bemoaned the fact that there was but a single push mower for the entire camp. Internees constructed a reservoir and canal to feed irrigation water to the camp. They collected granite from the Sierra Nevada and large, jagged volcanic rocks from the White Mountains, using the rocks to create hardscape features such as borders, wading pools, and walls. Other found materials were arranged and molded into arbors, clotheslines, barbecue grills, picnic tables, fences, and even garden borders made of tin cans.

Firebreaks between barracks were transformed into community spaces. One firebreak victory garden was subdivided into plots for which families paid membership dues. Nonmembers could work in the garden on a communal basis. Recreational facilities such as baseball diamonds, football fields, a judo building, and a platform for kendo and outdoor theaters also sprang up in the firebreaks. Still standing on the camp's western edge, Manzanar's fenced cemetery and its monument has become perhaps the single-most identifiable symbol of the internment camp experience.

Manzanar is Spanish for apple orchard, and on the WRA site were remnants of a farming community that had been abandoned by the 1930s. Internees nurtured and incorporated long-neglected apple and pear trees into their open spaces. Jeanne Wakatsuki Houston remembers moving with her parents "to block 28, right up next to one of the old pear orchards. That's where we stayed until the end of the war, and these trees stand in my memory for the turning of our life in the camp, from the outrageous to the tolerable."[35]

The *Manzanar Free Press* credited William Katsuki, a Bel Air area gardener, with the first ornamental garden at his barracks home in block 24. He began construction in April 1942 (the first evacuees arrived March 21). It included a small pond made of granite from the Sierra Nevada, miniature bridges, and Joshua trees from Death Valley, sixty-five miles to the southeast (the Inyo County newspaper editorialized against such trips while gas rationing was in effect). Many oth-

At Manzanar, Dorothea Lange photographed the victory garden plots, which lay in the vast open spaces between blocks of barracks.

ers soon followed Katuski's lead, including Tak Moto, whose rock garden in block 15 was the first residential rock garden mentioned in any of the block manager's daily reports. Houston remembers her father planting succulents and moss and hauling stones from the desert for their doorway garden.

The mess halls became the location for Manzanar's most elaborate gardens. The garden at the block 22 mess hall has taken on almost legendary status, as have the individuals involved in its creation. Hawaii-born Harry Ueno managed a fruit stand in Los Angeles before the war and was a mess hall cook in block 22. Akira Nishi, along with his brother Kuichiro, owned a San Fernando Valley nursery specializing in roses. In July 1942 Ueno had the idea of building a pond at the mess hall entry so "people can enjoy it while they are waiting for the mess hall bell to ring to line up." When Ueno and others began digging the hole, Akira Nishi offered to draw up a plan. Many people also joined the effort, which included hauling rocks weighing up to two tons that were destined to be sitting places outside the mess hall. The plan called for twenty-four bags of cement to line the bottom of the pond, but camp policy restricted them to ordering three sacks at a time.

The product of a great deal of coordinated volunteer labor, the mess hall garden at block 22 in Manzanar was a carefully constructed delight for internees waiting to enter the hall for meals. In the center is a tall dead tree trunk.

Internees jokingly referred to the pond as the Three-sack Pond; it was also known as Otaba no Ike, after the source of sacred water at Kyoto's famed Kiyomizu Temple.[36]

The completed block 22 garden measured over 25 by 110 feet and was encircled by small stones. The centerpiece of the garden was a figure-eight pond with a concrete pathway across its neck. The lower pool had a small island. Large and small stones bordered most of the pond. The water was pumped into a "wishing well" built by George S. Takemura so that it overflowed and tumbled into the pool. These were popular in the first Japanese-style gardens in the nineteenth century in North America. At the north end of the gardens, a ring of stones outlined a tree.

Ultimately, almost every block had its own garden. Landscape contractor Henry Nishi, Kuichiro's son, remembers the block 22 gardens as "nothing really special," but in the fall of 1942 the garden won first prize in a reader's poll in the *Manzanar Free Press*'s Best Garden Contest.[37] There was great cooperation but also competition among the blocks and builders.

This first and highly visible pond-making effort at block 22 sparked a flurry of garden construction. Ueno thinks that seventeen or eighteen ponds were ultimately built. In August, the block 34 manager reported that "the men in our block are hard at work on building a fish pond and garden in front of the mess hall."[38] At block 15 Roy Suguwara, a former gardener, and Kuichiro, a former flower grower, designed and constructed a pond there. Acquiring cement was still a problem, and block managers' reports note the theft of hundreds of sacks.

Each garden was unique, but gardens outside mess halls and the camp hospital shared common features. Typically there were a rectangular perimeter of small stones framing a watercourse and a shaped pond as the central design feature. Gathered and carefully chosen stones bordered the ponds. Ponds were made more enticing with small islands, bridges, waterfalls, cascades, or fountains. Internees stocked the ponds with carp. Given the camp's dimensions and the standard location in the blocks, most gardens were of similar size and had a north–south orientation. But they were also privy to a common symbolic language derived from Japanese garden tradition.

Manzanar's mess hall garden at block 34, San-shi-en ("3–4 garden"), won second place in the garden competition. It is a Momoyama hill-and-pond-style garden in three levels, with a rise of stones and water source leading to a watercourse flowing into a lower pool. These gardens have their origins in China in Taoist and Buddhist beliefs. The garden is meant to evoke peace, prosperity, pleasantness, and long life. The rock arrangements symbolize the Taoist's "immortal isles"; believed to be islands off the coast of China or Korea, they were thought to be the dwelling places of people (*hsien*) who have the secrets of everlasting youth. Traditionally, the *hsien* traveled throughout the immortal isles on the backs of beautiful cranes, and within these mystic islands all the creatures were white, every flower was fragrant, and all the fruits brought immortality to those who ate them. Originally these were floating isles, but they were then fixed in space on the backs of tortoises.

The hill and stones to the north (center middle ground in the photo on p. 185) represent Mount Shumisen, in Buddhism, said to be the highest mountain and the sacred mountain at the center of the universe, where the Buddha is enthroned. The sun, moon, and planets rotate around Mount Shumisen, which supports the heavens and is surrounded by nine mountain ranges and eight seas. The watercourse begins at these stones, following a channel to pools below (foreground). The upright stones symbolize cranes, and there is a large flat turtle rock as well (foreground). Although the forms in the garden mirror the shapes of animals, they also carry other subtle meanings. The steepness and jaggedness of the crane island combine the three forces often represented in garden compositions, with elements that are horizontal (earth), diagonal (man), and vertical (heaven). Turtle rocks and islands suggest ancient, worn mountains and also offer symbolic protection from natural disasters and proper control of rivers. When found together, crane and turtle (*tsuru-kame*) represent an ageless vitality.

At another level, the block 34 garden is also a miniaturized landscape of the transition from mountains to stream, river valley, and finally plain. As in all the gardens at Manzanar, this transition is visible by lifting one's eyes to the mountains of the Sierra on the western horizon. Japanese gardens use the idea of *shakkei,* or borrowed scenery, and many of Manzanar's gardens capitalize on distant views or even draw the eye toward specific peaks or ranges.

The hospital gardens and parks at Manzanar combined elements of hill and pond gardens with both traditional stroll and tea gardens. A composition of winding paths and pauses leading through a sequence of carefully unfolding pictures, stroll gardens are meant to be seen in progression. The choreographed movement is intended to highlight one's awareness of the garden and its sensory experience. Nitaro ("William") Ogami was hospital grounds foreman and gardener. His son, Arthur, remembers his father spending much of his time working at the hospital: "He would take his crew, and they would furnish trucks and tools, and they would drag them up to the foothills and the mountains. They would pick up rocks, shrubs, trees, whatever he needed to use in the landscaping."[39] There were rock circles around trees, planting beds around buildings, pathways, stepping stones, ramps and stairs, retaining walls, and a concrete bench beautifully crafted to simulate wood. Used by both patients and staff, the central elements of the hospital garden were a pond and watercourse over fifty feet long. The water began its journey in a concrete and rock basin, then cascaded along a serpentine channel down over three modest falls into a twenty-foot-long basin that was about five feet lower than the small hill. The length of the stream was marked on both sides by a careful arrangement of stones of varying sizes. Almost midway along the waterway, a path of concrete and stepping zones cut through the garden, allowing a classic view up and down the waterway.

One of several areas at Manzanar transformed into parkland,

The mess hall garden at block 34 at Manzanar expressed Taoist and Buddhist principles and beliefs. The photograph faces north.

Cherry Park was the area next to the children's village, where orphans lived. F. M. Uyematsu of Montebello, California, donated a thousand trees from his prewar nursery stock for the project, but water constraints limited how many of these could be planted. The park included a wisteria trellis over a watercourse, a teahouse, and a lawn. Landscape gardener William Katsuki supervised the project. North Park benefited from a shady grove of cottonwoods that had been part of a ranch on the site. As movement beyond the fences was progressively permitted, two South Parks were also constructed that took advantage of large shade trees and creekside locations. These supplemented a popular picnic area in the camp's southwest corner, where Bairs Creek cut across the camp boundary.

Merritt Park, however, was the site at Manzanar most photographed by visitors, such as Ansel Adams and Dorothea Lange, as well as by camp photographer Toyo Miyatake and the camp staff. Although in theory cameras were not permitted in camp, in practice many photographs were taken. As National Park Service landscape architect Anna Tamura notes, Merritt Park provided "a scenic and photogenic place to mark the passage of major life events, such as birthdays, weddings, and farewells to soldiers. These scenic places allowed internees to celebrate these passages without fear of poisoning a lifetime of these memories with reminders of their imprisonment."[40]

Construction on Merritt Park began in a firebreak in 1942. The camp's showcase garden was first named Rose Park, later renamed Pleasure Park and finally Merritt Park in honor of Ralph Merritt, the relocation camp administrator who was director from late 1942 until Manzanar was dismantled in 1946. Tak Muro supervised construction, but the design is credited to a collective enterprise orchestrated by the Nishi brothers, Akira and Kuichiro. The densely planted one-acre park eventually included ponds with islands, bridges, waterfalls, and a teahouse. The first plantings included domestic roses grafted onto native rootstock by rose expert Kuichiro. The WRA supported the project and even paid the builders between $16 and $19 a month for their work.

The design of Merritt Park was an adaptation of a Japanese stroll garden. At the park's entrance were two large upright stele, which internees had harvested from near Yosemite. One stele was inscribed in Japanese: "To the memory of fellow Japanese immigrants . . . [who, although ushered to] this place with the breaking of friendly relations

Merritt Park at Manzanar included this pool and bridge, shown here in 1943.

between the two countries, have come to enjoy this quiet, peaceful place." The park was dedicated "for the enjoyment of the people and to the memory of the time of our residence here."[41] A pond was fed by water that cascaded over a turtle-shaped rock dividing the water into two waterfalls. Another stone was placed to suggest a turtle swimming in the pond. The park offered a fine display of craftsmanship in the park's benches, bridges, and rock arrangements. The rustic teahouse was constructed from natural materials. Tree stumps roped together marked the area of the teahouse and the path.

Henry Nishi thought of his father's garden work that "it was just something he liked to do. Something he loved to do. Something for the betterment of the camp." Reflecting on the paradox that Merritt Park represented, Jeanne Wakatsuki Houston wrote, "sometimes in

Kuichiro Nishi (right) helps as a fellow internee uses Manzanar's only mower to groom the lawn in Merritt Park, 1943.

the evenings you could walk down the raked gravel paths. You could face away from the barracks, look past a tiny rapids toward the darkening mountains, and for a while not be a prisoner at all. You could hang suspended in some odd, almost lovely land you could not escape from yet almost didn't want to leave."[42]

As artistic and cultural expressions, the internment camp gardens were rich in meaning. They combined aspects of classic Japanese garden practice, the Japanese American garden traditions that had evolved in the prewar West Coast, with responses to the conditions at each camp. Gardens are always adaptations to specific environments. At Manzanar and all the camps, a language of design that had developed in another landscape was both constrained and liberated by the necessity to employ local plants and rocks. These were gardens in a desert landscape unlike the more Mediterranean environment of Los Angeles or the fecund greenery of Puget Sound, and certainly in a more arid landscape than anything in Japan. In most cases ample water was supplied by irrigation from systems largely built by the internees. Thus, the gardens had an affinity to oasis gardens found in desert landscapes throughout the world. They presented a dramatic contrast to their surroundings and a respite from extreme conditions.

Garden making in the camps was the domestication of an inhospitable environment. Camps were "home," but only for an indeterminate period. Internees worked to create a cultural setting that fostered a semblance of normalcy under abnormal and unjust conditions. Gardens offered the dignity of work, opportunities for the expression of individual creativity, and a shared cultural identity. The beauty of the gardens offered solace and a contrast with an alien environment. However admirable and beautiful these creations, the frame delineates and completes the picture. The "wall" for all of these gardens was a barbed-wire fence with guard towers, their searchlights and guns pointed inward—as we have seen for ghetto residents, POWs, and civilian internees. All of these gardens, grand and small, were acts of resistance, directed toward the maintenance of cultural integrity and self-respect. They were tangible symbols of hope that helped people survive their internment, fostered their mental and physical health, and were a demonstration of psychological and also political defiance. The gardens further offered an assertion of cultural identity that contrasted dramatically with the conditions of internment and the withholding of basic American freedoms. In a sense the gardens were the anticamp, a subversive response to internment, where individual and collective gestures were a way of denying the camp administration and environment. Like George Eisen's protective cloak (see chapter 3), they are part of the struggle to transform "camp" into something else.

As with the other gardens we have examined, gardens constructed by Japanese American internees also fulfilled more prosaic garden functions. They were the sites for growing plants for food and pleasure; they were places to sit, gather, work, and play. They were places that ameliorated the extremes of climate through the making of an amenable microclimate. Plantings and structures offered comfort and shade and relief from the heat and dust. Interned at Crystal City, a Justice Department internment camp in south Texas, the Reverend Kenko Yamashita, a Soto Zen bishop who came to the United States in 1938, said, "Japanese farmers couldn't sit and just watch it [the barren soil], so they put gardens in front of their houses. They grew eggplants and cucumbers; so sometimes we had fresh cucumbers."[43] Gardens have deep meanings, but they are also about the simple and equally profound pleasure of a fresh cucumber.

Internees' desire to connect to a more familiar nature was powerful. Arthur Kleinkopf was impressed by three Japanese ladies who he drove out of camp one day in October 1942. It was their first trip out of Minidoka in six months. "They were thrilled beyond words by the sight of trees, flowers, and green fields. One lady said, 'Mr. Kleinkopf, I'd just like to get out of the car, walk over to one of those trees, touch it, and put my arms around it.' A lump came into my throat as I tried, somewhat unsuccessfully, I'm sure, to understand, because only those who have experienced the sufferings and longings of a minority group whose members have been evacuated from their homes and all that home holds dear, can ever fully understand the feelings of the lady who wanted to caress the tree."[44]

Gardens provide a way to domesticate space. Evacuees took the empty WRA framework and filled it to make it into their homes, the domestic environment where personal and family lives were enacted. Control over one's environment is not just over space; it also implies the ability to control one's social and psychological environment. Garden making (and other forms of construction in the camps) was a way of taking possession through labor, design, creativity, use, and cultural signification. For people who had just been dispossessed of their homes, belongings, careers, and daily lives, this was particularly important. The tangible physical result was a form of communication — we did this, and this is who we are.

Gardens are capable of carrying a wide range of meaning. The actions of the garden makers imposed an order on the camps that was theirs, not the WRA's. The gardens were beautiful but also an expression of anti-institutionalization. In a dehumanized and alien setting, internees humanized the camps by introducing familiar garden features. The practice began at the assembly center, where people were dehumanized immediately by being confined to places made for — and recently populated by — animals. Although internees had little opportunity to bring personal property with them, they could possess

Residents of this barracks at Manzanar pose at the entrance garden.

the gardens. Because size was not critical, the smallest space could be appropriated: residential barracks gardens ranged from only two by four feet to as large as twenty by forty.

The gardens were part of homemaking, and the meaning and expression of "home" was different for each of the resident generations. For the Issei, it was a memory, often of childhood homes in Japan as well as the homes they had made in America. For Nisei, it was an imagined and idealized cultural home in Japan as well as their American homes, which often had gardens in a Japanese style. For Kibei it was homes in both places. All the gardens were a combination of Japanese cultural heritage and American experience set primarily in the landscape of the American West. The gardens were signs of normalcy and "mementos of home" for the residents, people *Newsweek* described as not only transferred but also "transplanted."[45]

Henry Nishi reports that at Manzanar, people had more time to study and to transmit Japanese traditions, such as garden making.

According to WRA policy, all meetings and publications at the camps had to be in English, and Japanese was spoken only in the privacy of the barracks. This undermined whatever sense of "home" internees might have been able to imagine in the camps. Under such conditions, garden making allowed internees to make very public statements using the garden language of their culture.

Domestication also implies a calming or quelling of something wild. Plunked down in rudimentary buildings surrounded by an alien wilderness, internees were understandably stressed by the sudden change and by the environment. Kleinkopf perceptively noted that "the impact of the emotional disturbances as a result of the evacuation procedures, plus the dull dreary existence in a desert region surely must give these people a feeling of helplessness, hopelessness, and despair which we on the outside do not and will never fully understand."[46] The gardens played a role in relieving the stress of camp life by acting as mental oases. Although the internees were not combatants in the war, like POWs they too needed to sustain their morale. The government supported this homemaking for its own reasons: first, the WRA preferred an active, occupied population; second, it took a paradoxical pride in camp beautification, as we already saw POW and civilian camp commandants do in Germany and Asia during World War II.

Garden making also allowed internees to identify with the historic western experience. The camps were essentially frontier communities in wild landscapes, which internees "civilized" with their frontier gardens. The first issue of the *Minidoka Irrigator* (note that irrigation is an instrument of landscape domestication and transformation) editorialized:

> Minidoka, as we know it now, is a vast stretch of sagebrush stubble and shifting, swirling sand—a dreary forbidding, flat expanse of arid wilderness. Minidoka in September of 1942 is the sort of place people would normally traverse only to get to another destination. We are not here by choice. We, the ten thousand, then, can have but one resolve; to apply our combined energies and efforts to the grim task of conquering the elements and converting a wasteland into an inhabitable community. Our obligation to ourselves is to wrest the nearest approximation of normalcy of an abnormal situation. Our goal is the creation of an oasis. Our great adventure is a repetition of the frontier struggle of pioneers against the land and the elements.

T. AKIYAMA (2-10-A)

Tomo Akiyama, an Issei dye works operator from Seattle, built this garden at Minidoka.

Minidoka internees seemed ready to take this to heart. The Reverend Taro Gato combined the complexities of both spiritual and patriotic sentiment in this statement from the *Topaz Times:* "Topaz is more than just an engineering marvel. It is more than just an isolated settlement for evacuees. It is the sum total of dreams, deep thinking, courage, and faith — it is a living personality. Topaz is born of the great Mother America. We are again the pioneers, blazing the road into the wilderness of our social frontiers. Not that we alone march, but that we follow the ever guiding pillar of the divine wisdom and light — it is our strength."[47] The task was clear to the internees at all the camps: make this a "home" in the way the pioneers domesticated the American West in the past century.

In a depersonalized institutional environment, the ability to personalize one's environment assumes a larger importance, as houses and gardens, generally symbols of self, also become tools of community expression. The picture was typical of people moving into a new community, where individual actions are ways of both personalizing one's territory and simultaneously making an offering to the community. When forty-eight-year-old Tomo Akiyama, a dye works operator from Seattle, was asked why he made his Minidoka garden even though it was not a permanent home, his answer was recorded in Robert Hosokawa's garden report: "This was a means of bettering the quality of life during that interim, no matter how short or long. It gave pleasure to his spare moments and made life more livable. At the same time it contributed to the community as a whole."[48]

Gardens are the product of labor, but garden work generally represents the more pleasurable aspects of labor. The satisfaction of creating something out of raw materials recurs at each stage of garden making, from conception through harvest. Even unskilled gardeners feel a sense of control over their materials and a sense of satisfaction as they monitor the progress of their planting or a construction project as it develops.

The Japanese American community was used to hard work. Keeping busy and active was a way of maintaining self-respect, and pride in one's work was important. Imprisoned at Poston, Hanayo Inouye said, "We were Japanese after all . . . so no one spent lazy days. Some people planted various kinds of trees in the compound, and between the trees we grew vegetables and other things."[49]

Arthur Ogami, the son of Nitaro Ogami, the creator of Manzanar's hospital gardens, emphasized that garden building kept people busy with something useful and productive, which he thought was especially important for the Issei. He added that garden making was also "just a natural thing to be doing. When you have the manpower and people to do it. For their own pleasure, for the camp itself. They took a lot of pride in whatever they were doing."[50]

Arthur Kleinkopf admired the variety of tin vessels that were used as sprinklers. "I watched one Japanese man sprinkle his garden. He had a two-quart can with nail holes in the bottom. Near the top on one side was a hole about an inch in diameter and another hole on the opposite side of the same size but slightly lower so that when a 3-foot stick was run through the holes, the can made a good dipper and sprinkler combined."[51] The internees responded to necessity and deprivation with an improvisatory sensibility toward materials.

Gardens are an outlet for creativity and artistry. Perhaps the recognition of beauty and the human desire to create things and places of beauty are heightened by ugly conditions. Almost as if it were a reflex, beautification of their surroundings began immediately at the assembly centers. At Tanforan Yoshiko Uchida said, "We all worked constantly to make the windswept racetrack a more attractive and pleasant place." He noted that what had been a junk pile was transformed into a colorful garden, and he admired the park created in the racetrack's infield: "It wasn't much, but it was one of many efforts made to comfort the eye and heart." Uchida is clear about the connection between "the eye," or the perception of beauty, and "the heart," or the sense of well-being, even health, that beauty can impart. These creations were good for both the soul and sight.[52]

Camp residents were aware of the contribution beauty made to their lives. The *Gila News-Courier* praised WRA regional director E. R. Fryer's attention to camp beautification: "It is evident that people living under the physical drawbacks of the centers need the stimulation of environmental order and beauty to help them in the difficulties they are encountering." The administration seemed aware that beauty was essential for people's morale and of "inestimable, though intangible, value." The *Topaz Times* was particularly generous in praising the role of women:

> Though Nature wasn't generous with Topaz in giving out her verdant gifts, the women here have combated the ugliness and drabness of the surroundings by directing their creative impulses towards the beautification of the home. . . . Artificial flowers fashioned from crepe and wax paper, and crocheting thread, with its vibrant color and personality, enhance the rooms of any apartment. But flowers contrived by art is an inferior substitute for the genuine blooms. We, who have lived near the rolling green hills of California with its lush poppies and wild plants, the scented gardens, immaculate lawns and thriving flower beds of the bay area, yearn for Nature's expression of greenery. Happily, though on a small scale, we can induce greenery to grow near the windows of our barracks.[53]

Although many internees could no longer practice their occupations, artists were very active in the camps as practitioners and teachers. Artists have a keen eye for recognizing the qualities of their surroundings, and in the camps they captured the sublime vistas and dramatic grandeur to offer solace or to comment wryly on their condition. But all the internees, not just the artists, could glean something from the observation of nature. Machiye Maxine Nakamura, for example, noticed: "A saguaro bloomed this spring, that queen of the desert, thriving stately where no nourishment is visible. It had this message to me that even in this seared land many things will bloom. One must stand above the saguaro to see its beauty, so I, too, must climb beyond the present difficulties, and search for that possible beauty that may come out of this thorny existence here."[54]

While the conditions in camps were not the horrendous landscapes of battlefield trenches, the artistry in the internment camps has affinities with the trench art of the war. Both were expressions of art where it was least expected, and its creation brought solace to its creators and a sense of surprise and wonder to those who viewed it.

In his poem "Children of Camp," Lawson Fusao Inada, who was at camps in Arkansas and Colorado, expresses the paradox. In a place of incarceration, stripped of poetry and joy, people still made poetry, art, and gardens.

> The people made poetry
> With their very own hands —
> Little gifts of scrap
> For precious loved ones,
> Friends, elders, children.
>
> There was no poetry in camp.
> But the people made it so.
> With hands, vision, hearts,
> The people made it so.[55]

Art, in all its forms, visual, musical, literary, was not a luxury or a frill, but an imperative and perhaps even a necessity. At Heart Mountain, when Shoji Nagumo "thought about children being raised in the desert without grass or trees," he "was sure they would become human beings who would not feel joy or pleasure in anything. They might even grow up not understanding the beauty of nature."[56] This concern encouraged him to work to beautify the camp and to organize the camp's victory garden.

How was it possible for Japanese Americans to maintain a sense of cultural identity and self-respect in the face of imprisonment and vilification by their adopted — or native — country? At Tule Lake, Hiroshi Kashiwagi felt that "in addition to the physical confinement, there was [a] fence around our spirit, and this imprisonment of the spirit was the most ravaging part of the evacuation experience."[57] Under camp conditions, certain underlying traits and behaviors came to the fore. Strategies of resistance and survival, both conscious and unconscious, merged; complementary Japanese cultural attitudes fostered the internees' adjustment to conditions while simultaneously working to subvert the intentions of the government. *Shikata ga nai* — it cannot be helped — is an acceptance of fate and situations that allowed people to deal with the situation. At the same time the internees displayed *gaman,* which connotes perseverance, fortitude,

Minidoka residents tend the block 26 garden.

or stamina. These traits were coupled with a tradition of working together as a community.

In the camps, cultural identity could be reinforced not only through shared underlying values but also in cultural practices that united individuals from disparate communities in both Japan and the United States. Japan has a venerated tradition of garden art honed over many centuries. That expertise and history of appreciation accompanied immigrants to North America. The gardens "made familiar the strange land" of the camps by continuing a cultural legacy. Garden making was a way for Japanese immigrants to assert their heritage while also adjusting to American culture. In the camps, traditional Japanese garden elements were integrated into miniature front yards, Japanese vegetables were planted in victory gardens — and there were many more baseball fields than judo rings. This was a continuation of a process that began with the first immigrants from Japan. As art historian Kendall Brown has noted, "By grafting part of their cultural heritage to their new home in the form of gardens, these Issei put down literal and figurative roots. By creating something Japanese in America, they made themselves into Japanese Americans."[58]

In the prewar Little Tokyos of the West Coast, certain institutions were de facto community centers. The Maneki restaurant in Seattle's international district was such a place; the restaurant garden was a sanctuary where people could be themselves. Paradoxically, in the camps — which were also ethnic ghettos — this was possible, as well. There was a continuity of the social functions of gardens and parks, and in the camps these were the venues for traditional cultural activities such as ceremonies, weddings, and festivals. According to Tama Keiki Tochihara, who has studied the Issei gardens of Seattle, the gardens were simultaneously cultural sanctuaries and an adaptation to a new setting.[59]

At the 1979 pilgrimage to Tule Lake, Richard Oyama read his "Poem for the Survivors of Tule Lake," which includes the lines, "And so you survived, / And thrived, to raise / A garden from / A desert land."[60]

Although the phrase *spiritual resistance* is often applied to the European ghettos of World War II, it holds true for Japanese American internment camps as well. The quality of *gaman* is akin to resistance. One can even perceive a certain stubbornness in camp behavior. Thrust into this unbearable and ugly situation, the internees not only withstood it but did so with honor and transformed what was ugly into something beautiful. With much pride, Uchida found that people at Topaz "endured the hardship of the evacuation with dignity, stoic composure, disciplined patience, and an amazing resilience of spirit. I think they displayed a level of strength, grace, and courage that is truly remarkable."[61]

Camp garden makers resisted their incarceration in many ways. Their first act was to appropriate land without permission. After having been stripped of their own land and possessions, they now staked a claim to their new surroundings. When negotiations with the WRA for permissions were unsuccessful, they sometimes ignored the regulations. Internees transformed scrounged and gathered materials into art as they constructed gardens within the confines of the camp. This was the anticamp, where acts of cultural identity could be construed as subversive to those in power. Arthur Ogami reflected that "the gardens expresses that just because we're here, we have to do something to refresh our feelings. I think that the gardens is something that they want to express that there is hope for peace and freedom. And you can go to these gardens and feel it."[62]

Jeanne Wakatsuki Houston saw her father emasculated by his new circumstance, but most coped and even defied authorities, sometimes drawing strength and solace from the inhospitable but powerful landscape around them. The view to the mountains was important, especially for the Issei. Houston observed that Mount Whitney, which was visible from Manzanar, reminded Papa of Fujiyama, that is, it gave him the same kind of spiritual sustenance. The tremendous beauty of those peaks was inspirational, as so many natural forms are to the Japanese (the rocks outside our doorway could be those mountains in miniature). They also represented those forces in nature, those powerful and inevitable forces that cannot be resisted, reminding man that sometimes he must simply endure that which cannot be changed. . . . What had to be endured was the climate, the confinement, the steady crumbling away of family life. But the camp itself had been made livable.[63]

The resilience of plants was mirrored in the fortitude and determination of the population. When Toyo Suyemoto complained to his mother about camp life, she replied, "'Spring will come again.' I burst out, 'But it won't be the same spring!' 'No,' she continued, 'not the same spring, but another spring, a new spring.'" On the train en route to Manzanar, Yoriyuiki Kikuchi identified with the geraniums he noticed on the side of the Los Angeles River, later writing a poem recalling the experience: "Uprooted, thrown in a pile, side of the road. / But remember, rise again and full bloom once again."[64] Internees were evoking images of oppression, defiance, and survival similar to those used by Jewish ghetto residents in Europe in the same war.

The growth of gardens was echoed in the life of camp residents. In Tim Toyama's play *Independence Day* (later filmed as *Day of Independence*), which takes place during a baseball game played in a camp on July 4, Zip, a teenage Nisei, receives a letter from his Issei father, who has returned to Japan. The letter includes a poem from his father, where he likens his son to a pine tree growing in the garden.

> In the desert, a garden,
> Alive.
> Spring has come again.
>
> In the garden in the desert
> A stream,
> Water from winter's melted snow,
>
> I put my hand in the flowing water,
> And feel winter's melted tears between my fingers.
>
> In the garden in the desert,
> A young pine tree grows.
> My son.[65]

In Shinto tradition, the landscape is filled with spirits called *kami* who inhabit elements of the natural world. Stones are particularly important vessels for *kami*. Jeanne Wakatsuki Houston thought that the rock gardens would outlive the barracks, roads, and towers of Manzanar, and that the camp's enduring physical legacy would be its stone gardens. Because she saw "each stone . . . [as] a mouth, speaking for a family, for some man who had beautified his doorstep," she found such stone gardens "enduringly human." In Houston's short story "Rock Garden," Old Man Morita befriends a young girl, Reiko, at Manzanar. He teaches her to meditate and takes her to what she immediately understands to be a special place, a garden hidden behind a bamboo with a "brilliant white lake of tiny pebbles." The old man teaches her "Rock, water, plant, wood all same. You, me, rock same." Here Reiko learns to rake the pebbles and help him "garden his rocks."[66]

SIX 🌿 Postwar
Gardens after the War

How do we bury the dead
stacking up on the patio against
    our picture window? I can barely see
over the last body blown here by another cluster bomb —
every forty minutes, every twenty, every ten, every five,
every four every three every two
every one —
I can no longer see into the garden.

MERMER BLAKESLEE, "How Do We Bury the Dead?"

THE DEFIANT WAR GARDENS we have examined were short-lived, but their duration is not at all proportional to their meaning. In fact, their brief life spans may magnify their significance as we turn to the fate of these war gardens and what the places are like now. That gardens rarely outlive their makers (at least in their original form) is just one of the reasons change is at the essence of garden meaning and experience.

Gardens require tending, and without that attention they begin their slow return from a place of culture back to nature, where its rules, cycles, and imperatives are paramount. After the battle, nature returned, on its own or assisted by human activity. Sometimes the restoration of a natural state was rapid, with a single season's growth obscuring the marks of people on the land. War's effect on humans, too, varied in the duration of the impact: for some individuals the wartime events were forgotten or repressed, never to emerge consciously; for others, the thoughts of their time of distress and horror never left them, and they remained traumatized for a lifetime, even affecting their children. The second generation of Holocaust survivors also suffers in ways different from their parents. Post-traumatic stress disorder is now recognized as a common affliction among war survivors.

As J. B. Jackson has said, "The landscape is history made visible." The land remembers, but the return of nature after war blurs and eventually obliterates the death and destruction that dwelled on the land. Is the reappearance of vegetation an obscuring — a forgetting — or a healing? Shiloh park ranger Paul Hawkes feels that wars leave "ghost marks" on the landscape.[1]

One of the more insidious remnants of warmaking are land mines. These ghost marks are in a sense ghost makers, as well, because they still contain the potent power of a war ended long ago to maim and to kill. Around the world, millions of active mines hidden beneath the soil of former battlefields and no-man's-lands remain deathtraps (a British television documentary on landmines was titled *The Devil's Gardens*). The beauty of the nature that has returned to these places of destruction belies the remaining potential for death still resident in the ground.

Some battlefields — the safe ones — become sites of commemoration and are even converted into a form of garden or park. The actual experience of the land, its fields and hills, its dimension, and the resonance of its spirit can bring visitors closer to a realization of what war was like in this place. This happened "here" is an extraordinarily powerful emotional catalyst. When the dead are interred at or near where they fell, the graves remind visitors of the events that transpired in what is otherwise a peaceful location.

In the context of town or village life, cemeteries are not tragic places; they are merely part of the cycle of life. Predictable cemeteries are ones where you expect to lie when you die, where you expect your family and descendents to mourn — and to some extent a predictable cemetery is one where you expect to find one. The chaos of war, however, felled soldiers before their time and in places never intended to be graveyards. The cemeteries of the war dead — both military and civilian — are poignant reminders of the break in continuity caused by war.

After World War I the French designated an area too dangerous for resettlement as the Zone Rouge. Most of this area was eventually made habitable, but around Verdun it was replanted as forest because the number of dead and unexploded shells made the area unsafe for agriculture. Unexploded shells and bombs, along with bones and the detritus of war, continue to be unearthed by farmers' plows along the 475-mile Western Front. Revisiting sites along that deadly line, Jack Beatty observed, "The loveliness of Tyne Cot [a cemetery near Ypres] is a sort of reaction formation against the memory of hell. . . . The transfigurations of territory. They serve to remind us that the civi-

This 1917 photograph was originally captioned "Where pastoral peace once more reigns in a fiercely contested battlefield."

lization said to have been destroyed by the Great War, that 'old bitch gone in the teeth' of Ezra Pound's bitter postwar poem, still remembers how to mask death with beauty."[2]

Even during World War I, soldiers revisited the sites of earlier battles. Edmund Blunden describes a tragic, teasing interlude that evokes both a peaceful prewar past and the wished-for postwar condition. In 1917 Blunden and companions passed through the sites of previous battlefields. At Albert, the site of horrendous fighting, he writes, "We view Albert, pretty well revived, its tall chimneys smoking, its rosy roofs renewed and shining, and all about it the fields tilled, and young crops greening. The mercy of nature advances. Is it true?" He passes countryside that would soon be devastated. He reflects that "fortunate it was that at the moment I was filled with this simple joy. I might have known the war by this time, but I was still too young to know the depth of its ironic cruelty. No conjecture that, in a few weeks, Buire-sur-Ancre would appear much the same as the cataclysmal railway cutting by Hill 60, came from that innocent greenwood."[3]

In France in May 1916, Second Lieutenant Stephen Hewett wrote in a letter of the endless work of making war and its devastation on the land, which nevertheless was no match for the inexorable movement of nature: "The trenches which in February were grim and fea-tureless tunnels of gloom, without color or form, are already over-arched and embowered with green. You may walk from the ruins of a cottage, half-hidden in springing green, and up to the Front line trenches through a labyrinth of Devonshire lanes. Before the summer comes again children will play between the trenches as in a garden, hide in strange hollows where old fragments of iron peep out from a wilderness of poppies and corn flowers."[4] Hewett envisions a future in which the debris of war is seamlessly incorporated into the coun-tryside and into the lives of the next generation.

Rudyard Kipling, whose son died in the war, described a visit to an unnamed town in France that had been shelled and destroyed. Looking up a long street, he wrote, "one perceived how the weeds, to whom man's war is the truce of God, had come back and were well established the whole length of it, watched by the long perspective of open, empty windows."[5]

When Steven Graham visited the Somme in the fall of 1920, he found "trees not quite dead but sprouting green from black trunks and then to blasted trees dead to the core. . . . The terrible battle area of Passchendale, all pits, all tangled with corroded wire—but now as if it were in tumultuous conflict with Nature. . . . The stagnancy has not dried up, but festers still in black rot below the rushes. Double shell-holes, treble shell-holes, charred ground, great pits, bashed in dug outs, all overgrown with the highest of wild flowers."[6]

Steven O'Shea, who walked the Western Front in the 1990s, noted that the ground still bore the "scar of the front," making him conclude that the "earth had not yet recovered from the Great War." At the Somme he saw "the crazy upheaval of heavily shelled land. There is really nothing more evocative of the war than this frozen violence. All the woods in this region have the same obscene, unnatural floors. . . . like some slow-moving sea monster."[7] These tortured landscapes evoke real horror. Most often, however, modern visitors to battlefields remain ignorant and innocent of the history of the bloodied ground beneath their feet.

The most compelling feature of all these descriptions is the unstoppable power of nature to subvert the human-tortured land-scape back into a natural form.

There has long been a Jewish cemetery in Warsaw, once the second largest Jewish city in the world, which the Nazis turned into the

A small cemetery on Serre Road in the Somme.

Warsaw ghetto. In the prewar cemetery, there would have been a few trees only in the section where nonorthodox, or more assimilated, Jews were buried. Once the area was ghettoized, residents would have valued those few trees highly, since green nature was rare in the ghetto.

In the Jewish tradition, mourners place a small stone atop the grave marker as a sign they have visited. But when the cycle of life is interrupted by war, all of those expectations are shattered: Who will visit your grave? Who will lay a stone for you? The few stones atop the headstones in the Warsaw cemetery are poignant reminders of the horrible effectiveness of the Nazi plan to annihilate Jews from Poland. Most were probably placed by nonfamily members, like me, who wanted to honor mass graves and the graves of extraordinary individuals. Today there are still a few burials from Poland's minuscule Jewish community and from relatives who wish to be interred in this hallowed ground, but the meager numbers of these newer graves dramatize the difference between Poland before the war and Poland after. All the graves now lie under a dense canopy of trees that rose after the war.

Most images that survived the Warsaw ghetto are of the life — and death — in the streets. They show brutality, starvation, and acts of spiritual resistance. Walking the site of the ghetto today, it takes concerted effort to ignore the modern housing blocks and new streets and imagine the area as it looked during the war, with the crowded streets and courtyards of the ghetto, the crowds who filled the street, even in the winter. I was born three years after the Warsaw ghetto uprising was quelled and the ghetto razed. I knew the history and the site from written descriptions, maps, and photographs. I know that I am stepping on ground where thousands died, that the sidewalk I am walking on is where people stepped over starving children and around dead bodies. I know that here soldiers rounded up families. I know that death was rampant. I know that the sewers beneath the streets were passages for smugglers and escape routes for the few. I know that the full spectrum of human emotions happened *right here:* unthinkable horror, acts of unimaginable courage, the loss of all faith, and flashes of awareness of a divine presence.

I know that on this ground a few people planted seeds to grow food to keep people and their hopes alive. I know that few survived and that fate was random. I know that I am honored to be part of this tradition. In the cemetery, I place a small stone on a gravestone, careful to choose one that has had no visitors.

Jean Gittins revisited Stanley in Hong Kong a year after regaining her freedom.

She had told her companions from Australia about her garden and took them to the site. "Stopping by our block of flats I tried to get my bearings, but something was different. I looked and I looked. Puzzled and astonished, I couldn't understand why there was not a trace of the garden. I could not believe that in less than twelve months the undergrowth had taken over — my garden was no more."[8]

The fecundity in Asia, the rush of nature toward chaos, did not take long to overcome the relatively minor changes in landscape that gardening produced.

By the end of World War II, almost half the Japanese American population of the relocation camps had been relocated east of the line that demarcated the "exclusion area." On December 17, 1944, three years after Pearl Harbor had been bombed, the exclusion order was lifted and the camps were designated to be closed within a year. The process of dismantling the camps and returning internees home began, but for many that home no longer existed. The next stage of their travails was just beginning.

In his diary May 21, 1945, Arthur Kleinkopf, education superintendent at Minidoka, duly noted that internees continued their garden activity, and he was surprised that "in spite of all the efforts being made to relocate the people as fast as possible, they are planting gardens and making great preparations for harvesting the planted crops this fall." By October, after the internees had been relocated from Minidoka, he noticed, "many beautiful flowers are still growing around the barracks. The chrysanthemums and the asters are at their best. Each day I pick a bouquet of these and take them to the office. There are several small patches of strawberries too. Quite frequently I gather a handful of strawberries for lunch." At the end of November he made a last trip to the residential area before the physical dismantling would begin, noting that "many beautiful chrysanthemums [were] still blooming."[9]

For this brief period the internment camp gardens continued to flourish after the internees were once again relocated, but gardens, especially in the desert, need to be tended, and soon the Minidoka gardens, and the gardens at other internment camps, would revert to their natural state.

By December 1946 the *Los Angeles Times* would show photos of the demolition of Manzanar and of Merritt Park "overrun with weeds and the once-verdant nursery . . . being returned to the desert."[10] The camps were demolished, the buildings relocated, and the land abandoned. The National Park Service has excavated a few gardens at Manzanar, but the former camp still shows signs of gardens everywhere. Surviving are arrangements of stones, a depression where a pool might have been, upraised rocks, trees that must have been planted just more than a half-century ago, rusting tin cans that bordered a bed, and even wood slowly decaying in the desert.

Such shards of the internment experience are poignant signs of the lives of those who struggled to maintain their dignity and culture and somehow get on with their lives in a place that, against their will, would be their temporary home. The remnants evoke the life that was present there. The dirt streets and wooden barracks are long gone, but

All that remains of block 34 at Manzanar are these hardscape features.

remaining are the barracks "welcome mats" — the entry walks, a line of stones or slab of concrete leading, now, from nowhere to nowhere. Many of the hardscape features are decorated, and some have names, addresses, dates, or handprints. The cottonwoods and Chinese elms planted by the internees remain, as do the abandoned Manzanar fruit trees that were incorporated into the camp's children's village.

Similar traces of life are present at other camps. At Gila River the stones and ponds of earlier gardens are still discernable. The surviving garden features prompt an awareness of both the fragility and the endurance of the gardens on the land.

Since 1969 there has been an annual pilgrimage to Manzanar. There have been similar pilgrimages to other camps by the survivors, their families, and others in solidarity with their experience. The National Park Service, along with the Manzanar Committee, has been discussing the possibility of reconstructing one of the gardens. If done properly, the site of a single garden with growing plants and flowing water will honor the artistry and meaning of these creations.

Minidoka had many skilled designers, but the design and fate of the Kogita garden in particular is fascinating. Before the war, Seattle res-

Yasusuke Kogita poses in his Minidoka garden; the stones have endured several relocations and now reside in a family garden.

ident Yasusuke Kogita had elaborate gardens at his home and work. In Minidoka he scoured the landscape for materials, including hauling a one-ton rock to the camp for his garden. Internees called it "stove-pipe rock" because of its hollow interior. In the garden he planted willows from Seattle, sagebrush that he bonsaied, and plants from the Sears Roebuck catalog. Overflow from the laundry supplied water for two fishponds. In the course of her research on Minidoka, Anna Tamura interviewed Yasusuke's sons, Ted and Paul, who said of their father's garden that it was "a part of him" and that it helped him endure his captivity and idleness. When the camp closed, Kogita did not leave that part of him in Minidoka. He had the garden transported to Seattle, where he reconstructed a portion of the garden in front of a hotel he owned. It is the known example of a camp garden transferred from one place to another. The symbolism is provocative: Kogita had been uprooted from his home and life in Seattle. The garden he constructed in Minidoka, like many others, was a recollection of other places, a way to assuage the conditions of the camp, but also an attempt to put roots down in a place they all hoped would only be temporary. That garden was then uprooted and brought to Seattle.

Only Kogita knew whether this reconstructed garden was a reminder of the camp and its indignities or a source of pride of what he had accomplished under those dire circumstances; perhaps it was both things to him. Kogita's son Paul ultimately became the caretaker of the stones, moving them to the garden of his home in Seattle. Few who see the house know the story of these stones' journey from the Idaho wilderness or the Minidoka garden. The rocks are now family heirlooms, according to Anna Tamura.[11]

In Shinto belief, the spirits of one's ancestors, or *kami,* are said to reside in places and natural elements. Stones were favored vessels for their residence. It is easy to think of the stones of camp gardens as the embodiment of the spirit of those who lived and left their imprint on the landscape of the camps in the 1940s.

Nature always returns and eventually obscures evidence of human action. It may happen within one season or it may take generations, but eventually culture becomes compost.

SEVEN ❧ Digging Deeper
The Spirit of Defiant Gardens

GARDENS MEAN MANY THINGS, and we have seen that hardship and stress accentuate these meanings. In times of crisis or difficulty, gardens have the potential to offer more than we have expected. We discover their latent capacities to provide us with forms of sustenance we had not imagined. Since gardens are so commonplace and gardening is so familiar, most of us take them for granted. Many of us have a friend or relative whose company we appreciate or find congenial, who then responds with unexpected aid or depth of compassion in a crisis. Gardens are like that: comfortable companions whose capacities lie dormant, awaiting a crisis to release their potential.

This book has taken us to gardens made by victims — soldiers, prisoners, and internees — who refused to be victimized. We have found that defiant gardens are places of peace, and they are symbols of peace. In the midst of conflict and war, these places take on the role of a truce, where combatants and innocent bystanders enjoy a temporary cessation of hostilities. Like a truce, the garden represents a desired condition, anticipating a time of peace and normalcy.

Defiant gardens surprise us by their presence and persistence. These are gardens against the odds. The fact that they *seem* out of place is indeed part of their appeal; ultimately, however, these gardens reveal themselves to be supremely adapted to the specifics of their condition. Defiant gardens first astonish by their mere presence, and then they astonish when we recognize the sheer force of will and effort that created and sustained them. Such gardens are interrogative places, prodding us to ask questions: how could that happen, who made this, *how* did they do it? This book explores what gardens have meant to people in the most extreme of situations, listening to the voices and words of garden makers themselves. I hope you have, among the words and pictures, also heard the gardens speak, for while they are inanimate they are not mute. In fact, what they have to say to us is quite inspirational.

Gardens embody a paradox. We associate gardens with nature, but they are a manifestation of human dominion over the natural world. Garden writer Henry Mitchell explains the inherent temerity that is required of all gardeners, these people who wrestle with weather, soil, and pestilence to make something grow. "Defiance," he says, "is what makes gardeners."[1] In an extreme situation beyond an individual's control, such as is common during war, the manifestation of the human ability to wield power over something is a potent reminder of our ability to withstand emotional despair and the forces of chaos. Gardens domesticate and humanize dehumanized situations. They offer a way to reject suffering, an inherent affirmation and sign of human perseverance. In contrast to war, gardens assert the dignity of life, human and nonhuman, and celebrate it.

In looking at gardens made during the horrors and tribulations of the twentieth-century world wars, we have examined the meaning and significance of gardens particularly in terms of life, home, hope, work, and beauty: gardens are alive, they are a connection to home, they embody hope, and they are places of work and the sites of artistry. These are commonplace themes, but the meaning of each is magnified by the context of war and the garden's defiant response to conditions. The gardens speak to us, as do garden accounts found in diaries, memoirs, testimonies, and images. They all testify to a depth of garden meaning amplified through hardship, a meaning that may lie latent in all garden creation, awaiting a catalyst to bring it to conscious awareness.

As human beings we identify with nature's vitality; it is alive, like us. By employing the materials of nature, gardens connect us to its forces. Biologist E. O. Wilson has hypothesized the concept of biophilia, which posits that humans "explore and affiliate with life." He sees this biophilic tendency as a product of our evolutionary history, suggesting that ultimately "our existence depends on this propensity, our spirit is woven from it, [and] hope rises on its currents."[2] According to Wilson, biophilia anchors our relationship with nature. In war, where death is omnipresent and the fragility and preciousness of life are immediate, our connection to the life forces inherent in nature shifts from an implicit one to an explicit one.

Our species history is integral to our landscape history. Our species history suggests an innate genetic response and predisposition toward certain landscapes to their fitness for our survival. We approach places positively, or try to avoid others, based on our species needs. As researchers have noted, even after our survival needs are satisfied, they persist as an ingrained aesthetic preference. Certain landscapes have a capacity to reduce stress and tension, and this physical calming is demonstrated physiologically by lower blood pressure and reduced muscle tension. The evidence is strong that time spent in natural settings accomplishes this, as well as the simple act of viewing — even short-term visual contact can be beneficial. Essayist Alain de Botton believes that "we may see in nature certain scenes that will stay with us throughout our lives and offer us, every time they enter our consciousness, both a contrast to and relief from present difficulties. [Wordsworth] termed such experiences in nature 'spots of time': 'There are in our existence spots of time, / That with distinct pre-eminence retain / A renovating virtue . . . / That penetrates, enables us to mount, / When high, more high, and lift us up when fallen.'"[3]

From the long evolutionary perspective, our landscape preference and experience is that of a "survivor's landscape," one that ultimately sustained life. It is part of what makes us human. In the gardens of war and defiance there is an emergence of this realization from the genetic and unconscious level to one of consciousness and action. Francis Cogan called the gardens of civilian internees "patches of survival."[4]

Most of the time, nature is an expected element in our daily lives, so we take it for granted. It is a pleasant backdrop: the grass beneath our feet, the green of trees, the sounds of birds, the produce on the table. What state of mind provokes our awareness of the natural world around us (the warmth of the sun on a cold day, a burst of floral color, or the grandeur of a tree) and its power (crashing surf or a plant pushing through concrete)? If we are imprisoned and deprived of contact with the natural world, the immediate result is that what we previously took for granted rises in importance — and in some way represents the whole of our condition. Indeed, recall the eagerness of soldiers in World War I to find signs of life wherever they might emerge in the desolate trenches.

Having escaped to the Aryan side of Warsaw in World War II, Stanislaw Sznapman wrote about the dramatic contrast between two adjacent worlds: "Far beyond the ghetto walls you can see treetops covered with the vernal green, fields and gardens are bustling with springtime chores. The world is so beautiful, but we aren't allowed to see it; we aren't allowed to be in a field or garden. Everything in our world is gray, covered with dust, littered with trash."[5] The desire to connect with something living when nature itself has been banished is profound. Author George Eisen tells the story of a young girl in the Warsaw ghetto whose sister's dying wish was to have something green close by. Risking her life, she sneaked under the wall to the Aryan side to fetch a single leaf. Returning to her imprisonment, she placed the leaf in a glass by her sister's bed.

In "Simple Things," Lieutenant Alan Campbell, a prisoner at Oflag 4C in Germany, laments his deprivation from a beneficent nature: "We lack the mould of Nature's hand, / Those simple things that mean so much, . . . Here Nature is fettered: dead. / Four walls can only maim."[6]

The presence of living plants sustained people during war, but the inexorable force of nature to press on, grow, reproduce, and survive also promised a *continuation* of life. Glimpses of nature in turn inspired people and strengthened their resolve to survive. In Borneo, Agnes Newton Keith was permitted a daily guarded walk on the beach. It was an "escape from hell into heaven." She "believed then that walk was the only thing that kept me sane. In the end I learned that it isn't the outward circumstances which determine what one can endure, but something in oneself which either breaks, or stays intact, under strain. It isn't the difference in strain, it's the difference in the tensile strength of people."[7]

In his diary, POW Giovanni Guareschi contemplated nature's power to rejuvenate: "The earth, too, seems to be overpowered and dead. Surely it is impossible that it should ever flower again . . . suddenly a cataclysm reduces all the buildings to rubble and men cart the rubble away. Here, now, is a field of waving grain. . . . There, where the ears of wheat are heavy and golden, were torture chambers in which prisoners died of sheer terror . . . earth, like death, purifies everything. Earth, which is the end of all, is the eternal source of life."[8] He sees in the destruction of human-constructed buildings the innate possibility of nature to return, reiterating the central feature of nature, which is life itself.

For many the link to nature has a transcendental and spiritual power. In Elizabeth Vaughan's July 23, 1944, diary entry at Santo Tomas, she recorded: "Freshly washed little leaves, twisting and turning themselves in the sunshine, to shake off the rain which falls from them in glistening drops like pearls cast off one at a time. Below the trees the bright pools of water, then a pearl falls into the pool, setting forth a series of laughing ripples on the surface of the water, touching off a faint musical chime which tingles a series of notes from high treble to bass as the pearl slips down the notes of the musical scale of the bottom of the pool. Such is a corner of Santo Tomas on a bright Sunday morning after two weeks of unceasing rain. Such freshness in nature is the countenance of the Lord." Nature had interrupted the reality of Vaughan's imprisonment and the uncertainty of her future to remind her of the continuity of life. When she received an eight-month-old copy of the *Red Cross News* it triggered "the sudden memory of the red hills and streams of Georgia. . . . How fickle is the mind — and how interchangeable the emotions of hatred and love, though internment has made me like certain types of people less and [made me] love nature the more. For nature is kind, and humanity is not always so."[9]

Andy Goldsworthy's Garden of Stones Holocaust memorial is a powerful expression of how manmade war can be overcome by inextinguishable life. On the rooftop of the Museum of Jewish Heritage in lower Manhattan, the Holocaust memorial consists of trees growing out of eighteen boulders weighing between three and ten tons each. The artist had drilled a hole into each boulder and planted a dwarf chestnut oak in each cavity. In Hebrew numerology the number eighteen symbolizes *chai,* Hebrew for *life,* and the tree of life is a common Hebrew image; the living trees emerging from the inanimate stones suggest survival, resilience, and hope. Goldsworthy anticipates that trees will die, and he suggests that a dead tree be left in the grove, but also that survivor's children replant the acorns from the trees.

Not just a dwelling, home is also where one is from, in that way standing as a symbol of self and stability. Making a garden can be a way of making a new home, lending a literal dimension to the metaphor of putting down roots. Gardens can both help make an alien environment familiar and act as a "homing" device that takes us back in mem-

In the 1990–91 Gulf War, a green tarp held down by sandbags is transformed into a "lawn," with a sign warning "stay off." The tent city that comprised this U.S. Air Force Base at Al Khary, Saudi Arabia, was completely dismantled after only five months.

ory to a desired destination. Every garden contains inherent references to "other places, events, and themes," an aspect that garden historian John Dixon Hunt calls "re-presentation."[10]

In both their physical and psychological dimensions, gardens can sometimes remind people of where they came from or commemorate such places. They can evoke a place of the past or a desired future — sometimes they are one and the same. American soldiers' gardens in Saudi Arabia during the first Gulf War (1990–91) looked like caricatured versions of front yards, but they nevertheless offered their makers the solace and pleasures of domesticating a desert landscape into a vision of home during a time of great anxiety and danger. Soldiers were in an unfamiliar, sandy, harsh, desert landscape devoid of vegetation. They applied their imagination and remarkable ingenuity to the problem of how to transform their temporary quarters into "home" using only available materials. They bordered gardens with shell coverings, crafted fences out of pallets, and stacked sandbags as enclosures. They put up signs announcing who they were and how far they were from home, poignantly demonstrating their efforts to make a military encampment into an American streetscape.

The conical plastic covers of shells border the entry walk to this tent at the U.S. Air Force Base at Al Khary in the first Gulf War.

In decorating their barracks and tents inside and out, soldiers expressed both their individuality and their membership in a larger community. While combining expressions of individual identity, gardens also collectively contribute to the formation of group identity. These can be gestures ranging from the modest, such as mowing the lawn or displaying holiday decorations, to grander and bolder statements.

At Stalag Luft 3 in Germany, POW Peter Langmead's poem "'Wicks' or the Result of Thinking in Bed" voices the role the garden played in his yearning to be out of the war and home again: "Let the world rush by, on destruction bent / And I'll watch, from the gate where I lean." As if to acknowledge that some essential part of him remained at home in England, Langmead signed his poem with dual addresses: Sagan, the location of the camp where he was imprisoned; and his actual "home" address, Wicks Farm, Gratfton, Arundel, Sussex.[11]

Carrying memories of home, people often try to re-create or at least recapture aspects of their origins in a new setting. This is particularly dramatic for immigrants and is accentuated by their being thrust into an alien culture and environment. This type of garden

Italian POWs at the 16th Garrison Battalion POW detention camp in Hay, New South Wales, Australia, created this garden, which featured their model of the Coliseum in Rome.

making can also function as an act of adaptation, as demonstrated by the gardens of Russian and Ethiopian immigrants in Israel in the 1990s. Thousands resided temporarily in caravan communities that offered adequate shelter but were modest and short-term accommodations. In this situation individuals and families made gardens with minimal and scavenged materials, often never to see them reach fruition, for everyone moved on to permanent housing.

Most modern migrants move from the countryside and small, rural communities to metropolitan centers. Since that change can be daunting, any links to their previous home can facilitate the transition. Charles Lewis tells of a transplanted southerner who planted in New York City a traditional southern garden, including okra and cotton. Thinking beyond the pleasure she herself took in these familiar plants, and understanding the ability of the garden to transmit culture, she labeled the plants for neighborhood children because "it is important for children to know the names of all the plantings, even

Garden of Russian and Ethiopian immigrants in Haifa, Israel (1993). Stones provide borders for beds, and plastic containers, metal cans, and tires serve as planters.

some they don't see up here."[12] Another New York City example is found in the casitas, which are constructed by members of the Puerto Rican community. Fragments of the rural Puerto Rican landscape reconstructed in the city's vacant lots, casitas express an adaptation to urban life while reminding residents of home.

Such garden constructions can happen in places even more improbable than vacant city lots. The urban landscape of road overpasses, cheek-by-jowl buildings, bridges, and alleys, also offers ideal circumstances for secreting gardens in plain sight. In the summer of 1990, Daniel Pérez, an immigrant from the Dominican Republic, planted corn in the traffic islands of upper Broadway in New York. In this surprising setting the corn thrived. Pérez said he "wanted to beautify the streets," and that his "little farm" was "a recollection, a memory, of how things are back home."[13] Similarly, in the traffic island near his apartment in Eugene, Oregon, seventy-two-year-old Thakorbhai Patel planted a garden of plants familiar to him:

A casita in New York City evokes memories of the Puerto Rican homes of the immigrants.

turmeric, bhindi, baby eggplant, and peppers. He had carried the seeds and cuttings from his native India. Patel's modest personal saga is enacted by millions of immigrants and refugees around the world as they endeavor to use gardens to re-create and remind them of home.

Home is the first link in the chain to establish community. One step beyond individual gardens are communal gardens, which help create a sense of being home but also have a defiant aspect. We admire urban dwellers, especially the poor and disenfranchised, who wish to garden, because their success is dependent on their resourcefulness in making or co-opting a place, marshaling scarce resources, and establishing the garden in an inhospitable environment. The urban garden is in some ways an offering to a community along the lines of a charitable donation. The transformation of empty lots and derelict spaces into gardens is striking, and "against all odds" is a common description of the accomplishment.

Groups like SLUG (San Francisco League of Urban Gardeners), BUG (Boston Urban Gardeners), Seattle's Pea Patch program, New York City's GreenThumb program, and Green Guerillas have orchestrated the urban community gardening phenomena into a movement in their respective communities and even internationally. Such programs initially involved allotment gardens, but as the movement matured, many groups expanded beyond their origins and incorporated a full range of garden possibilities: play areas, children's gardens, fountains, miniparks, places of commemoration and memorial, art, even classic garden features such as labyrinths and gazebos. They have also developed innovative solutions to composting, irrigation, security, and construction, and encouraged an exceptional and ingenious range of local artistry and craft in everything from paving to tiles, using recycled and scrounged materials. As a result of these efforts, vacant lots in depopulated inner cities are being reclaimed both by volunteer plants and through the purposeful activity of human volunteers, urban farmers.

Pride in accomplishment boosts self-esteem and confidence, and success affords a sense of control, and enhances social and community bonds. Garden vandalism is uncommon in these urban gardens, for there is respect for the effort and broad appreciation of the result. In New York housing projects, the gardens have become special places in the social life of the community. They are where commemorative pictures were taken and where weddings and graduations occurred, a sure sign of affection for a place. The announcement for an Open Garden Day in the San Francisco Bay Area in 1997 showcasing innovative urban garden projects proclaimed that "these projects, which include community gardens, school gardens, market gardens, job training gardens, and demonstration gardens, serve a variety of community needs. They produce food and provide beauty in the urban landscape; they are places of refuge and learning; they are oases where people in the community gather to work and relax in a natural setting."[14]

Cities often have had an adversarial approach to urban gardeners, but they have gotten better at recognizing the benefits of individual and community action. The Seattle Department of Transportation sponsors a gardening contest that "welcomes streetside garden stewards and those that enjoy steward efforts" for the city's traffic circles. In a neighborhood undergoing gentrification in Portland, Oregon, the Jardin des Anarchistes was inspired by the graffiti tag, "gardens not galleries."

Landscape architect Diana Balmori and photographer Margaret Morton recorded society's most fleeting gardens — the gardens of homeless persons in New York City — in their book *Transitory*

Jimmy relaxes in his garden on the Lower East Side, New York City, ca. 1992.

Gardens, Uprooted Lives. Their work causes us to question what we have understood to be the most basic garden facts. How can places, which by their nature grow, often slowly, be temporary? Does a garden need to be rooted? These are gardens built from a profound desire of individuals to make a home despite incredible odds. Their studies show gardens offering a full range of garden functions and meaning. They are places of personal pleasure, sites for meals, work places, territorial markers, ritual centers, collections, and expressive displays. These intensely used places take imaginative and maximum advantage of minimal materials and space. They are powerful reminders of the multiple forms of sustenance and meaning that gardens offer. Inevitably these gardens are destroyed, not by the elements but by human intervention: bulldozers, eviction, or fire. Their short-lived existence only emphasizes their power.

Halina Birenbaum was a teenager when she was sent from the Warsaw ghetto to the Majdanek concentration camp, where she worked as a slave laborer. Even there the power of contrast and the imagery of a garden contributed to a sense of hope.

> Sometimes we worked in fields only a stone's throw from a village hut — armed SS sentries cut us off from freedom. Then I used to look with envy and longing at children playing freely in the peasant's gardens, at the hens pecking the dust, the people bustling about. . . . I just could not comprehend that there still existed another world in which people were allowed to move around open spaces not cordoned off with barbed wire and in which children played! But at the same time the faith quickened in me that we too at some future time be people. The existence of life outside the camp, the sight of the bright sky and green fields alleviated the tragedy of the camp. . . . Here in the open fields, closer to people's houses, it was easier to hope.[15]

Hope is not just an emotion but a force. Janusz Korczak, the director of the orphanage in Warsaw, called hope the "crutch of illusion essential to the survival of human dignity." On the one hand that illusion could be a necessary support, on the other hand it could be a willful deception that functioned as a defense mechanism. That hope was baseless for all but the few survivors does not diminish the force of the emotion or desire, and what it may have meant to people at the moment. Korczak's final diary entry of August 4, 1942, reads: "I watered the flowers, the poor orphanage plants, the plants of the Jewish orphanage. The parched soil breathed with relief."[16] Korczak accompanied his charges into the gas chambers.

In times of personal, social, or cultural despair, the garden sustains hope. The German philosopher Ernst Bloch writes that hope is the "counter-emotion against anxiety and fear" and "the most human of all mental feelings." In historical "images of hope," the archetypes of the Golden Age and paradise, the idea is given imaginative form in what Bloch calls "wishful landscapes." These are also the foundational images and ideals of garden creation. But for Bloch such landscapes are not just about image and ideal: "hope is . . . ultimately a practical, militant emotion, it unfurls banners."[17]

The French philosopher Gabriel Marcel formulated a concept of hope based upon his observations of persons imprisoned during World War II. In the prisoners he saw something representative of the entire human condition: that we are all in a state of captivity and that we all are prisoners of despair. Hope, he said, is "the act by which the temptation to despair is actively overcome." Hope is preparation for the future, whose positive energy nourishes our actions. Author Rebecca Solnit posits that "hope just means another world might be possible, not promised, not guaranteed. Hope calls for action; action is impossible without hope. . . . To hope is to give yourself to the future, and that commitment to the future makes the present inhabitable." We are always anxious about what may come, but Bloch asserts that "hope extinguishes anxiety."[18] The resonance of these attributes of hope with garden making is striking.

Marcel recognized the characteristics of hope as humility, patience, nonacceptance, and active waiting. Hope is not naive optimism. Hope has certain predictable traits or habits: persistence, resourcefulness, courage. The playwright Tony Kushner, author of *Angels in America,* has said, "Hope is not this bubbly, fizzy emotion that rises up in you. It's a very tough thing. You have to work to find it. You have to work to drive it through despair. It's not real hope unless it's gone through despair. Hope that has survived an encounter with the terribleness of life. There's a certain Jewish faith that on the other side of despair there is something worth working toward. Justice will arrive. . . . Moshiach [Messiah] arrives constantly, we're just not ready. It doesn't just happen — it's something we have to also bring about."[19] This view of hope as being what we go through before justice is delivered echoes the meaning behind the gardens ghetto residents and other World War II civilian internees struggled to create and nurture, tragically often in vain.

Gardens are inherently optimistic. The gardener has faith that what is planted will grow, and that as plants mature they will be cared for. When visiting the ruins of Manzanar long after the war, Gary Okihiro pondered a gnarled cherry tree: "Someone must have planted this tree, I knew. Someone must have had faith in the future."[20]

New York Times garden columnist Anne Raver takes an expansive view of gardens and often reports the efforts of urban gardeners. In writing about a patch of wild petunias in Brooklyn she notes, "Were they part of some lush perennial border I wouldn't give them a glance. It's their existence in this wasteland that makes them so striking. . . . You can find signs of such invincible spirits all over the city — and across the country — if you look for them." She finds the work of the city gardeners, where plants are grown in impossible places, "literally stuffed into pockets of earth," to be "emblems of the gardeners' courage." Of El Jardín del Paraíso, a community garden on New York's Lower East Side, urban gardener Julie Kirkpatrick says, "you need a ray of hope and you find it seeing what can grow out of rubble." The intent of a community gardening project in the South Bronx was to displace drug dealers. A project in landscape and social reclamation, it was modeled after a similar project in Harlem, the Success Garden. Reporter Tony Hiss found that "both hope and fear [are] deeply embedded in this garden site, to some extent they have intertwined."[21]

Kathy Pilgrim is one of the founders of Voices in the Wilderness, a peace group, who was imprisoned for trespassing at a missile silo site in the Midwest. She planted corn on the missile silo site as a gesture symbolizing Isaiah's prophecy of swords being turned into plowshares. The architect Daniel Liebskind, who designed the post–September 11 reconstruction on the World Trade Center site, included Gardens of the World in his original design, with gardens placed within his 1,776-foot-high Freedom Tower. When asked why he had included gardens in his design, Liebskind responded that "gardens are a constant affirmation."[22]

Gardens can also be a form of consecration. An aspect of hope is that of solace, the giving of comfort, especially to those who are grieving or wounded. Memorial gardens can offer solace and comfort. The mechanism may seem mysterious, but perhaps it is the sense of refuge, of calm and peacefulness, or just the quiet and the connection to nature — to life. In urban neighborhoods across the United States there are street gardens described as "peace gardens" and "grieving gardens," which are memorials to those killed by violence. Similar gardens, which are akin to shrines, abound on roadsides for the victims of car accidents throughout the world.

After September 11, 2001, Matthew Arnn, working for the U.S. Forest Service in New York, began the Living Memorial project, a national planting project already in hundreds of communities. Having observed rescue workers sitting in Battery Park City under ash-covered lindens, Arnn noticed that "the trees were shrouded in ash, but they still offered solace and an opportunity to get away from the pile." Arnn was inspired by E. B. White's essay "Here Is New York," about an old willow in Turtle Bay. White observed a "battered tree, long suffering and much climbed, held together by strands of wire but beloved of those who know it. In a way it symbolizes the city: life under difficulties, growth against odds, sap-rise in the midst of concrete, and the steady reaching for the sun." Nadia Murphy, a horticulturist married to a firefighter in the Rockaways, a neighborhood that lost eighty people on September 11, 2001, understands that "planting a garden is an act of faith that you will be there to take care of it — or someone will." The Rev. Lyndon F. Harris of St. Paul's Chapel, Trinity Episcopal Church, which had been protected by sycamores from the morning attack, saw a sparrow making a nest out of debris. Anne Raver was struck by the symbolism. "It is the sparrow, not the phoenix, that is rising from the ashes in New York. It is the weeds poking out of ground zero. It is people planting trees. These acts combined become a form of healing that transcends, yet never forgets, a single life lost."[23]

In landscape terms, hope has often been embodied in ideas of the pastoral. The pastoral in its literary and garden forms is a retreat into the past, into nostalgia and often into the country, physically or symbolically. There is a danger that the garden becomes a trite palliative, a mask, and that working in the garden reflects an abdication of involvement and responsibility. At the extreme, the garden seems cowardly. One of the paradoxes of the pastoral is that it is not always based on an urge to get away from something. The garden may represent a desire to have a different kind of involvement. Hope is not passive, but in its "refusal of fatalism [it is] an active non-capitulation," according to author Joan Nowotny. Similarly the garden can be assertive: it can be about survival and sanity. The pastoral can be conceived of as a movement toward an ideal. Hope, says Verena Kast, "draws on a hidden vision of the better."[24] To extend that concept to the garden, we might say that gardens take that hidden vision and make it visible by

In the immediate aftermath of September 11, 2001, memorial gardens sprang up in New York, most dramatically in Union Square. This photo was taken September 13.

Garden in the mostly dry moat of Theresienstadt. The image is from the Nazi propaganda film *Der Fuehrer Schenkt den Juden eine Stadt* (The Fuehrer Gives the Jews a City), shot in September 1944.

giving it shape, form, and life. The peace that the garden may offer is not merely the absence of conflict found in quiet and tranquillity but is a positive assertive state. So too the garden is not only a calm retreat and welcome respite, but also the assertion of a proposed condition, a model of a way of being and of physical form.

The pastoral vision always implies a contrast. Most often that contrast has been between urban and rural worlds. The power of the imagery and perhaps the depths of its meaning derive in part by the dimensions of the contrast. At the Majdanek extermination camp, Halina Birenbaum was assigned to weeding the grass between the two rows of electrified barbed wire that divided the women's and the men's camps. Just touching the wire meant death, and some hurled themselves into the wire to terminate their suffering. As the weeders worked between the wires, the German guards left them alone. In this gap Birenbaum found that she "could sit and rest, picking at the weeds and grass. . . . I preferred this work to any other. Here I had the peace I longed for."[25] This is a horrifying pastoral vision of a bizarre respite, weeding green grass hemmed in by a deadly electrical current and the prospect of death.

Hope can also be perverted and used as propaganda, communicating false impressions of actual conditions. Gardens are not immune from being put to nefarious purposes. This book does not include gardens that are perversions of the garden's promise of life and hope, despite the fact that they may have offered comforts. At Treblinka the main street of the lower camp was an 800-meter-long stage set bordered with flowers and garden beds. Charlotte Delbo, a Frenchwoman imprisoned at Ravensbruck, told of going through a gauntlet of SS men with aprons filled with earth to make an SS garden. Primo Levi tells us that at Auschwitz there was an SS "village" with houses, gardens, children, rabbits, and dogs. The paths were paved with human bones.[26]

Theresienstadt (Teresin) was a Nazi "model ghetto" built in an old fortress town near Prague. This was a show camp, with show gardens just outside the fortress embankments. The gardens were SS property worked by Jews. Workers were forbidden to eat the produce; those who were caught doing so were sent to Auschwitz. For a visit by the International Red Cross in June 1944, buildings were painted, new barracks built, and gardens planted within the walls. The reality was that Theresienstadt was a deportation site to extermination camps; 33,000 died there and 85,000 more died in Auschwitz.

Garden is a verb as well as noun. The activity can carry equal, or even greater meaning and significance than the place itself. Defiant gardens are the product of defiant gardening, assertive and deliberate actions. The mental and physical work of gardening has satisfaction and rewards attuned to the many and varied processes of garden creation, and to the whole panoply of gardens, uses from aesthetic satisfaction to a setting for leisure. Not everyone finds pleasure in each of these stages, but almost everyone finds gratification in some aspect.

Work affords individuals a livelihood and a way to contribute to society, but we are less conscious of work's other functions. Defiant gardens of all kinds emphasize work's broader meaning. Work can be

Huts at the No. 14 Convalescent Depot at Trouville, France, August 16, 1918.

productive, but it is also a way to keep one's mind and body occupied. It fosters a sense of dignity, self-respect, and identity. Garden work can provide a sense of purpose; it is an act that provides relief from monotony, idleness, and restlessness — it can be something "to do."

Work itself can have a therapeutic value. The conditions of defiant gardens accentuate the difficulty of each stage of garden making. Aspects of gardening that are taken for granted under normal conditions loom to the fore. Land has to be set aside, soil needs to be prepared and fertilized, seeds must be collected, plots have to be carefully monitored against intrusion by pests and people, plants have to be tended and the harvest carefully gleaned. All of this work can comfort the psyche and even enhance the physical health of the workers. There is a sense of dignity and self-respect inherent in garden labor. Gardening can be a "natural" antidepressant, alleviating stress and acting as a mental escape, placing individuals in a different state of mind. The practice of horticultural therapy provides insight into the mechanisms for how this operates.

Inherent in the life rhythms of plants are a steadiness and predictability that offer comfort, especially in stressful circumstances, such as war. Gardens also foster a form of nonverbal communication

Vegetable cultivation by the troops, near Fruges, France, July 14, 1918.
Note the German scarecrow with arms uplifted in a pose of surrender.

among a person, plant, and place. They offer an opportunity to nurture. Journalist Robin Herbst notes that adversity can breed art: "Sometimes the maker begins less with a clear vision than an obsession to work something out through the sweat of the brow. So it is with gardens." Herbst cites the example of Connie Umberger's Nantucket garden, which was motivated by the suicide of her twenty-nine-year-old daughter. Umberger recalls her grief: "When I found that I couldn't do anything — I can't tell you why or how, one just comes to these things — I found that digging seemed to help. . . . It was one of those things you think of as a mindless activity, but actually it was more than mindless. In fact it was just the opposite, because my mind was doing the digging. Not in any conscious way: I didn't even understand what was happening. I never thought, 'Oh gosh, this digging is really good for me.'"[27] Umberger's garden is an embodiment of the nonverbal, almost instinctual healing that gardening can offer as physical labor that effects a psychological change.

For active persons, work is an essential aspect of personal identity. Skilled gardeners take pride in their expertise and accomplishments, from fine flowers to abundant produce. Having an understanding of the gardening process, knowing what might grow, and being resource-

Mrs. T. Arima's garden at block 7 at Jerome Relocation Center, Arkansas. The plans included a pool for goldfish.

ful in gathering materials are deeply satisfying, and the final satisfaction is in the result, be it consuming the product — the literal fruit of one's labor — or enjoying the place and its attributes.

Roman Kent wrote about the arduous and time-consuming labor in the gardens in the Lodz ghetto, and the gift this work offered residents:

> Slowly but surely, we learned how to toil and utilize every inch of the land more and more efficiently. To achieve our objectives not only required hard work, but also involved many hours of our time to daily work in the field. We had to rake, water, and weed properly in order to give our vegetables the best chance to grow. Since the earth was not particularly fertile, this task was even harder to accomplish.
>
> To my surprise, in spite of the heavy load I had to carry, I became very fond of working in the field. Even though it was only temporary relief, for the time that I was there I could forget about the daily problems of ghetto life we were forced to endure and our unfortunate situation in general.[28]

Women work in a garden in the Kovno ghetto while children look on.

In "Blessings of the Earth," an essay probably written by Lodz ghetto chronicler Josef Zelkowicz, the author takes the view that life in the ghetto taught Jews things both good and bad, placing gardens squarely on the positive side of the ledger. Zelkowicz's reasoning goes beyond the gardens as a source of food. He describes Jews as historically alienated from nature and even willfully ignoring its beauties, a people who have extolled a "head" life at the expense of a "hand" life. He wrote: "The public threw themselves at the land as if it was a piece of roasted meat. Those who had never seen a plant in their lives are today gardeners. He who had always believed that butter grew in the ground because when he was in his summer-house he saw the peasants bringing butter wrapped in green leaves, is today himself a peasant, working his plot of land himself."

Zelkowicz constructs a fascinating and almost humorous dialogue between "head" life and "hand" life. He says that peasants traditionally didn't bother to ask why things had to be done a certain way, since they worked based on experience and tradition, but neophyte Jewish gardeners, not having that background, incessantly asked questions:

"— *Why* is it better to water cucumbers when it is sunny and between 10:00 and 3:00 in the afternoon?

"— *Why* does one have to tie garlic shoots?

"— *Why* have you placed stakes near your tomatoes?"

Of the Jews who were new to gardening, Zelkowicz speculates, "maybe he demonstrates with his bowed posture that field work does not require any head, but only healthy hands and strong legs, but finally, he can't shed his own skin that easily. In the end, the character of a people changes only through evolution — The Jew who has always lived a head-life can't suddenly overnight go over entirely to a 'hand' or 'leg' life. Even when it comes to farmwork, he needs his head; he needs to understand to work; he must know the *why*."[29]

Jean Gittins, imprisoned at Hong Kong's Stanley Camp, wrote that "not only was our diet improved by the added vitamins, but the joy of achievement more than compensated for the effort. Above all, fruitful occupation gave meaning and purpose to our lives." Garden work can be individual or collective; each has its distinct satisfactions, but gardening together fosters a sense of community. Also at Stanley, William Sewell found that the additional food the garden yielded was "bare compensation; the real reward of a constant job was an occupied mind and greater chance of physical health. The spirits of the men began to improve. Being in a gang gave a sense of co-operation and friendship."[30]

Scale is not important — a single sprouting seedling, a lone tree, can be an inspiration, especially under difficult conditions. Environmental psychologists Rachel and Stephen Kaplan refer to tiny efforts as being "micro-restorative environments." They identify four factors that contribute to the restorative experience: being away, which can be an actual escape or a sense of being away; fascination, something that holds one's attention; extent, an "explorable" world or a feeling of being removed from the everyday; and compatibility between personal needs and the place.[31] Gardens can provide all of these.

Nelson Mandela, in his autobiography *Long Walk to Freedom,* speaks of a garden he nurtured during his years of imprisonment. He is explicit about its meaning. "A garden was one of the few things in prison that one could control. To plant a seed, watch it grow, to tend it and then harvest it, offered a simple but enduring satisfaction. The sense of being the custodian of this small patch of earth offered a small taste of freedom." The BBC television show *Ground Force,* which constructs gardens for people, built a garden for Mandela at his home in South Africa. When interviewed about his new garden, Mandela said he was "essentially a country boy . . . who was very happy to see . . . a blade of grass . . . a leaf of a tree." He noted that decades of imprisonment hadn't obliterated that part of him. *Ground Force* also contributed to the development of a prison vegetable garden project by Seeds for Africa based at the University of Kent. The first garden was at the Kabwe Maximum Security prison in Zambia in 2000, with plans for five more in Tanzania.[32]

Prisoners are often put to work at something that has the arduous dimension of slave labor or a chain gang or the more enlightened and even liberating and rehabilitative aspect of a prison garden. Prison gardens were originally where prisoners grew their own food and worked farms, but more recently they have been incorporated into rehabilitation programs. Since 1978 the National Gardening Association has established prison garden programs and facilitated the expansion of existing projects. The programs have many benefits. The work itself is relief from idleness and stress, a chance to be outdoors and a temporary relief from confinement. The work also offers opportunities for self-expression and personal achievement, enhances self-esteem, and allows prisoners to assume some responsibility. Homer Williams, an inmate at the Men's Correctional Institution in Hardwick, Georgia, says that "having a chance to go outside and work at something I enjoy means a lot to me. It gives me a chance to get rid of some or most of my bad feelings that build up in prison." The prisoners at New York City's Rikers Island Prison produce 30,000 pounds of vegetables per year. Although this supplements their diet in a healthy way, the psychological benefit to the inmates is more important. Inmate Frederick Lewis said of working in the garden, "It's like serenity. . . . There's a sense of freedom."[33]

America's now-abandoned maximum-security prison, Alcatraz, is also home to gardens that were constructed before the prison became a federal prison. Alcatraz Island was originally a fort and military prison, with gardens built for the officers' families after the Civil War. When still a military prison, Alcatraz housed inmates imprisoned for generally minor offenses, and for a century, such prisoners constructed much of the island, including gardens. Free on the island, they beautified Alcatraz into something of a garden spot. After 1933, when the prison was transferred to the jurisdiction of the Federal

Leyhill prison inmates designed the Garden of Hope, displayed at the 2004 Chelsea Flower Show.

Bureau of Prisons, it became home to the nation's most notorious criminals and prisoners still tended the gardens. The warden's secretary, Freddie Reichel, promoted gardening and even received help from the California Horticultural Society. "On 'the Rock,' little grew uninvited or untended. Only human tenacity enabled plants to flourish. In this sense, the gardens of Alcatraz are testaments to the human spirit, to the desire to create life and beauty even in a forbidding environment. Perhaps this above all is what makes these gardens so inspiring — and so touching."[34]

The British film *Greenfingers* tells the story of a group of prisoners in an experimental garden program who create their first garden at the Hampton Court Palace Flower Show. The film is based on true events at Leyhill Open Prison in Gloucester, a minimum-security prison with extensive gardens that are open to the public. The gardeners' work has won medals at the Chelsea Flower Show. Their 2000 entry, Time the Healer, showed nature encroaching on an abandoned industrial landscape and healing it with wildflowers. Their 2004 exhibit, the Garden of Hope, showed a "war-torn cottage" overlooking a bomb-cratered garden. Director Joel Hershman describes *Greenfingers* as being about second chances and redemption; the garden restores the makers as much as they restore the landscape.

Near Boesinghe, Belgium, an Army Service Corps member paints trees on the waterproof sheeting covering the side of his hut, January 28, 1918.

Gardens counterbalance the ugliness of war, but clearly the weight is not equal. The destructive power of war and its wanton killing, death, and destruction can only be temporarily and modestly restrained. The garden's calm and security are ultimately only a respite from war's terror. But the garden can function as a reminder of a peaceful prewar period and look ahead to a longed-for postwar time, when domesticity and simple pleasures will prevail and the "ugliness of war" would be replaced by the beauty of creation.[35] Homer, Augustine, and Proust all saw beauty as lifesaving not in a literal sense but in its affirmation of life and its quality to uplift the spirit.

The devastation of war filled people with disgust. But the observation and awareness of beauty is a precondition for its creation, and indeed wartime observers found beauty in startling situations, as we've already seen in the incongruities of war. During winter in Flanders, Phillip Gibbs observed that "in its first glamour of white the snow gave a beauty even to No-Man's Land, making a lace-work pattern of barbed wire, and lying very softly over the tumbled ground of mine-fields, so that all the ugliness of destruction and death was hidden under this canopy. The snowflakes fluttered upon stark bodies there, and shrouded them tenderly. It was as though all the doves of peace were flying down to fold their wings above the obscene things of war."[36]

Critic Elaine Scarry characterizes beauty as having a sacred as well as a life-saving quality: "Beauty quickens. It adrenalizes. It makes the heart beat faster. It makes life more vivid, animated, living, worth living." During war, this quality would be even dearer and appreciated with a greater intensity. Gibbs notes that "one of the paradoxes of the war is that beauty lived but a mile or two away from hideous squalor." Any artistic endeavor, including a garden, could be an act of "aesthetic redemption," what historian Jay Winter describes as the "retrieval of beauty from the carnage of war." But the context was never forgotten. In the spring of 1916, Captain Theodore Percival Cameron Wilson felt that "even the beauty of Spring has something of purgatory in it — the sort of purgatory a madman may know who sees all beautiful things through a veil of obscenity."[37]

Even in the most extreme situations, people not only see beauty; they seek it and will create art that celebrates beauty and life. In writing about Theresienstadt and its artists, Milan Kundera asks, "What was art for them? A way of claiming the full array of emotions, of ideas, of sensations, so that life should not be reduced to a single dimension of horror." Oskar Singer lauded the work of Lodz ghetto gardeners. "If yields should be recorded under these circumstances," he said, "then one must testify (or certify or recognize) that the small farmers in the ghetto are great poets."[38]

In "Greenwood Trees at Ruhleben," the author contrasted the beauty of the English landscape with their meager copse.

A Devonian vale seen from its head where the water springs, a fruit-laden dell at the foot of the Alps, a Sussex wood beneath a Sussex sun, all are like, but, forgive me is I say it, none so beautiful as this copse of ours. If you are religious, it is the very breath of God which has sown richness in the place; if you are an artist, it is your idol among the masters who has designed it; if you are a philosopher, it is the triumph of life which has effected it; if you are a mystic, it is that glimpse beyond the sacred veil for which you thirst . . . you think that the Earthly Paradise of Dante cannot have been more gently luxurious in its charm. New leaves hang like butterflies upon the subtle etching of the branches; the maiden hair foliage of the beech, the small green flowers of the willow, the evanescent crimson silk of the aspen, soon to lie scattered on the ground, all cluster together in a divine dream.[39]

From the trenches, artist Paul Nash wrote home, "It sounds absurd, but life has a greater meaning here and a new zest, and beauty is more poignant. I never feel dull or careless, always alive to the significance of nature who, under these conditions, is full of surprises for me."[40]

In the Polish town of Bielitz, Gerda Klein's family had an enormous garden that she played in as a child and described as "my paradise." She also tended the graves in the Jewish cemetery, "to be in touch with nature, growth and beauty." After months of hiding in a cellar from the Germans, disregarding the risks, she sneaked back to the garden of her home for a final time. Finally captured, she was shuffled from work camp to work camp; her last camp was Grünberg, a place Klein describes as "cruelty set against a background of beauty. The gentle vineyard-covered hills silhouetted against the sapphire sky seemed to mock us." Each morning two thousand girls were marched to the factory. In the factory courtyard were star-shaped flower beds, exquisite rose gardens, and beds of tulips, lending a touch of "beauty against the grim reality." Klein craved something beautiful. "Day after day," she says, she "had to resist the desire to run out of line and touch those beautiful blossoms." One morning on their daily march, a crocus had broken through the concrete and was sprouting. The mass of girls parted, and silently "hundreds of feet shuffled around it" to avoid trampling the flower.[41]

As an adult, whenever she smelled roses Klein would recall her childhood garden as well as the "roses in Grünberg which we had not been allowed to touch." Years after the war, Klein returned to her childhood garden in Bielitz when Poland was still under Communist control. She found it to be reduced to a pile of rubbish and rubble, but even this delighted her: "It was horrible and really made me feel good" — she thought that it would have been too painful for her if it had remained as beautiful as it was when she was a child.[42]

In Santo Tomas, Frederick Stevens observed that in the midst of the worst privation in the camp, people found beauty in the flowers in their camp: "Here and there, in gay carnival-like colors, vivid tropical plants dot the landscape. Morning glories fought for a place on the nipa roofs, tall cana lilies rioted in the small gardens blooming in 'the magic gardens where there was no garden yesterday.'" But for Stevens the distinction between spiritual and physical sustenance never abated; he also observed that "no amount of beauty could dull the hunger."[43]

At Kuching Alice Keith recalled, "How we did long for beauty:

beauty of sight, sound, odor, beauty of thought! We dreamed of hearing symphonies again — opera, jazz — or whatever meant beauty of sound to the dreamer. We dreamed of beautiful flowers, places, sights, beautiful clothes: in our dreams we smelled perfumes, and fragrances, gingerbread, the sea, and the flowers. The scent of roses and violets haunted me, night after night I put myself to sleep remembering it. And day to day I smelled latrines." When Keith enumerated the things she had lost in captivity, her list noted "the entire absence of beauty, either physical in our surroundings, or emotional in our living."[44]

Alice Walker's essay "In Search of Our Mothers' Gardens" explores the extraordinary spiritual and creative lives of African American women. Walker writes of the artistry in her own mother's garden: "A garden so brilliant with colors, so original in its design, so magnificent with life and creativity, that to this day people drive by our house in Georgia — perfect strangers and imperfect strangers — and ask to stand or walk among my mother's art." Observing her mother in the garden, Walker writes, "It is only when my mother is working in her flowers that she is radiant, almost to the point of being invisible — except as Creator: hand and eye. She is involved in work her soul must have. Ordering the universe in the image of her personal conception of Beauty."[45]

It might seem almost sacrilegious to impose aesthetics on these gardens, but there are appeals to these gardens in their character and form. A defiant garden aesthetic has deep roots. David Reason in his essay "A Hard Singing of Country" notes how "there is an extensive web of traditions that seek to capture the essence of humanity in the emblematic garden: gardens are good to think." He adds, "I hanker for those other gardens: fragile and furtive, lurking below gratings of abandoned coal chutes and sprouting like wart-hairs from the tops of walls. Growth that is rank, untidy, invasive and unplanned is hearteningly independent, cheeky and chirpy in finding its niche." Defiant gardens border on Edmund Burke's formulation of the sublime, an aesthetic response founded on the paradoxical pleasure afforded at being some distance from phenomena that ultimately instill fear and might bring pain. Defiant gardens offer a bit of that distance, perhaps even more profoundly for they are a *direct* response to the sublime definers of privation, terror, and difficulty. They have a similar capacity for the sublime's most potent attribute, that of astonishment. This is not a claim that the terror of nature in storms and volcanoes, which are the products of natural forces, equals that of the terror of bombs and bullets, a human creation. Robert Graves wrote of the Great War that "War was return of earth to ugly earth, / War was foundering of sublimities. / Extinction of each happy art and faith / By which the world had still kept head in air."[46]

Gardens are planned, constructed, and cared for, and the results are carefully monitored. Here lies the foundation of an aesthetic sensibility, an eye that registers subtleties and appreciates form, pattern, and a multiplicity of meanings. They are the most profound reminders that the urge to transform one's surroundings for personal benefit is a basic human aspiration. Gary Okihiro included in this group internment camp artists and gardeners, mostly "'ordinary' people for whom the creative act, both before and during the war, was a way of coping, of healing, of living. . . . As artifacts, art from the camps speaks to us today of ingenuity, rare abilities, and imagination, and also of unrelenting persistence, quiet strength, and simple dignity. The ordinary is truly extraordinary."[47] Garden art often reflects a remarkable democracy and accessibility.

On a spit of land on England's south coast is a remarkable garden created by the British painter, theater designer, and filmmaker Derek Jarman that exemplifies all our garden themes of life, hope, home, work, and beauty. On the shingle beaches and estuary of Dungeness, within sight of a nuclear power station, Jarman worked his garden from 1986 until his death from AIDS in 1994. In this forbidding landscape he created an oasis among the windswept stones.

Jarman's garden is organized concentrically from the house, Prospect Cottage, outward to the surrounding shingle landscape. The periphery is loosely bordered with pointed stakes, a defensive palisade of sorts that recalls the ruins of a fortification. The garden is within this border but is almost indistinguishable from the surrounding landscape, for the same species are found on both sides. Within the staked border, the detritus of the coast has been collected and reconfigured. Their subtle tones are punctuated by the addition of colorful flowers, ordered and tended, highlighted and concentrated. The shingle stones evoke a Zen sand garden where they are raked into patterns. A closer look reveals small, mandala-like constructions that invite contemplation. Each composition is a self-contained creation that is part of an overall order and vision.

The garden is filled with found objects: beach debris, driftwood,

Derek Jarman's garden
in Dungeness, England.

stones, and metallic objects, including fragments of wartime mines
and shell casings. The repeated contrast of traditional garden materials and military artifacts is a significant aspect of the garden. Pointed
shapes and tools stand vertically amid a landscape that is round and
weathered. Everything is rusty, found, used, and yet somehow evokes
an arranged collection. Dangerous objects have been tamed as screw
pickets to support barbed wire, and clots of that icon of no-man's-land
are shaped into iron sculptures. Metal junk, driftwood, rusty and broken pieces from some industrial use, and weathered bones echo blossoms. These inanimate sculptural artifacts become organic. In
Jarman's gardening journal, he described his garden as "very good
therapy." Like the garden, its value to him "just grew rather than
being planned."[48] In his journal he also refers to his garden as a paradise, magical site, treasure hunt, his Eden, and his Gethsemane.

As I write and as you read this, war rages on and defiant gardens are created somewhere in the world. It has always been so. In 2004 soldiers

In July 2004, Army Warrant Officer Brook Turner, the camp cook, trims his grass with scissors in a camp north of Baghdad, Iraq.

from North Dakota of the 141st Engineer Combat Battalion stationed near Tikrit, Iraq, planted gardens with seeds donated from home. Sergeant Bob Syverson and Staff Sergeant Bill Poukka planted sunflowers. Syverson said of the garden, "I thought it'd be kind of [a] homey touch over here," and revealing a true connection to the landscape of home, he added, "It'd be nice if there was a lawn to mow, too."[49]

Sergeants Justin Wanzek and Carl Quam Jr. decided to plant a garden because "we were missing home, farming, and the joy of growing something." Neither their Meals Ready to Eat (MREs) nor the supply trucks arriving at their Forward Operating Base (FOB) supplied fresh vegetables, which proved a strong motivation to plant produce. Garden hoses and sprinklers were ill adapted to local conditions, so the soldiers adopted local irrigation and planting techniques, and they learned from local practice how to plant in this arid, sandy environment. They were pleased "just to grow something green out here." Quam described their North Dakota garden experience as "good family time and maybe in a way, the garden helped me kind of cope with missing them. I caught myself drifting back to home with the four of us all spending quality family time in our garden." These soldiers' gardens were made in their limited spare time that Quam described as follows: "At the time of garden prep, planting, weeding and watering, Sgt Wanzek and myself, along with the rest of our crew, were running 4–6 combat patrols a week, in 100–140 degree weather. When we came back to our area, we had a hard time getting motivated to work and weed, but we did. Like I said, it was good therapy

Sergeants Justin Wanzek and Carl Quam Jr. pose with their corn crop at FOB Speicher in Iraq.

to relax after a day of dodging roadside bombs, RPGs and escorting semi trucks full of unexploded ordinance over the worst stretch of road in northern Iraq."[50]

Warrant Officer Brook Turner had his wife send him grass seed from home. He missed the green of Hawaii, where he lives, and of his native Oregon. He said, "Usually after work I will water the back yard and listen to the radio barefoot, and just relax and feel the cool grass. I thought if I planted some grass I could still do that in a silly kind of way." His seeds were eaten by ants, but undeterred he somehow managed to acquire strips of sod that he watered three times daily.[51]

When hostilities cease, the opposing lines of conflict that were no-man's-lands present rare opportunities. After the Camp David accords in 1978, the international border between Israel and Egypt was moving every few months to its final demarcation. At El Arish in the northern Sinai, at a border crossing that everyone knew would be gone in a short period, some anonymous person or persons, using the

The creators of this Sinai garden knew their work would be ephemeral but nevertheless painstakingly assembled this mandala-like formation from found rocks.

few meager materials available, largely rocks, and importing a few plants, constructed a mandala-like garden. In this harsh and tenuous landscape, the garden beautified and offered a concrete manifestation of desire.

The World Conservation Union and the World Commission on Protected Areas are fostering the development of protected trans-boundary areas as well as international peace parks. The Iron Curtain snaked across all of Eastern Europe throughout the Cold War. Because people were forbidden to enter in many areas, especially in Berlin the area along the wall became a de facto wildlife preserve. Since 1989 proposals have been put forward for a European greenbelt to replace the course of the Iron Curtain with green, as a unifying sym-bol of peace. The proposal projects the urban greenbelt idea, essen-tially a protected garden zone surrounding a city, onto the continen-tal scale. A first conference of a working group to launch the project was held in September 2004.

Similarly, in Korea, the 151-mile-long demilitarized zone between North and South Korea has been uninhabited since the cease-fire of 1953. The Seattle landscape architectural firm of Jones and Jones, through the U.N. Development Program, investigated one area adjacent to the DMZ for ecologically sound and sustainable development. Their proposals for a biosphere reserve pointedly do not respect the current political boundaries but cut across the DMZ and capitalize on the fifty-year dearth of development in the region. Their proposals include a reunification parkway as well as a series of eco-villages and ecotourism for the area. In a beautiful twist, endangered cranes, which symbolize peace in many cultures, now inhabit the DMZ, which remains one of the world's most extensively mined areas.

The *New York Times* reported a teacher in Sarajevo, Bosnia, and Herzegovina, as saying in spring 1994: "The other day, I could not believe my eyes. I saw a wisteria bloom near my house that I had known all my life but had not seen for the past two years. It was a source of tremendous joy to me." As did residents of the Warsaw ghetto, residents of Sarajevo had planted "war gardens" that appropriated parks and every available scrap of land.[52]

Between 1992 and 1995, Sarajevo, a city once renowned for its peaceful relationships among different ethnic and religious communities, witnessed the killing of 10,000 civilians (including 2,000 children) and the wounding of 50,000. This massive human catastrophe ran alongside urbacide, the willful destruction of a city, where the soccer field became a graveyard and minefields remain commonplace.

That war has ended, or, perhaps more accurately, at least reached a state of truce maintained by U.N. peacekeepers. In its aftermath has arisen a remarkable garden effort. In 2000 the American Friends Service Committee established the Community Gardening Association in Bosnia and Herzegovina. Directed by Sarajevo native Davorin Brdanovic, the gardens have multiple objectives. They are an attempt at resocialization and reconciliation, they offer material assistance for the families by providing food and some produce to sell, and they also provide a form of work therapy and education, especially for children. Their physical presence is powerful symbolically, as gardens have been created in former minefields and killing grounds. The Central Garden in Kula, for example, was built in a former minefield. Because the ground had not been treated with pesticides, once the mines were removed, it was certified as an organic field!

Residents must be approved to join the gardening project, and each

Garden of the Community Gardening Association of Bosnia and
Herzegovina led by Davorin Brdanovic (to the left). Resocialization
of former enemies is a basic goal of the garden.

garden must be multiethnic, with Serb, Croat, and Bosnian participants. By the end of 2003, the project had ten gardens with over a
thousand participants from 252 families. Although most gardens are
devoted to vegetables, they yield intangible benefits, as well. One garden is at a children's home for war orphans. Here, says Brdanovic, the
children "come and garden and feel wonderful," for all the playgrounds or parks in the area were destroyed. Another garden is by
design not multiethnic: the garden in Misevici is reserved for Bosnian
women from Srebrenica and their children. The garden is part of a
refuge house for these women, most of whom had been raped during
the hostilities. "The garden [is the] only place we don't think about
what happened to us," say the women.

Because while in the gardens people are "all gardeners," says
Brdanovic, "not Serbs, Croats, Catholics," the gardens allow residents to put aside their thoughts and difficulties for a time.[53] The
Sarajevo gardens further express a garden paradox: they operate at
both ends of the time spectrum by being planted for the future (and
therefore expressive of hope), and by hearkening back to a more
peaceful time, either an actual or an idealized past. In Sarajevo these

gardens both attempt to let the society move on and attempt to re-create the prewar peace among the city's diverse inhabitants.

Psychologist Abraham Maslow theorized that people have a hierarchy of needs, where the more basic needs must be satisfied before the issues of the next level can be properly addressed. Maslow portrayed these as a pyramid. Gardens have a place at both the base of the pyramid, the level of physical survival, and at the apex, the level of self-actualization. The act of garden making, and the meaning that people derive from gardens, prompts us to question Maslow's premise, because gardens satisfy our needs and desires at all levels, from physical survival to the highest levels of art and cultural achievement.

Let us return briefly to Genesis. The story of the Garden of Eden is one of basic human questions: of mortality and immortality, knowledge, ethics, social, and environmental relations. In Genesis 2:9 we find, "From the ground the Lord God caused to grow every tree that was pleasing to the sight and good for food." In its first commentary about Eden, the Bible places aesthetics first, before the basic sustenance of life. These two aspects of gardens, Edenic or not, seem to be inevitably linked in all gardens.

The aesthetic value of gardens supports their image as a place of escape and refuge; on the other hand the sustenance value links gardens to the role they play in building hope and preserving one's values and ideals even amid unimaginable horrors. An exchange among the members of CIAM (Congrès Internationaux d'Architecture Moderne), the founding collaborative organization of modernist architects, expresses the dual sides of the garden and its possibilities. Polish architect Jersey Soltan, a member of CIAM, reports that the organization had a saying in the 1930s, when Europe was in the grip of rising fascism: "How can one think about roses when the forests are burning?" The group of course had an answer to its own question: "How can you not plant roses when the forests are burning?"[54] Gardens always ask us this most elementary question. For the forests are always burning, and we always both need and want to plant roses.

Directory of Prisoners and Internees

Henri Barbusse (1873–1935), French novelist and journalist

Max Bassler (1895–1916), killed on the Somme

Edmund Blunden (1896–1974), became a fellow of Merton College, Oxford

Christian Creswell Carver (1887–1917), died in Flanders

Phillip "Tubby" Clayton (1885–1972), cofounder of the Toc House

Leslie Coulson (d. 1916), killed in France

Lothar Dietz (1889–1915), killed near Ypres

Richard Donaldson (1896–1918), killed in France

Ludwig Finke (1893–1915), killed on the Western Front

Philip Gosse, became a naturalist and doctor

Robert Graves (1895–1985), poet, fought on the Western Front

Willy Holscher (1893–1917), killed in Champagne

Tom MacDonald, no data available

Harold Macmillan (1894–1986), wounded on three occasions; Prime Minister of Great Britain, 1957–63

John Masefield (1878–1967), served in the Red Cross in France and at Gallipoli

Rudolf Moldenhauer (1894–1914), killed on the Western Front

Paul Nash (1889–1946), enlisted in the Artists' Rifles, serving at Ypres on the Western Front

Friedrich Oehme (1897–1916), killed on the Western Front

Wilfred Owen (1893–1918), killed in France one week before the
armistice

John Oxenham (1852–1941), author of poem on the memorial
plaque at the entry to Newfoundland Memorial Park

Kurt Rohrbach (1893–1916), killed on the Somme

Siegfried Sassoon (1886–1967), poet and author wounded and
decorated in the war; author of the 1917 "Soldier's Declaration"

Hans Spatzl (1891–1917), killed on the Western Front

Friedrich Georg Steinbrecher (1892–1917), killed in Champagne

Robert Sterling (1893–1915), killed at Ypres

Georg Stiller (1895–1915), killed on the Western Front

Bernard Lewis Strauss (1883–1917), killed in France

Neville Talbot (1879–1943), cofounder of the Toc House named in
honor of his brother Gilbert, who was killed at Hooge

Gotthold von Rohden (1895–1915), killed in Champagne

Arthur Graeme West (1891–1918), killed at Bapaume

Henry Willamson (1896–1980), fought at the Battle of the Somme
and at Passchendaele, where he was seriously wounded

Theodore Percival Cameron Wilson (1889–1918), killed in France

GHETTO GARDENS

Bielsko, Poland

Janik (Jonah) Fuchs, survived the war; emigrated to Israel

Gerda Klein (1924–), Holocaust survivor of the Bielsko ghetto and
slave-labor camps in Marzdorf, Landshut, and Gruenberg;
emigrated to the United States in 1946

Kovno, Lithuania

Ilya Gerber (1924–1944), died in the Holocaust

William Mishell (d. 1994), liberated from Dachau in April 1945, he
emigrated to the United States, where he took an engineering
degree from New York University

Esther Mishkin (c. 1922–), participated in the mass illegal
immigration to Israel; later emigrated to the United States

Abraham Tory (1909–), emigrated to Israel

Lodz, Poland

Abraham Biderman (1924–), survived Auschwitz and Bergen-
Belsen; emigrated to Australia

Sylvia Glas-Weiner, teacher, Holocaust survivor

Leon Hurwitz (d. 1944?), killed at Auschwitz

Roman Kent (1920s–), survivor of the Lodz ghetto and Auschwitz, Mertzbachtal, Dornau, and Flossenburg concentration camps

Irena Liebman, survived Auschwitz, lives in Israel (1925–)

Dr. Israel Milejkowski, physician, Holocaust survivor

Oskar Rosenfeld (1884–1944), killed at Auschwitz

Henryk Ross (1910–1991), Holocaust survivor; emigrated to Israel

Stefania Ross, Holocaust survivor; emigrated to Israel

Mordechai Chaim Rumkowski (1877–1944), killed at Auschwitz

Simha Bunim Shayevitsh (1907–1944), died in the Holocaust

Oskar Singer (1898–1944), died in the Holocaust

Jozef Zelkowicz (1897–1944), died in the Holocaust

Nachman Zonabend, Holocaust survivor; settled in Sweden

Majdanek, Poland

Halina Birenbaum, see entry at Warsaw

Ravensbrück, Germany

Charlotte Delbo (1913–), resistance fighter, survivor of Auschwitz and Ravensbrück

Theresienstadt, Czechoslovakia

Frantisek Bass (1930–1944), killed in Auschwitz

Vilna, Lithuania

Herman Kruk (1897–1944), died in the Holocaust

Warsaw, Poland

Stanislaw Adler (d. 1946)

Mary Berg (1924–), released from the ghetto in 1944; emigrated to the United States

Halina Birenbaum (1928–), survivor of Warsaw ghetto, Auschwitz, Majdanek, Ravensbrück, Neustadt-Gleve; emigrated to Israel

Hershele Danieliwicz (d. 1941), starved to death, Warsaw ghetto

Janina David (1931–), Holocaust survivor, playwright

Stefan Ernest, presumed dead 1943

Peretz Hochman, Holocaust survivor

Chaim Kaplan (1880–1943), killed at Treblinka

Jan Karski (1914–2000), member of the Polish undergound

Janusz Korcazk, (1981–1942), killed at Auschwitz

Abraham Lewin (1893–1943), killed at Auschwitz

Rabbi Isaac Nissenbaum (1868–1943), murdered in Warsaw
Emmanuel Ringelblum (1900–1944), shot and killed in the Warsaw
   ghetto
Dawid Sierakowiak (d. 1944), died of TB in the Warsaw ghetto
Marek Stok, Holocaust survivor; emigrated to Brazil
Helena Szereszewska, Holocaust survivor
W. Szlengel (1914–1943), perished in the Warsaw ghetto uprising
George Topas (1924–), Holocaust survivor of Majdanek
Yitzhak ("Antek") Zuckerman (1915–1981), a leader of the Warsaw
   ghetto uprising; founder of the Ghetto Fighter's Kibbutz
Sara Zyskind, ghetto survivor

BARBED-WIRE GARDENS

World War I

Western Front
James Farrant
Horace Gilliland
Douglas Lyall Grant
Edouard V. Isaacs
André Warnod

Ruhleben, Germany
Israel Cohen
J. Davidson Ketchum
E. L. Wright

European Theater, WWII
Alan Campbell
John Cordner
Brian Filliter
Giovanni Guareschi
A. D. M. Hilton
David James
Peter Langmead
Odell Meyers
Phillip Miller
C. I. Rolfe
David Westheimer
Norman (Cy) L. Widen

Asian Theater, WWII

Borneo
Agnes Newton Keith

Changi, Singapore
Murray Griffin
P. H. Romney

Indonesia
Dr. Richard Philps

Santo Tomas and Los Baños, Manila
G. H. Bissinger
Alice Franklin Bryant
William Cheney Bryant
A. V. H. Hartendorp
Pat Hell, killed at Los Baños
Karen Kerns Lewis
Carl Mydans
Margaret Sams
Elizabeth Vaughan

Stanley, Hong Kong
Bill Faid, died at Stanley
Jeanne Faid
Jean Gittins
Ancil Nance
Elizabeth Nance
William Sewell
Horner Smith

STONE GARDENS

Crystal City, TX

Kenko Yamashita

Descoigne, BC, Canada

Frank Kadowaki
Fujitaro Kubota
Takeo Nakano
Fuji Takaichi

Gila River, AZ

Sam Fukuda
Charles Kikuchi
Roy Marubayashi
Gene Oishi
Y. Tomita
Kenichi Zenimura

Granada (Amache), CO

Lawson Fusao Inada
Wataru Ishisaka
Atsushi Kikuchi
Lili Sasaki

Heart Mountain, WY

Bill Hosakawa
Toro Ino
Amy Uno Ishi
Estelle Ishigo
Shoji Nagumo

Manzanar, CA

Jeanne Wakatsuki Houston
William Katuski
Mr. Kayahara
Yoriyuiki Kikuchi
Mr. Kubota
Mr. Murakomi
Tak Muto
Kango Nakamura
Akira Nishi
Henry Nishi
Kuichiro Nishi
Arthur Ogami
Nitaro (William) Ogami
Roy Suguwara
George S. Takemura
Harry Ueno

Minidoka, ID

Tomo Akiyama
Reverend Taro Gato
Yoshio Hamamoto
Robert Hosokawa
Riyozo Kado
C. Misuki
C. Natsuhara
Mr. Nitta
Arthur Ogami
Nitaro Ogami
Eddie Sato
Moto Takahashi
Buneyomen Wada

Poston, AZ

Suikei Furuya
Isamu Noguchi
Lawrence Sasano
Mr. Sato
George Sogioka

Rohwer, AR

Sada Murayama
Henry Sugimoto

Topaz, AZ

Don Akamatsu
H. Hayashi
Nobuo Kawabata
G. Matsuma
S. Neishi
Chiura Obata
Mine Okubo
Toyo Suyemoto
Tom Takaki
Kango Takamura
Yoshiko Uchida

Tule Lake, CA

Hiroshi Kashiwagi

Notes

ONE. WAR AND GARDENS

Sources for this chapter in addition to those already identified here include Abrioux, *Ian Hamilton Finlay*; Craig and Egan, *Extreme Situations*; Hedges, *War Is a Force That Gives Us Meaning*; Hill and Wileman, *Landscapes of War*; J. B. Jackson, "Landscape as Seen by the Military"; Keegan, *Face of Battle*; Keegan, *History of Warfare*; Keegan and Darracott, *Nature of War*; Koch, *Rise of Modern Warfare*; Marx, *Machine in the Garden*; McClung, *Architecture of Paradise*; Moore, Mitchell, and Turnbull, *Poetics of Gardens*; Mukerji, *Territorial Ambitions and the Gardens of Versailles*; Pollan, *Second Nature*; Riley, "From Sacred Grove to Disney World"; Schama, *Landscape and Memory*; Shepard, *Man in the Landscape*; Sontag, *Regarding the Pain of Others*; and Thacker, *History of Gardens*.

1. Sassoon, *Siegfried's Journey*, 119.
2. Kincaid, "Sowers and Reapers," 41.
3. Frye, *Stubborn Structure*, 101.
4. Eisen, *Children and Play in the Holocaust*, 8.
5. Lewis, *Green Nature Human Nature*, 54.
6. McHarg, *Quest for Life*, 47, 59.
7. Eisen, *Children and Play in the Holocaust*, 5.
8. Jekyll, *Home and Garden*, 32.
9. Duff, "High Country Gardens," 331.
10. Tamaviaartumik — Finn Larsen's Photo Exhibition of the Gardens of Greenland, www.garden.gl/english/projekt.htm, accessed 1 Sept. 2005.
11. Inturrisi, "Roman Spring of Ancient Stones."
12. Editorial, *New York Times*, 11 Nov. 1994.
13. The term *ruderal* is derived from *rudus*, *ruderis* (Latin: debris, mortar); see Mills, *Ruderal Plants in Manhattan*. On Chatto's garden, see Penelope Hill, "Planting Revolution in the Modern Garden."

14. This and the preceding quotations in Kaplan and Kaplan, *Experience of Nature*, 165–76, 171, 177–200.

15. Hunt, *Greater Perfections*, 13. See also Riley, "From Sacred Grove to Disney World."

16. Sackville-West, *Garden*, 14–15.

17. S. Hynes, "In the Whirl and Muddle of War," 22. J. H. Fabre quoted in Schlebecker, *Whereby We Thrive*.

18. Fussell, *Doing Battle*, 183. Machiavelli, *Prince*, 59.

19. Horwitz, *Confederates in the Attic*, 170, 385.

20. P. Nash, *Outline*, 194.

21. For Khe Sanh, see Hasford, *Short-Timers*, 146. For Vietnam statistics, see Westing and Pfeiffer, "Cratering of Indochina," 25, 28.

22. S. Hynes, "In the Whirl and Muddle of War."

23. Hillman, *Terrible Love of War*, 65.

24. Eisen, *Children and Play in the Holocaust*, 8.

TWO. TRENCH GARDENS

Sources for this chapter in addition to those already identified here include Audoin-Rouzeau and Becker, *14–18*; Barnett, *The Great War*; Beatty, "Along the Western Front"; Brown, *Imperial War Museum Book of the First World War*; Chapman, *Haven in Hell*; Chasseaud, *Topography of Armageddon*; Donavan, *Hazy Red Hell*; Ferro, *The Great War*; Graham, *Challenge of the Dead*; Graves, *Good-Bye to All That*; S. Hynes, *Soldier's Tale*; Keegan, "There's Rosemary for Remembrance"; Kipling, *France at War*; Leed, *No Man's Land*; Messenger, *Trench Fighting 1914–1918*; Nobbs, *On the Right of the British Line*; Sassoon, *Siegfried Sassoon Diaries*; Sassoon, *Siegfried's Journey*; Sassoon, *War Poems of Siegfried Sassoon*; Sherriff, *Journey's End*; A. J. P. Taylor, *Illustrated History of the First World War*; and Warnke, *Political Landscape*.

1. Blunden, *Undertones of War*, 27.

2. Sassoon quoted in Fussell, *The Great War and Modern Memory*, 41.

3. Cited in O'Shea, *Back to the Front*, 16.

4. Strauss in Housman, *War Letters of Fallen Englishmen*, 269.

5. Macquarrie, *How to Live at the Front*, 127.

6. Willamson, *In Spite of All Rejoicing*, 68, 219. Weintraub, *Silent Night*, 150.

7. J. Ellis, *Eye-Deep in Hell*, 30. The title of Ellis's book comes from a poem by Ezra Pound.

8. Macquarrie, *How to Live at the Front*, 142. MacDonald MS, 45.

9. O'Flaherty, *Return of the Brave*, 124. Sillitoe in Chasseaud, *Topography of Armageddon*, 4.

10. J. Ellis, *Eye-Deep in Hell*, 24.

11. Soldier quoted in Dyer, *Missing of the Somme*, 98. Gosse, *Memoirs of a Camp Follower*, 103. Blunden, *Undertones of War*, 173. Blunden was now an intelligence officer. Barbusse quoted in Dyer, *Missing of the Somme*, 120.

12. Blunden, *Undertones of War*, 42.

13. O'Shea, *Back to the Front*, 155, 158, 164.

14. Blunden quoted in Brown, *Tommy Goes to War*, 11. Blunden, *Undertones of War*, 123.

15. Gibbs, *Now It Can Be Told*. Fussell, *The Great War and Modern Memory*, 136.

16. Barbusse quoted in Dyer, *Missing of the Somme*, 115.

17. Oxenham, *High Altars*, 30. Carver in Housman, *War Letters of Fallen Englishmen*, 68.

18. Owen, *Wilfred Owen*, 156. Groom, *Storm in Flanders*, vii.

19. Masefield quoted in Dyer, *Missing of the Somme*, 120. Owen, *Wilfred Owen*, 155.

20. Owen, *Wilfred Owen*, 156. Blunden quoted in Fussell, *The Great War and Modern Memory*, 259.

21. T. MacDonald manuscript, 71, IWM. Oehme in Witkop, *German Students' War Letters*, 288. Oxenham, *High Altars*, 59. Gibbs, *Now It Can Be Told*, 400.

22. Willamson, *In Spite of All Rejoicing*, 124. *Totenlandschaft* in Dyer, *Missing of the Somme*, 117. Masefield quoted in Dyer, *Missing of the Somme*, 126. J. Ellis, *Eye-Deep in Hell*, 75.

23. Stallworthy, *Oxford Book of War Poetry*, 223.

24. Gosse, *Memoirs of a Camp Follower*, 108. Groom, *Storm in Flanders*, vi.

25. Graves quoted in Fussell, *The Great War and Modern Memory*, 170. Oehme in Witkop, *German Students' War Letters*, 288. Montfort letters. Gosse, *Memoirs of a Camp Follower*, xiv.

26. Saunders, *Trench Art*, 115. Nottingham in Housman, *War Letters of Fallen Englishmen*, 202.

27. Groom, *Storm in Flanders*, 169.

28. Ibid., 72–72. See also Gosse, *Memoirs of a Camp Follower*, 26. Fussell, *The Great War and Modern Memory*, 51. Philps, *Prisoner Doctor*.

29. Owen, *Wilfred Owen*, 179.

30. Blunden, *Undertones of War*, 53, 119.

31. Mosse, *Fallen Soldiers*, 108.

32. Willamson, *In Spite of All Rejoicing*, 202. Blunden, *Undertones of War*, 33.

33. P. Nash, *Outline*, 196. S. Hynes, *War Imagined*, 197. Blunden, *Undertones of War*, 250.

34. P. Nash, *Outline*, 196.

35. Spencer, *War Scenes I Shall Never Forget*, 20.

36. Dietz in Witkop, *German Students' War Letters*, 62–63.

37. *Illustrated London News*, 8 May 1915, 25 Sept. 1915.

38. Von Rohden in Witkop, *German Students' War Letters*, 156. Donaldson in Housman, *War Letters of Fallen Englishmen*, 111. Holscher in Witkop, *German Students' War Letters*, 301.

39. Gibbs, *Now It Can Be Told*, 85.

40. On potatoes, see Ashworth, *Trench Warfare*, 131. P. Nash, *Outline*, 188.

41. "Adrian" barracks were temporary structures. Taft, *Service with Fighting Men*, 349–52.

42. Gosse, *Memoirs of a Camp Follower*, 175.

43. Witkop, *German Students' War Letters*, 269.

44. Oxenham, *High Altars*, 52.

45. Saunders, *Trench Art*, 16.

46. Fink and Stiller in Witkop, *German Students' War Letters*, 94 and 126. Blunden, *Undertones of War*, 148.

47. Blunden, *Undertones of War*, 82.

48. Major R. S. Cockburn, unpublished MS, 44, IWM.

49. P. Nash, *Outline*, 187. De Lapradelle and Coudert, *War Letters from France*, 11–12.

50. Housman, *War Letters of Fallen Englishmen*, 263.

51. The word *Blighty* is a corruption of the Hindustani *bilaik*, foreign country, especially England. Brophy and Partridge, *Songs and Slang of the British Soldier*, 100.

52. Gibbs, *Now It Can Be Told*, 153. Willamson, *In Spite of All Rejoicing*, 80.

53. Clayton, *Tales of Talbot House*, 72.

54. Steinbrecher in Witkop, *German Students' War Letters*, 325. Willamson, *In Spite of All Rejoicing*, 172. Moldenhauer in Witkop, *German Students' War Letters*, 16.

55. Cockburn, 107, IWM. O'Flaherty, *Return of the Brute*, 82.

56. Blunden, *Undertones of War*, 88, 72, 165.

57. Gosse, *Memoirs of a Camp Follower*, 68.

58. In Witkop, *German Students' War Letters*, 362.

59. Spatzl and Bassler in Witkop, *German Students' War Letters*, 304 and 234.

60. Dyer, *Missing of the Somme*, 12.

61. Ibid., 13.

62. Kenyon quoted in Longworth, *Unending Vigil*, 34.

63. Dyer, *Missing of the Somme*, 130.

THREE. GHETTO GARDENS

Sources for this chapter in addition to those already identified here include Bard, *Forgotten Victims*; Bartoszewski, *Warsaw Ghetto*; Bauer, *They Chose Life*; Berenbaum, *World Must Know*; Browning, *Path to Genocide*; Corni, *Hitler's Ghettos*; Crowley, *Warsaw*; Czerniakow, *Warsaw Diary of Adam Czerniakow*; Dawidowicz, *War against the Jews*; Dobroszycki, *Chronicle of the Lodz Ghetto*; Elias, *Triumph of Hope*; Georg, *In the Warsaw Ghetto*; Gilbert, *Holocaust Journey*; Grossman, *With a Camera in the Ghetto*; Gutman, *Jews of Warsaw*; Huberband, *Kiddush Hashem*; Katz, *Poland's Ghettos at War*; Kermish, *To Live with Honor and Die with Honor!*; Korczak, *Ghetto Diary*; Langer, *Art from the Ashes*; Lanzmann, *Shoah*; Lewin, *Cup of Tears*; Mishell, *Kaddish for Kovno*; Pernitz, *Memories of a Wartime Teenager*; Spiegel, *Ghetto Kingdom*; Tushnet, *Uses of Adversity*; Unger, *Last Ghetto*; U.S. Holocaust Memorial Museum, *Hidden History of the Kovno Ghetto*; U.S. Holocaust Memorial Museum, *Historical Atlas of the Holocaust*; Volavkova, *I Never Saw Another Butterfly*; Zelkowicz, *In Those Terrible Days*; and Zuckerman, *A Surplus of Memory*.

1. Glas-Wiener, "The Children's Garden," *Children of the Ghetto*, 160–70. The story is told by Sheva Glas-Wiener.

2. Ringelblum, *Notes from the Warsaw Ghetto*, xvi.

3. This collection details the evolution of a garden bureaucracy and communicates the more intimate aspects of garden creation; see entry in bibliography.

4. Ernest in Grynberg, *Words to Outlive Us*, 334. Diarist quoted in Adelson and Lapides, *Lodz Ghetto*, 439.

5. Engelking, *Holocaust and Memory*, 22.

6. Jackson quoted in Cole, *Holocaust City*, 16, 21.

7. Grynberg, *Words to Outlive Us*, 3.

8. Lodz was in an area where the ultimate goal was the removal of the Polish population and repopulating the area with Germans resettled from the Balkan states.

9. Hochman, *Daring to Live*, 39.

10. M. Kaplan, *Between Dignity and Despair*, 226. Szereszewska, *Memoirs from Occupied Poland*, 46. Ringelblum, *Notes from the Warsaw Ghetto*, 233. Stok in Grynberg, *Words to Outlive Us*, 37. Ringelblum, *Notes from the Warsaw Ghetto*, 130.

11. Zelichower in Grynberg, *Words to Outlive Us*, 243.

12. Karski, *Story of a Secret State*, 330.

13. Ernest in Grynberg, *Words to Outlive Us*, 306.

14. "Psychosis of decline" in Engelking, *Holocaust and Memory*, 37. Sierakowiak, *Diary of Dawid Sierakowiak*, 59, 14.

15. Adelson and Lapides, *Lodz Ghetto*, 35 (Liebman), 94 (Hurwitz), and 212 and 272 (Rosenfeld).

16. G. W. Klein, *All But My Life*, 74.

17. This and the preceding quotations in Zyskind, *Stolen Years*, 156–59, 164.

18. Sierakowiak, *Diary of Dawid Sierakowiak*, 94. Biderman, *World of My Past*, 50.

19. David, *Square of Sky*, 101. Ringelblum, *Notes from the Warsaw Ghetto*, 259. Zelkowiocz in Adelson and Lapides, *Lodz Ghetto*, 278.

20. Biderman, *World of My Past*, 166.

21. Engelking, *Holocaust and Memory*, 96.

22. This and the preceding quotation in M. Berg, *Warsaw Ghetto*, 59, 144.

23. Sierakowiak, *Diary of Dawid Sierakowiak*, 152, 154.

24. Biderman, *World of My Past*, 140.

25. Shayevitsh in Adelson and Lapidus, *Lodz Ghetto*, 250–62. The last line quoted here links the poem to Chaim Nachman Bialik, "City of Slaughter," about the Kishinev pogrom of 1903, and its line "The sun shines, the acacia blossoms and the slaughterer slaughters."

26. Ringelblum, *Notes from the Warsaw Ghetto*, xix.

27. Roland, *Courage under Siege*, 50. Ringelblum, *Notes from the Warsaw Ghetto,* 146.

28. C. A. Kaplan, *Scroll of Agony*, 243, 256. Siedman, *Warsaw Ghetto Diaries*.

29. Eisen, *Children and Play in the Holocaust*, 39.

30. "Fantasy gardens" in Jan Jagielski, interview by the author, 16 March 2004. Engelking, *Holocaust and Memory*, 42. Engelking calls it a "minor" difference between the ghetto and the rest of Warsaw that in the ghetto there were no trees, grass, or greenery, and that all parks and open spaces were outside the walls. I disagree, and the testimonies seem to, as well.

31. Hochman, *Daring to Live*, 77 (in Hebrew, *gan* means both garden and park; in this context, when Hochman refers to the fact that there was "not even a single garden," I believe he means there were no parks). C. A. Kaplan, *Scroll of Agony*, 292–93.

32. Ringelblum, *Notes from the Warsaw Ghetto*, 165. The Judenrat was helpful, but there were significant political divisions and rivalries in the ghetto, as Ringelblum noted in his diary: "When the Toporol organization held a public meeting for the purposes of agitation, the first question posed by the audience was 'Do you have any connection with the Council administrations [the Jewish council]?'" That is, the council was seen by many as playing favorites.

33. Ibid., 276.

34. Birenbaum, *Hope Is the Last to Die*, 11. Wilner in Grynberg, *Words to Outlive Us*, 472. Ringelblum, *Notes from the Warsaw Ghetto*, 187.

35. Topas, *Iron Furnace*, 50.

36. This and preceding quotations in M. Berg, *Warsaw Ghetto*, 61, 137, 62, 61.

37. David, *Square of Sky*, 132. M. Berg, *Warsaw Ghetto*, 147.

38. M. Berg, *Warsaw Ghetto*, 227.

39. Szereszewska, *Memoirs from Occupied Poland*, 51.

40. Hurwitz in Adelson and Lapides, *Lodz Ghetto*, 38.

41. Ibid., 38.

42. Adelson and Lapides, *Lodz Ghetto*, 136. Sierakowiak, *Diary of Dawid Sierakowiak*, 86.

43. Litsmanstadt Ghetto, YIVO.

44. Rosenfeld in Adelson and Lapides, *Lodz Ghetto*, 311–15.

45. Singer in ibid., 306. Sierakowiak, *Diary of Dawid Sierakowiak*, 210.

46. Kent, *Ghetto Years*.

47. Singer, "Something about Horticulture in the Ghetto," Ghetto Fighter's House Archive.

48. Dobroszycki, *Chronicle of the Lodz Ghetto*, 243.

49. Ibid., 243. Eisen, *Children and Play in the Holocaust*, 42.

50. Dobroszycki, *Chronicle of the Lodz Ghetto*, 344.

51. This and the preceding quotations are Rosenfeld quoted in ibid., 407, 480, 483.

52. Kent, interview with the author, 22 April 2004.

53. Dobroszycki, *Chronicle of the Lodz Ghetto*, 491.

54. Singer in ibid., 492.

55. Rosenfeld quoted in ibid., 515.

56. Esther Mishkin, interview with the author, 8 Dec. 2003.

57. Holzman testimony, Shoah Foundation Interview Code 15947.

58. Mishell, *Kaddish for Kovno*, 87, 392 (Tory, *Surviving the Holocaust*, 229, places these same events in the summer of 1942).

59. Tory, *Surviving the Holocaust*, 116. Tory's diary is a remarkably complete record of the Kovno ghetto.

60. This and the preceding quotation in Tory, *Surviving the Holocaust*, 86–87, 99, 115.

61. Gerber in Zapruder, *Salvaged Pages*, 339.

62. Doctorow, *City of God*, 67.

63. Rudashevski, *Diary of the Vilna Ghetto*, 16.

64. Jewish slogan in Rudavsky, *To Live with Hope*, 60. C. A. Kaplan, *Scroll of Agony*, 244. Adler, *In the Warsaw Ghetto*, 255.

65. Zelkowicz, "Blessings of the Earth," Zonabend Collection, YIVO 896.

66. Pile as cited in Cole, *Holocaust City*, 22. "Head life" in Zapruder, *Salvaged Pages*, 192. Trunk, *Jewish Responses to Nazi Persecution*, 14.

67. Milejkowski in Adelson and Lapides, *Lodz Ghetto*, 184. Rosenfeld quoted in Engelking, *Holocaust and Memory*, 186.

68. Silkes quoted in Eisen, *Children and Play in the Holocaust*, 83. Stok in Grynberg, *Words to Outlive Us*, 21.

69. Adler, *In the Warsaw Ghetto*, 261.

70. Nissenbaum in Rudavsky, *To Live with Hope*, 5.

71. Adelson and Lapides, *Lodz Ghetto*, xii–xiv, 513.

72. Engelking, *Holocaust and Memory*, 133.

73. Sznapman in Grynberg, *Words to Outlive Us*, 191.

74. Shayevitsh in Adelson and Lapides, *Lodz Ghetto*, 216–30.

75. Kruk, *Last Days of the Jerusalem of Lithuania*, 522.

FOUR. BARBED-WIRE GARDENS

Sources for this chapter in addition to those already identified here include Archer and Federowich, "The Women of Stanley"; E. B. Berg, *Behind Barbed Wires*; Carlson, *We Were Each Other's Prisoners*; Cogan, *Captured*; Cohen and Taylor, *Psychological Survival*; R. Jackson, *Prisoners*; Roland, *Long Night's Journey into Day*; Vourkoutiotis, *Prisoner of War and the German High Command*.

The chapter epigraph is from I. Cohen, *Ruhleben Prison Camp*, 128.

1. Gilliland, *My German Prisons*, xi.

2. Dennett, *Prisoners of the Great War*, 13.

3. Rolf, *Prisoners of the Reich*, 29. Bailey, *Prisoners of War*, 13. Bischof and Ambrose, *Eisenhower and the POWs*, 18–20. The sources vary in statistics, but the loss of life was staggering no matter what numbers are used.

4. Doyle, *Voices from Captivity*, 170.

5. This and the preceding quotations in McCarthy, *Prisoner of War in Germany*, 53.

6. Myers, *Thrice Caught*, 101.

7. This and the preceding quotation in Havers, *Reassessing the Japanese Prisoner of War Experience*, 11, 31.

8. Keith, *Three Came Home*, 47.

9. Dancocks, *In Enemy Hands*, xiv.

10. Myers, *Thrice Caught*, 111.

11. Foy, *For You the War Is Over*, 75. Canadian quoted in Vance, *Objects of Concern*, 205.

12. Gilliland, *My German Prisons*, 254.

13. Warnod, *Prisoner of War*, 29–33. Moynihan, *Black Bread and Barbed Wire*, 26.

14. Ketchum, *Ruhleben*, 153. Ruhleben camp newspaper gardening column, ca. 1916. Ketchum, *Ruhleben*, 17.

15. Taft, *Service with Fighting Men*, 217.

16. Vischer, *Barbed Wire Disease*, 49–52. Durand, *Stalag Luft III*, 213. Bailey, *Prisoners of War*, 22.

17. Taft, *Service with Fighting Men*, 220, 222.

18. Vischer, *Barbed Wire Disease*, 9.

19. Warnod, *Prisoner of War*, 29–33. *Lager Echo* quoted in Vischer, *Barbed Wire Disease*, 31. Taft, *Service with Fighting Men*, 221.

20. Westheimer, *Sitting It Out*, 209. Bryant, *Sun Was Darkened*, 168.

21. Vischer, *Barbed Wire Disease*, 49. Taft, *Service with Fighting Men*, 221. Vischer, *Barbed Wire Disease*, 57.

22. Myers, *Thrice Caught*, 107. Ketchum, *Ruhleben*, 32. Moynihan, *Black Bread and Barbed Wire*, xii. Myers, *Thrice Caught*, 37–38.

23. Hoffman, *In the Prison Camps of Germany*, 3. Guareschi, *My Secret Diary*, 99, 75. I. Cohen, *Ruhleben Prison Camp*, 189–90.

24. Weiss quoted in Bird, *American POWs of World War II*, xvii.

25. Wood, *Detour*, 47–49.

26. Moynihan, *Black Bread and Barbed Wire*, 83. Hoffman, *In the Prison Camps of Germany*, 4. Wright, Wright Papers, IWM, 4 Aug. 1917. I. Cohen, *Ruhleben Prison Camp*, ix, 110.

27. Rolf, *Prisoners of the Reich*, 26.

28. Gilliland, *My German Prisons*, 253. McCarthy, *Prisoner of War in Germany*, 27.

29. Myers, *Thrice Caught*, 38.

30. I. Cohen, *Ruhleben Prison Camp*, 190.

31. Warnod, *Prisoner of War*, 68+. Bailey, *Prisoners of War*, 22.

32. Warnod, *Prisoner of War*, 117.

33. Ketchum, *Ruhleben*, 3, 21, 65.

34. I. Cohen, *Ruhleben Prison Camp*, 60, 110. Ketchum, *Ruhleben*, 229.

35. Ketchum, *Ruhleben*, 195. I. Cohen, *Ruhleben Prison Camp*, 150.

36. "Territorial" in Ketchum, *Ruhleben*, 184. Medal craze and ark in I. Cohen, *Ruhleben Prison Camp*, 129, 201. Bezalal in Exodus 35:30.

37. Ketchum, *Ruhleben*, 249.

38. Morgan, *P.O.W.*, xv, 173.

39. Durand, *Stalag Luft III*, 253.

40. Bryant, *Sun Was Darkened*, 147. Mydans, *More than Meets the Eye*, 73.

41. Hoffman, *In the Prison Camps of Germany*, 34–37, 39, 131.

42. Taft, *Service with Fighting Men*, 293. McCarthy, *Prisoner of War in Germany*, 65.

43. Wright Papers, IWM, 23 May 1915, 20 June 1915, 9 June 1916.

44. Stibbe, *Reminiscences of a Civilian Prisoner*, 20; see also Wright Papers, IWM, 24 Aug. 1917.

45. Wright Papers, IWM, 4 Aug. 1917.

46. Foy, *For You the War Is Over*, 93. Myers, *Thrice Caught*, 110.

47. Rolfe Papers, IMF.

48. Westheimer, *Sitting It Out*, 166, 236.

49. Durand, *Stalag Luft III*, 165–66.

50. Filliter quoted in Dancocks, *In Enemy Hands*, 87.

51. Durand, *Stalag Luft III*, 29.

52. James, *Prisoner's Progress*, 56.

53. Westheimer, *Sitting It Out*, 87–96.

54. Havers, *Reassessing the Japanese Prisoner of War Experience*, 106.

55. Philps, *Prisoner Doctor*, 74–75, 110–13.

56. This and the preceding quotations in Gittins, *Stanley*, 102, 104, 112–13.

57. Elizabeth Nance, interview with the author, January 2005.

58. This and the preceding quotations in Sewell, *Strange Harmony*, 112, 114.

59. G. Nash, *That We Might Live*, 37. Johansen, *So Far from Home*, 34.

60. Hartendorp, *Santo Tomas Story*, 14. Vaughan, *Ordeal of Elizabeth Vaughan*, 42.

61. Hartendorp, *Santo Tomas Story*, 25. An internee at Santo Tomas, Hartendorp's accounts of Bacolod are secondhand.

62. Johansen, *So Far from Home*, 44.

63. Vaughan, *Ordeal of Elizabeth Vaughan*, 56, 272.

64. Bryant, *Sun Was Darkened*, 157–58.

65. Vaughan, *Ordeal of Elizabeth Vaughan*, 56. Vaughan, *Community under Stress*, 21. Vaughan, *Ordeal of Elizabeth Vaughan*, 201.

66. Sams, *Forbidden Family*, 212.

67. G. Nash, *That We Might Live*, 202, 161.

68. Keith, *Three Came Home*, 229, 262.

69. Ibid., 17. Bryant, *Sun Was Darkened*, 36.

70. Guareschi, *My Secret Diary*, 84. Westheimer, *Sitting It Out*, 50.

71. Gittins, *Stanley*, 149. Sewell, *Strange Harmony*, 99. Sams, *Forbidden Family*, 191.

72. Gilliland, *My German Prisons*, 29.

73. Vance, *Objects of Concern*, 3.

74. Havers, *Reassessing the Japanese Prisoner of War Experience*, 103.

75. Ketchum, *Ruhleben*, 211.

76. Vaughan, *Ordeal of Elizabeth Vaughan*, 284, 292.

77. Lewis in Nova and Lourie, *Interrupted Lives*, 103. Bryant, *Sun Was Darkened*, 180.

78. Keith, *Three Came Home*, 177.

79. Vischer, *Barbed Wire Disease*, 84.

80. Guareschi, *My Secret Diary*, 119. Vischer, *Barbed Wire Disease*, 9.

81. Report of the Committee of the Ruhleben Horticultural Society for 1917–18, Michael Pease file, IWM.

82. Warnod, *Prisoner of War*, 168. Gilliland, *My German Prisons*, 257.

83. Capt. A. D. M. Hilton papers, IWM.

FIVE. STONE GARDENS

Sources for this chapter in addition to those already identified here include Adams and Miyatake, *Two Views of Manzanar*; Burton and Farrell, *This Is Minidoka*; Burton, Bergstresser, and Tamura, *Minidoka Internment National Monument*; Daniels, *Concentration Camps USA*; Davis, *Behind Barbed Wire*; Embrey, Hansen, and Mitson, *Manzanar Martyr*; Ewan, *Land Between*; Higa, *View from Within*; Mackey, *Heart Mountain*; Myer, *Uprooted Americans*; Nakano, *Within the Barbed Wire Fence*; Obata, *Chiura Obata's Topaz Moon*; Slawson, *Secret Teachings in the Art of Japanese Gardens*; P. Smith, *Democracy on Trial*; Takeuchi, *Minidoka Interlude*; S. C. Taylor, *Jewel of the Desert*; Thomas, *Salvage*; Uchida, *Journey to Topaz*; and camp newspapers (*Gila News-Courier, Topaz Times*, and *Manzanar Free Press*).

1. Hirahara, *Greenmakers*, 25.

2. Burton et al., *Confinement and Ethnicity*, 33, 34.

3. Internment camps were also known as "concentration camps," a term that is technically correct. However, the most widely recognized term after the war has become "internment camps," to distinguish them from Nazi extermination camps. On terminology, see Burton, *Three Farewells to Manzanar*, 3; Ng, *Japanese American Internment during World War II*, xiii; Harth, *Last Witnesses*, 15; Burton et al., *Confinement and Ethnicity*, 18.

4. Quoted in Thomas, *Salvage*, 192.

5. Okubo, *Citizen 13660*, 97, 98–99.

6. This and the preceding quotations in Kikuchi, *Kikuchi Diary*, 55, 132, 203–4, 156.

7. Houston, *Farewell to Manzanar*, 29. Artist quoted in Thomas, *Salvage*, 523. Gesensway and Roseman, *Beyond Words*, 45.

8. Suyemoto quoted in Harth, *Last Witnesses*, 30. Uchida, *Desert Exile*, 105. Sasano quoted in Gesensway and Roseman, *Beyond Words*, 148.

9. Houston, *Farewell to Manzanar*, 40.

10. Horiuchi, *Dislocations*, 269. Thomas, *Salvage*, 402.

11. Williams, *Camp Dharma*, 195.

12. Thomas, *Salvage*, 250.

13. Ibid., 253. Takamura quoted in Gesensway and Roseman, *Beyond Words*, 123–24.

14. Tamura, "Interview with Henry Nishi."

15. Hosokawa, *Gardens*. See also Kleinkopf, "Relocation Center Diary," 2 Nov. 1942.

16. "Residents Urged to Beautify City," *Gila News-Courier*, 23 Sept. 1942.

17. Kadowaki quoted in Gesensway and Roseman, *Beyond Words*, 101. Tamura, "Interview with Arthur Ogami."

18. Ishigo, *Lone Heart Mountain*, 47.

19. Uchida, *Desert Exile*, 125.

20. "Beautification," *Topaz Times*, 30 Sept. 1943.

21. Okubo, *Citizen 13660*, 149. Uchida, *Desert Exile*, 138.

22. Kikuchi quoted in Gesensway and Roseman, *Beyond Words*, 48. Ishisaka quoted in Sherman and Katagiri, *Touching the Stones*, 60.

23. Sogioka quoted in Gesensway and Roseman, *Beyond Words*, 148.

24. Burton et al., *Confinement and Ethnicity*, 23.

25. Girdner and Loftis, *Great Betrayal*, 219.

26. This and the preceding quotations in Hosokawa, *Gardens*.

27. Kleinkopf, "Relocation Center Diary," 2 Aug. 1943. Quoted in *Minidoka Irrigator*, 1943, JAHM.

28. Kleinkopf, "Relocation Center Diary," 16 and 23 June, 1943.

29. Ibid., 14 March 1944.

30. *Minidoka Irrigator*, 1943. "Cactus Cutters Cautioned," *Gila News-Courier*, 21 Oct. 1942.

31. "Hunt Gets Face-Lifting Treatment; Dustbowl Becomes Desert Oasis" (editorial), *Minidoka Irrigator*, 1 May 1943.

32. Kleinkopf, "Relocation Center Diary," 21 June 1942.

33. Armor and Wright, *Manzanar*, xvii, quoting from Ansel Adams, *Born Free and Equal*. Adams's houseman Harry Oye was interned, which outraged Adams.

34. National Park Service, *Cultural Landscape Report for Manzanar National Historic Site*, 2. Hereafter cited as NPS, *CLR Manzanar*.

35. Houston, *Farewell to Manzanar*, 95.

36. Tamura, "Gardens below the Watchtower" (2004), 17. NPS, *CLR Manzanar*, 13.

37. Tamura, "Interview with Henry Nishi."

38. Burton, *Three Farewells to Manzanar*, 87–89.

39. Tamura, "Interview with Arthur Ogami."

40. Tamura, *Gardens below the Watchtower* (2002), 42.

41. Tamura, "Gardens below the Watchtower" (2004), 10.

42. Tamura, "Interview with Henry Nishi." Houston, *Farewell to Manzanar*, 99.

43. Interview with Kenko Yamashita, 10 Aug. 1978.

44. Kleinkopf, "Relocation Center Diary," 16 Oct. 1942.

45. Tamura, *Gardens below the Watchtower* (2002), 30. *Newsweek* cited in Okihiro, *Whispered Silences*, 194.

46. Kleinkopf, "Relocation Center Diary," 26 Sept. 1942.

47. *Minidoka Irrigator*, 10 Sept. 1942. *Topaz Times*, 17 Sept. 1942.

48. Hosokawa, *Gardens*.

49. Inouye quoted in Okihiro, *Whispered Silences*, 205.

50. Tamura, "Interview with Arthur Ogami."

51. Kleinkopf, "Relocation Center Diary," 2 June 1943.

52. Uchida, *Desert Exile*, 93.

53. "Colony Beautification," *Gila News-Courier*, 26 Sept. 1942. "Creative Beauty," *Topaz Times*, 24 April 1943.

54. Nakamura quoted in Gesensway and Roseman, *Beyond Words*, 26.

55. Inada, *Drawing the Line*, 112.

56. Hirahara, *Greenmakers*, 53–57.

57. Ross and Reiko, *Second Kinenhi*, 37.

58. Brown, *Japanese-Style Gardens of the Pacific West Coast*, 15. Brown, *Putting Down Roots*, 37–39.

59. Tochihara, lecture, University of Oregon, 4 April 2004.

60. Ross and Reiko, *Second Kinenhi*, 13.

61. Uchida, *Desert Exile*, 148.

62. Tamura, "Interview with Arthur Ogami."

63. Houston, *Farewell to Manzanar*, 98.

64. Suyemoto quoted in Harth, *Last Witnesses*, 34. Kikuchi quoted in Hansen, *Japanese American World War II Evacuation*, 205.

65. Toyama, *Day of Independence*.

66. Houston, "Rock Garden," 277–82. Although the camp is not named in the story, the history of the place identifies it as Manzanar.

SIX. POSTWAR

1. Horwitz, *Confederates in the Attic*, 176.

2. Beatty, "Along the Western Front," 109.

3. Blunden, *Undertones of War*, 265.

4. Hewett in Housman, *War Letters of Fallen Englishmen*, 138.

5. Kipling, *France at War*, 30.

6. Graham, *Challenge of the Dead*, 18.

7. O'Shea, *Back to the Front*, 5, 7, 94.

8. Gittins, *Stanley*, 162

9. Kleinkopf, "Relocation Center Diary," 21 May 1945, 1 Oct. 1945, 24 Nov. 1945.

10. Burton, *Three Farewells to Manzanar*.

11. Tamura, *Gardens below the Watchtower* (2002), 65–68.

SEVEN. DIGGING DEEPER

Sources for this chapter in addition to those already identified here include Appleton, *Experience of Landscape*; Balmori and Morton, *Transitory Gardens, Uprooted Lives*; Brdanovic, "Community Gardens in Bosnia"; Jarman, *Derek Jarman's Garden*; Jones and Jones, *Paju Ecopolis*; Kaplan and Kaplan, *Experience of Nature*; Kardiner and Spiegel, *War Stress and Neurotic Illness*; Monin and Gallimore, *Devil's Garden*; Raver, "From Rubble, Ingenuity Sprouts"; Segal, *Poetry and Myth in Ancient Pastoral*; Ulrich, "View through a Window May Influence Recovery from Surgery"; and Warner, *To Dwell Is to Garden*.

1. Mitchell, *Essential Earthman*, 3.

2. Wilson, *Biophilia*, 1. See also Lewis, *Green Nature/Human Nature*, 89.

3. Botton, *Art of Travel*, 151.

4. Cogan, interview with the author, 2004.

5. Sznapman in Grynberg, *Words to Outlive Us*, 318.

6. Campbell in Wood, *Detour*, 89.

7. Keith, *Three Came Home*, 57.

8. Guareschi, *My Secret Diary*, 129.

9. Vaughan, *Ordeal of Elizabeth Vaughan*, 285, 281.

10. Hunt, *Greater Perfections*, 76.

11. Rolfe notebook, IWM.

12. Lewis, *Green Nature/Human Nature*, 7.

13. Pérez quoted in Meyers, "Farmer Unearthed."

14. Untitled brochure, Open Garden Day (a project of the Center for Urban Education about Sustainable Agriculture [CUESA]).

15. Birenbaum, *Hope Is the Last to Die*, 88.

16. Korczak, *Ghetto Diary*, 113.

17. Bloch, *The Principle of Hope*, 75, 112.

18. Marcel, *Existential Background of Human Dignity*, 142. Solnit, *Hope in the Dark*, 5. Bloch cited in Kast, *Joy, Inspiration, and Hope*, 137–38.

19. Kushner quoted in Monde, "Soul on Fire," 39.

20. Okihiro, *Whispered Silences*, 123.

21. Raver, "Softening Gritty Urban Gray with a Little Green." "For Young and Old, a Pocket Paradise." Hiss, "Breaking Ground," 101.

22. Liebskind quoted in Raver, "This Stop."

23. Raver, "Honoring Loss with the Power of Green."

24. Nowotny, "Despair and the Object of Hope," 46. Kast, *Joy, Inspiration, and Hope*, 148.

25. Birenbaum, *Hope Is the Last to Die*, 88.

26. Clendinnen, *Reading the Holocaust*, 51, 149, 144.

27. Herbst, "For a Lost Child, Rooms of Flowers."

28. Kent, "Ghetto Years."

29. This and the preceding quotes in Zelkowicz, "Blessings of the Earth," translated by Roberta Newman, Zonabend Collection, YIVO 896.

30. Gittins, *Stanley*, 103–4. Sewell, *Strange Harmony*, 115.

31. Rachel Kaplan and Stephen Kaplan, "Restorative Experience: The Healing Power of Nature," in Francis and Hester, *Meaning of Gardens*, 238–43.

32. Mandela, *Long Walk to Freedom*, 926. Thornicroft, *Ground Force*.

33. Williams quoted in Flinn, *Prison Garden Book*, 39. Lewis quoted in Martin, "Gardens Flourish Behind Razor Wire."

34. Hart, *Gardens of Alcatraz*, vii.

35. Winter in Housman, *War Letters of Fallen Englishmen*, xviii.

36. Gibbs, *Now It Can Be Told,* 242.

37. Scarry, *On Beauty and Being Just*, 24–25. Gibbs, *Now It Can Be Told*, 115. Winter and Wilson quoted in Housman, *War Letters of Fallen Englishmen*, ix, 297.

38. Kundera, "Such Was Their Wager," 95. Oskar Singer, "Something about Horticulture in the Ghetto," Ghetto Fighter's House Archive.

39. "Greenwood Trees at Ruhleben," in *British Prisoner of War,* 90, Pope-Hennesey Papers, IWM.

40. Nash, *Outline*, 188.

41. Klein, interview with the author, 12 July 2004. Klein, *All But My Life*, 167, 171. Klein interview, 12 July 2004. Klein, *All But My Life*, 170–71.

42. Klein, *All But My Life*, 221. Klein interview, 12 July 2004.

43. Frederick Stevens quoted in Johansen, *So Far from Home*, 121.

44. Keith, *Three Came Home*, 213–14, 298.

45. Walker, *In Search of Our Mothers' Gardens*, 241.

46. Reason, "Hard Singing of Country," 71. Graves, "Recalling War," *Collected Poems*.

47. Okihiro, *Whispered Silences*, 209.

48. Jarman in Godwin, *Edge of the Land*, 121.

49. Syverson quoted in Dobler, "Soldiers Plant Gardens in Iraq's Sandy Soil."

50. E-mail from Quam to the author, 1 Feb. 2005. E-mail from Poukka to the author, 31 Dec. 2004.

51. Dobler, "Soldiers Plant Gardens in Iraq's Sandy Soil." "Soldier Grows Grass, Controversy."

52. R. Cohen, "Spring in Sarajevo Amid Lilacs Out of Dead Land."

53. This and preceding quotations from Davorin Brdanovic, interview with the author, 2004.

54. Jerzy Soltan, lecture at the Technion Israel Institute of Technology, Haifa, Israel, 1981.

Bibliography

INTERVIEWS AND TESTIMONIES

Brdanovic, Davorin. Interview by the author, 2004.
Cogan, Francis B. Interview by the author, 2004.
Fuchs, Janik ("Jonah"). Interview by the author, 2004.
Holzman, Nina. Shoah Foundation interview 15947.
Jagielski, Jan. Interview by the author, 2004.
Kent, Roman. Interview by the author, 2004.
Klein, Gerda. Interview by the author, 2004.
Mishkin, Esther. Interview by the author, 2003.
Nance, Elizabeth. Interview by the author, 2005.
Nishi, Henry. "Interview with Henry Nishi" by Anna Tamura, unpublished oral history, 2002.
Ogami, Arthur. "Interview with Arthur Ogami" by Anna Tamura, unpublished oral history, 2002.
Rubanek, Henryk. Testimony. Yad Vashem File 03/4307.
Topas, George. Shoah Foundation Interview 40322, 1997.

ARCHIVES

Densho Archive, Japanese American Legacy Project. Seattle, Washington.
Ghetto Fighter's House Archive (Beit Lohamei Haghetaot), Kibbutz Lohamei Haghetaot, Israel. Oskar Singer, "Something about Horticulture in the Ghetto" (30 May 1942), translated by Susan Anderson.
Imperial War Museum (IWM), London. Major R. S. Cockburn, unpublished manuscript. Captain A. D. M. Hilton Papers, POW No. 287, Oflag 8B, Germany papers. T. MacDonald, manuscript. Michael Pease WWI Ruhleben file, IWM Reports of the Committee of the Ruhleben Horticultural Society, 1917–18, Michael Pease File. Pope-

Hennesey Papers. C. I. Rolfe Papers. E. L. Wright Papers. G. D. H. Ross Papers. Letters: R. (Roland) Montfort, D. Lance Corporal.

Japanese American Historical Museum (JAHM), Los Angeles. *Gila News Courier*, 12 Sept. 1942–1 Jan. 1944. *Topaz Times*, 17 Sept. 1942–30 Dec. 1943.

Jewish Historical Institute (JHI), Warsaw, Poland.

Shoah Visual History Foundation, Los Angeles.

Toc House, Poperinghe, Belgium.

U.S. Holocaust Memorial Museum (USHMM), Washington, D.C.

Yad Vashem, Jerusalem, Israel. Survivors of the Emmanuel Ringelblum Archives.

(Nachman) Zonabend Collection, YIVO Institute for Jewish Research, New York. "Information for Small Gardeners: Garden Calendar for the Month of July," Litzmanstadt ghetto, 2 July 1943. Oskar Rosenfeld, "Sketches of Ghetto Life." Oskar Singer, "The Face of the Ghetto." Josef Zelkowicz, "Blessings of the Earth," translated by Roberta Neuman. This collection details the evolution of a garden bureaucracy and communicates the more intimate aspects of garden creation.

BOOKS AND ARTICLES

Abrioux, Yves. *Ian Hamilton Finlay: A Visual Primer.* Cambridge: MIT Univ. Press, 1992.

Adams, Ansel, and Tiyo Miyatake. *Two Views of Manzanar: An Exhibition of Photographs.* Edited by Graham Howe, Patrick Nagatani, and Scott Rankin. Los Angeles: Frederick S. Wright Art Gallery, UCLA, 1978.

Addie, Lieutenant Colonel J. H. Forrester, and Captain A. T. A. Dobson. "Agriculture behind the Lines in France." *Journal of the Ministry of Agriculture* 27, nos. 8–9 (Nov./Dec. 1921): 1–19.

Adelson, Alan, and Robert Lapides, eds. *Lodz Ghetto: Inside a Community under Siege.* New York: Viking, 1989.

Adler, Stanislaw. *In the Warsaw Ghetto 1940–43: An Account of a Witness, The Memoirs of Stanislaw Adler.* Jerusalem: Yad Vashem, 1982.

Alan of Lille. *Anticlaudianus, or The Good and Perfect Man.* Translation and commentary by James J. Sheridan. Toronto: Pontifical Institute of Mediaeval Studies, 1973.

Anderton, Stephen. "What Is a Garden?" *Garden*, Nov. 1997, 796–801.

Appleton, Jay. *The Experience of Landscape.* New York: John Wiley, 1975.

Archer, Bernice, and Kent Federowich. "The Women of Stanley: Internment in Hong Kong, 1942–1945." *Women's History Review* 5, no. 3 (1996): 373–99.

Armor, John, and Peter Wright. *Manzanar [Ringoen].* Photographs by Ansel Adams. New York: Vintage, 1989.

Ashworth, Tony. *Trench Warfare: 1914–1918, The Live and Let Live System.* New York: Holmes & Meier, 1980.

Audoin-Rouzeau, Stéphane, and Annette Becker. *14–18, Understanding the*

Great War. Translated by Catherine Temerson. New York: Hill & Wang, 2002.

Bailey, Ronald H., and the editors of Time-Life Books. *Prisoners of War.* Chicago: Time-Life Books, 1981.

Balmori, Diana, and Margaret Morton. *Transitory Gardens, Uprooted Lives.* New Haven: Yale Univ. Press, 1993.

Bard, Mitchell G. *Forgotten Victims: The Abandonment of Americans in Hitler's Camps.* Boulder: Westview Press, 1994.

Barnett, Correlli. *The Great War.* New York: Putnam, 1980.

Barth, Gunther. *Instant Cities: Urbanization and the Rise of San Francisco and Denver.* New York: Oxford Univ. Press, 1975.

Bartoszewski, Wladyslaw. *The Warsaw Ghetto: A Christian's Testimony.* Boston: Beacon, 1987.

Bassani, Giorgio. *The Garden of the Finzi-Continis.* Translated by William Weaver. New York: Harcourt Brace Jovanivich, 1977.

Bauer, Yehuda. *They Chose Life: Jewish Resistance in the Holocaust.* New York: American Jewish Committee, 1973.

Beatty, Jack. "Along the Western Front." *Atlantic* 258, no. 5 (Nov. 1986): 106–17.

Berenbaum, Michael. *The World Must Know: The History of the Holocaust as Told in the United States Holocaust Memorial Museum.* Boston: Little Brown, 1993.

Berg, Erik B. *Behind Barbed Wires: Among War Prisoners in Germany.* Rock Island, Ill.: Augustana Book Concern, 1944.

Berg, Mary. *Warsaw Ghetto, A Diary by Mary Berg.* Edited by S. L. Shneiderman. New York: L. B. Fischer, 1945.

Biderman, Abraham H. *The World of My Past.* Melbourne, Australia: AHB Publications, 1995.

Bird, Tom. *American POWs of World War II: Forgotten Men Tell Their Stories.* Westport, Conn.: Praeger, 1992.

Birenbaum, Halina. *Hope Is the Last to Die: A Coming of Age under Nazi Terror.* New, expanded edition. Armonk, N.Y.: M. E. Sharpe, 1996 [1967].

Bischof, Günter, and Stephen E. Ambrose, eds. *Eisenhower and the German POWs: Facts against Falsehood.* Baton Rogue: Louisiana State Univ. Press, 1992.

Bloch, Ernst. *The Principle of Hope.* Translated by Neville Plaice, Stephen Plaice, and Paul Knight. Cambridge: MIT Press, 1986.

Blunden, Edmund. *Undertones of War.* London: Robin Cobden-Sanderson, 1928.

Botton, Alain de. *The Art of Travel.* New York: Pantheon, 2002.

Brdanovic, Davorin. "Community Gardens in Bosnia." Lecture, University of Washington, 21 Nov. 2003.

Bring, Mitchell, and Josse Wayembergh. *Japanese Gardens: Design and Meaning.* New York: McGraw Hill, 1981.

Brophy, John, and Eric Partridge, eds. *Songs and Slang of the British Soldier: 1914–1918.* 3rd ed. London: Eric Partridge, 1931.

Brown, Kendall. *Japanese-Style Gardens of the Pacific West Coast.* Photographs by Melba Levick. New York: Rizzoli, 1999.

———. "Putting Down Roots: Prewar Japanese Gardens and Garden Builders." In *Greenmakers: Japanese American Gardeners in Southern California*, edited by Naomi Hirahara. Los Angeles: Southern California Gardener's Federation, 2000.

Brown, Malcolm. *The Imperial War Museum Book of the First World War.* Norman: Univ. of Oklahoma Press, 1991.

———. *Tommy Goes to War.* London: J. M. Dent & Sons, 1978.

Browning, Christopher. *The Path to Genocide: Essays on Launching the Final Solution.* New York: Cambridge Univ. Press, 1992.

Bryant, Alice Franklin. *The Sun Was Darkened.* Boston: Chapman & Grimes, 1947.

Burton, Jeffery F. *Three Farewells to Manzanar: The Archeology of Manzanar National Historic Site, California.* Publications in Anthropology 67. Tucson: Western Archeological and Conservation Center, National Park Service, 1996.

Burton, Jeffery F., and Mary M. Farrell. *This Is Minidoka: An Archeological Survey of Minidoka Internment Camp National Monument, Idaho.* Tucson: Western Archeological and Conservation Center, 2001.

Burton, Jeffery F., Laura S. Bergstresser, and Anna H. Tamura. *Minidoka Internment National Monument: Archeology at the Gate.* Tucson: U.S. Department of the Interior, 2003.

Burton, Jeffery F., et al. *Confinement and Ethnicity: An Overview of World War II Japanese American Relocation Sites.* Seattle: Univ. of Washington Press, 2002.

Carlson, Lewis H. *We Were Each Other's Prisoners: An Oral History of World War II American and German Prisoners of War.* New York: Basic Books, 1997.

Chapman, Paul. *A Haven in Hell: Talbot House, Poperinghe.* Edited by Ted Smith. London: Leo Cooper, 2001 [1930].

Chasseaud, Peter. *Topography of Armageddon: A British Trench Map Atlas of the Western Front, 1914–1818.* Lewes, East Sussex: Mapbooks, 1991.

Churman, Frank F. *The Bamboo People: The Law and Japanese Americans.* Del Mar, Calif.: Publisher's, 1976.

Clark, James, ed. *Urban Paradise: Gardens in the City.* Public Art Issues 3. New York: Public Art Fund, 1994.

Clayton, P. B. *Tales of Talbot House, Everyman's Club in Poperinghe and Ypres, 1915–1918.* London: Chatto & Windus, 1919.

Clendinnen, Inga. *Reading the Holocaust.* New York: Cambridge Univ. Press, 1999.

Cogan, Francis B. *Captured: The Japanese Internment of American Civilians in the Philippines, 1941–1945.* Athens: Univ. of Georgia Press, 2000.

Cohen, Israel. *The Ruhleben Prison Camp: A Record of Nineteen Months' Internment.* New York: Dodd, Mead, 1917.

Cohen, Roger. "Spring in Sarajevo Amid Lilacs Out of Dead Land." *New York Times,* 15 May 1994, international edition.

Cohen, Stanley, and Laurie Taylor. *Psychological Survival: The Experience of Long-term Imprisonment.* New York: Pantheon, 1972.

Cole, Tim. *Holocaust City: The Making of a Jewish Ghetto.* New York: Routledge, 2003.

Corni, Gustavo. *Hitler's Ghettos: Voices from a Beleaguered Society, 1939–1944.* New York: Oxford Univ. Press, 2002.

Craig, David, and Michael Egan. *Extreme Situations: Literature and Crisis from the Great War to the Atom Bomb.* Totowa, N.J.: Barnes & Noble Books, 1979.

Crowley, David. *Warsaw.* London: Reaktion, 2003.

Cupers, Kenny, and Markus Miessen. *Spaces of Uncertainty.* Wuppertal, Germany: Müller & Busman, 2002.

Czerniakow, Adam. *The Warsaw Diary of Adam Czerniakow: Prelude to Doom.* Edited by Raul Hilberg, Stanislaw Staron, and Josef Kermisz. Translated by Staron and the staff of Yad Vashem. New York: Stein & Day, 1979.

Dancocks, Daniel G. *In Enemy Hands: Canadian Prisoners of War 1939–45.* Edmonton, Canada: Hurtig, 1983.

Daniels, Roger. *Concentration Camps USA: Japanese Americans and World War II.* New York: Holt, Rinehart & Winston, 1971.

Daniels, Roger , Sandra C. Taylor, and Harry H. L. Kitano, eds. *Japanese Americans: From Relocation to Redress.* Seattle: Univ. of Washington Press, 1991.

David, Janina. *A Square of Sky: A Wartime Childhood in Poland.* New York: Penguin, 1981.

Davis, Daniel S. *Behind Barbed Wire: The Imprisonment of Japanese Americans during World War II.* New York: Dutton, 1982.

Dawidowicz, Lucy S. *The War against the Jews, 1933–1945.* New York: Holt, Rinehart & Winston, 1975.

De Lapradelle, A., and Frederic R. Coudert, eds. *War Letters from France.* New York: D. Appleton, 1916.

Dennett, Carl P. *Prisoners of the Great War: Authoritative Statement of Conditions in the Prison Camps of Germany.* Boston: Houghton Mifflin, 1919.

Dobler, Amy. "Soldiers Plant Gardens in Iraq's Sandy Soil." National Guard, www.ngb.army.mil/news/story.asp?id=1316, accessed 19 Nov. 2004.

Dobroszycki, Lucjan, ed. *The Chronicle of the Lodz Ghetto, 1941–1944.* Translated by Richard Lourie et al. New Haven: Yale Univ. Press, 1984.

Doctorow, E. L. *City of God.* New York: Random House, 2000.

Donavan, Tom. *The Hazy Red Hell: Fighting Experiences on the Western Front 1914–1918.* Staplehurst, U.K.: Spellmount, 1999.

Doyle, Robert C. *Voices from Captivity: Interpreting the American POW Narrative.* Lawrence: Univ. Press of Kansas, 1994.

Duff, Oliver. "Sundowner." "High Country Gardens." In *The Shepard's*

Calendar, Out of Town. Edited by Jeff Gordon. Christchurch, New Zealand: Shoal Bay Press, 1951.

Durand, Arthur A. *Stalag Luft III: The Secret Story.* Baton Rouge: Louisiana State Univ. Press, 1988.

Dyer, Geoff. *The Missing of the Somme.* London: Phoenix, 2001 [1994].

Eisen, George. *Children and Play in the Holocaust: Games among the Shadows.* Amherst: Univ. of Massachusetts Press, 1988.

Eisenman, Theodore. "Memory Never Stands Still." *Landscape Architecture,* June 2004, 114–17.

Elias, Ruth. *Triumph of Hope: From Theresienstadt and Auschwitz to Israel.* Translated by Margot Bettauer Dembo. New York: John Wiley, 1998.

Ellis, John. *Eye-Deep in Hell: Trench Warfare in World War I.* Baltimore: Johns Hopkins Univ. Press, 1976.

Ellis, William S. "The Gift of Gardening." *National Geographic* 181, no. 5 (May 1992): 52–81.

Embrey, Sue Kunitomi, Arthur A. Hansen, and Betty Kulberg Mitson. *Manzanar Martyr: An Interview with Harry Y. Ueno.* Fullerton, Calif.: Oral History Program, California State University, 1986.

Empey, Arthur Guy. *Over the Top.* New York: G. P. Putnam's Sons, 1917.

Engelking, Barbara. *Holocaust and Memory: The Experience of the Holocaust and Its Consequences: An Investigation Based on Personal Narratives.* Edited by Gunnar S. Paulsson, translated by Emma Harris. New York: Leicester Univ. Press, 2001.

Engelking, Barbara, and Jacek Leociak. *Getto Warsawskie: Przewodnik Po Niestniejacym Miescie.* (The Warsaw ghetto: Guide to the Non-existing City). Warsaw: Wydawnictwo IFiS Pan, 2001.

Ewan, Rebecca Fish. *A Land Between: Owens Valley, California.* Baltimore: Johns Hopkins Univ. Press, 2000.

Ferro, Marc. *The Great War, 1914–1918.* Translated by Nicole Stone. London: Routledge & K. Paul, 1973.

Fiset, Louis. *Imprisoned Apart: The World War II Correspondence of an Issei Couple.* Seattle: Univ. of Washington Press, 1997.

Flinn, Nancy. *The Prison Garden Book.* Burlington, Vt.: National Gardening Association, 1985.

Ford, Aleksander, director. *Border Street [Ulica graniczna].* Sarasota, Fla.: Polart 1995 [1948].

"For Young and Old, a Pocket Paradise." *New York Times,* 30 April 1989.

Foucault, Michel. "Of Other Spaces." *Diacritics* 16, no. 1 (1986): 22–27.

Foy, David A. *For You the War Is Over: American Prisoners of War in Nazi Germany.* New York: Stein & Day, 1984.

Francis, Mark, and Randolph T. Hester Jr., eds. *The Meaning of Gardens: Idea, Place, and Action.* Cambridge: MIT Univ. Press, 1990.

Frye, Northrop. *The Stubborn Structure: Essays on Criticism and Society.* Ithaca: Cornell Univ. Press, 1970.

Fuchs, Janik. *Field Post #27023.*

Fukuda, Kazuhiko. *Japanese Stone Gardens: How to Make and Enjoy Them.* Rutland, Vt.: Charles E. Tuttle, 1970.

Fussell, Paul. *Doing Battle: The Making of a Skeptic.* Boston: Little Brown, 1996.

———. *The Great War and Modern Memory.* New York: Oxford, 1975.

Georg, Willy. *In the Warsaw Ghetto: Summer 1941.* New York: Aperture, 1993.

George, Alice Rose, and Lee Marks, eds. *Hope: Photographs.* New York: Thames & Hudson, 1998.

Gesensway, Deborah, and Mindy Roseman. *Beyond Words: Images from America's Concentration Camps.* Ithaca: Cornell Univ. Press, 1987.

Gibbs, Phillip. *Now It Can Be Told.* New York: Harper, 1920.

Gilbert, Martin. *Holocaust Journey: Traveling in Search of the Past.* New York: Columbia Univ. Press, 1997.

Gilliland, Horace Gray. *My German Prisons.* Boston: Houghton Mifflin, 1919.

Girdner, Audre, and Ann Loftis. *The Great Betrayal: The Evacuation of the Japanese-Americans during World War II.* New York: Macmillan, 1969.

Gittins, Jean. *Stanley: Behind Barbed Wire.* Hong Kong: Hong Kong Univ. Press, 1982.

Glas-Wiener, Sheva. *Children of the Ghetto.* Translated by the author and by Shirley Young. Fitzroy, Australia: Globe Press, 1983 [1974 in Yiddish].

Godwin, Fay. *The Edge of the Land.* London: Jonathan Cape, 1995.

Goodman, Ellen. "All Tree Planters Know about Hope." *Eugene Register Guard*, 4 Dec. 1984.

Gosse, Philip. *Memoirs of a Camp Follower.* New York: Longmans, Green & Co., 1934.

Gough, Paul. "The Avenue at War." *Landscape Research* 18, no. 2 (1993): 66–77.

Grabitz, Helge, and Wolfgang Scheffer. *Letze Spuren* [Last traces]. Berlin: Hentrich, 1988.

Graham, Stephen. *The Challenge of the Dead.* London: Cassell, 1921.

Graves, Robert. *Collected Poems.* Garden City, N.Y.: Doubleday, 1958.

———. *Good-Bye to All That: An Autobiography.* Providence, R.I.: Berghahn, 1995 [1929].

Greening, Ross, and Angelo Spinelli. *How Our POW's Made "Little Americas" behind Nazi Barbed Wire . . . the Yankee Kriegies.* New York: YMCA, 1946?.

Gronso, Dale. *A Sense of History.* Master of Fine Arts Terminal Project, University of Oregon, 2002.

Groom, Winston. *A Storm in Flanders: The Ypres Salinet, 1914–1918: Tragedy and Triumph on the Western Front.* New York, Grove Press, 2002.

Grossman, Mendel. *With a Camera in the Ghetto.* New York: Schocken, 1977.

Grynberg, Michal, ed. *Words to Outlive Us: Eyewitness Accounts from the Warsaw Ghetto.* Translated by Philip Boehm. New York: Henry Holt, 2002.

Guareschi, Giovanni. *My Secret Diary, 1943–1945*. Translated by Frances Frenaye. New York: Farrar, Straus & Cudahy, 1958.

Gutman, Yisrael. *The Jews of Warsaw, 1939–1943: Ghetto, Underground, Revolt*. Translated by Ina Friedman. Bloomington: Indiana Univ. Press, 1982.

Handy, Mildred Tenny. "The Heavens Wept." Unpublished manuscript, Ghetto Fighters' House, Israel, 1981.

Hansen, Arthur, ed. *Japanese American World War II Evacuation Oral History Project*. Westport, Conn.: Meckler, 1991.

Hart, John, et al. *Gardens of Alcatraz*. San Francisco: Golden Gate National Parks Association, 1996.

Hartendorp, A. V. H. *The Santo Tomas Story*. New York: McGraw Hill, 1964.

Harth, Erica, ed. *Last Witnesses: Reflections on the Wartime Internment of Japanese Americans*. New York: Palgrave, 2001.

Hartman, Geoffrey, ed. *Holocaust Remembrance: The Shapes of Memory*. Cambridge: Blackwell, 1994.

Hasford, Gustav. *The Short-Timers*. New York: Bantam, 1979.

Havers, R. P. W. *Reassessing the Japanese Prisoner of War Experience: The Changi POW camp, Singapore, 1942–5*. London: Routledge, 2003.

Hayden, Dolores. *The Power of Place: Urban Landscapes as Public History*. Cambridge: MIT Univ. Press, 1995.

Hays, Frank. "The National Park Service: Groveling Sycophant or Social Conscience? Telling the Story of Mountains, Valley, and Barbed Wire at Manzanar National Historic Site." *George Wright Forum* 19, no. 4 (2002): 50–54.

Hedges, Chris. *War Is a Force that Gives Us Meaning*. New York: Anchor, 2003.

Helphand, Kenneth. "Battlefields and Dreamfields: The Landscape of Recent American Film." *Oregon Humanities*, 1990, 18–21.

———. "Defiant Gardens." *Journal of Garden History* 17, no. 2 (1997): 101–21.

———. "*Garden Is a Verb*." Review of *To Dwell Is to Garden* by Samuel Bass Warner, *Landscape Architecture* 77(6):32–33.

Herbst, Robin. "For a Lost Child, Rooms of Flowers." *New York Times*, 14 July 1994.

Hershman, Joel, director. *Greenfingers*. Columbia Tristar, 2000.

Higa, Karin M. *The View from Within: Japanese American Art from the Internment Camps, 1942–1945*. Seattle: Univ. of Washington Press, 1992.

Hill, Paul, and Julie Wileman. *Landscapes of War: The Archaeology of Aggression and Defence*. Charleston, S.C.: Tempus, 2002.

Hill, Penelope. "The Planting Revolution in the Modern Garden." *Topos*, 2001, 48–57.

Hillman, James. *A Terrible Love of War*. New York: Penguin, 2004.

Hirahara, Naomi. *Greenmakers: Japanese American Gardeners in Southern California*. Los Angeles: Southern California Gardener's Federation, 2000.

Hiss, Tony. "Breaking Ground." *New Yorker*, 26 Oct. 1992.

Hochman, Peretz. *Daring to Live.* Tel Aviv: Ministry of Defense Publishing House, 1994. Originally published in 1991 as *Le-ha`ez li-heyot.*

Hoffman, Conrad. *In the Prison Camps of Germany: A Narrative of "Y" Service among Prisoners of War.* New York: Association Press, 1920.

Horiuchi, Lynne. "Dislocations: The Built Environments of Japanese American Internment." In *Guilt by Association: Essays on Japanese Settlement, Internment, and Relocation in the Rocky Mountain West*, edited by Mike Mackey, 255–76. Powell, Wyo.: Western History Publications, 2001.

Horwitz, Tony. *Confederates in the Attic: Dispatches from the Unfinished Civil War.* New York: Pantheon, 1998.

Hosokawa, Robert. *Minidoka Report 9: Gardens.* War Relocation Authority Reports. Hunt, Idaho: Minidoka Relocation Center, 1943 or 1994.

Housman, Laurence, ed. *War Letters of Fallen Englishmen.* Philadelphia: Pine Street Books, 2002 [1930].

Houston, Jeanne Wakatsuki. "Rock Garden." In *Literature and the Environmnent: A Reader on Nature and Culture*, compiled by Lorraine Anderson, Scott Slovic, and John P. O'Grady, 277–82. New York: Longman, 1999.

Houston, Jeanne Wakatsuki, and James D. Houston. *Farewell to Manzanar: A True Story of Japanese American Experience during and after the World War II Internment.* Boston: Houghton Mifflin, 1973.

Howard, Michael. "Sadam's Routine: Gardening, a Muffin and Writing Poems." *Guardian Weekly*, 30 July–5 Aug. 2004, 7.

Huberband, Rabbi Shimon. *Kiddush Hashem: Jewish Religious and Cultural Life in Poland during the Holocaust.* New York: Yeshiva Univ. Press, 1987.

Humphreys, Helen. *The Lost Garden.* New York: Norton, 2002.

Hunt, John Dixon. *Greater Perfections: The Practice of Garden Theory.* Philadelphia: Univ. of Pennsylvania Press, 2000.

Hyams, Joseph. *A Field of Buttercups.* Englewood Cliffs, N.J.: Prentice Hall, 1968.

Hynes, H. Patricia. *A Patch of Eden: America's Inner City Gardeners.* White River Junction, Vt.: Chelsea Green Publishing, 1996.

Hynes, Samuel. "In the Whirl and Muddle of War." *New York Times Book Review,* 31 July 1988.

———. *The Soldier's Tale: Bearing Witness to Modern War.* London: Pimlico, 1997.

———. *A War Imagined: The First World War and English Culture.* New York: Atheneum, 1990.

Ignatieff, Michael. In *For Most of It I Have No Words,* edited by Simon Norfolk. Stockport, England: Dewi Lewi, 1998.

Inada, Lawson Fusao. *Drawing the Line: Poems.* Minneapolis: Coffee House Press, 1997.

Inturrisi, Louis. "The Roman Spring of Ancient Stones: A Wild Garden in the Colosseum." *New York Times,* 4 April 1993, 35.

Ishigo, Estelle. *Lone Heart Mountain.* Los Angeles: Japanese American
    Citizens League, 1972.
Jackson, J. B. "Landscape as Seen by the Military." In *Discovering the
    Vernacular Landscape.* New Haven: Yale, 1984.
———. *The Necessity for Ruins, and Other Topics.* Amherst: Univ. of
    Massachusetts Press, 1980.
Jackson, Robert. *The Prisoners, 1914–1918.* New York: Routledge, 1989.
James, David. *A Prisoner's Progress.* Edinburgh: William Blackwood & Sons,
    1947.
Jarman, Derek. *Derek Jarman's Garden.* Photographs by Howard Sooley.
    Woodstock, N.Y.: Overlook Press, 1996.
———. *Modern Nature.* Woodstock, N.Y.: Overlook Press, 1994.
Jekyll, Gertrude. *Home and Garden: Notes and Thoughts, Practical and Critical,
    of a Worker in Both.* New York: Longmans, Green & Co., 1900.
Johansen, Bruce E. *So Far from Home: Manila's Santo Tomas Internment Camp,
    1942–1845.* Omaha: PBI Press, 1996.
Jones, David. *In Parenthesis.* New York: Chilmark Press, 1962 [1937].
Jones and Jones. *Paju Ecopolis: Ecosystem Management Strategy.* Ministry of
    Science and Technology: Republic of Korea, 1998.
Kaplan, Chaim A. *Scroll of Agony: The Warsaw Diary of Chaim A. Kaplan.*
    Translated and edited by Abraham I. Katsh. New York: Macmillan,
    1965.
Kaplan, Marion. *Between Dignity and Despair: Jewish Life in Nazi Germany.*
    New York: Oxford Univ. Press, 1998.
Kaplan, Rachel. "Some Psychological Benefits of Gardening." *Environment
    and Behavior* 5, no. 2 (1973): 145–61.
Kaplan, Rachel, and Stephen Kaplan. *The Experience of Nature: A
    Psychological Perspective.* New York: Cambridge Univ. Press, 1989.
Kardiner, Abram, and Herbert Spiegel. *War Stress and Neurotic Illness.* New
    York: Paul B. Hoeber, 1947.
Karski, Jan. *Story of a Secret State.* Boston: Houghton Mifflin, 1944.
Kast, Verena. *Joy, Inspiration, and Hope.* Translated by Douglas Whitcher.
    College Station: Texas A&M Univ. Press, 1991.
Katz, Alfred. *Poland's Ghettos at War.* New York: Twayne, 1970.
Kaufman, Jason Edward. "Stones Full of Life and Memory." *New York
    Times,* 14 Sept. 2003, 35.
Keegan, John. *The Face of Battle.* New York: Viking, 1976.
———. *A History of Warfare.* New York: Vintage, 1994.
———. "There's Rosemary for Remembrance." *American Scholar* 66, no. 2
    (summer 1997): 335–48.
Keegan, John, and Joseph Darracott. *The Nature of War.* New York: Holt,
    Rinehart & Winston, 1981.
Keith, Agnes Newton. *Three Came Home.* New York: Time, 1965 [1946].
Keller, Ulrich, ed. *The Warsaw Ghetto in Photographs: 206 Views Made in 1941.*
    New York: Dover, 1984.

Kellert, Stephen R., and Edward O. Wilson, eds. *The Biophilia Hypothesis.* Washington, D.C.: Island Press, 1993.

Kent, Roman. "Ghetto Years." Unpublished manuscript, courtesy of the author.

Kermish, Joseph, ed. *To Live with Honor and Die with Honor!* Translated by M. Z. Prives et al. Jerusalem: Yad Vashem, 1986.

Ketchum, J. Davidson. *Ruhleben, a Prison Camp Society.* Toronto: Univ. of Toronto Press, 1965.

Kikuchi, Charles. *The Kikuchi Diary: Chronicle from an American Concentration Camp.* Edited by John Modell. Urbana: Univ. of Illinois Press, 1973.

Kincaid, Jamaica. *My Garden (Book).* New York: Farrar, Straus & Giroux, 1999.

———. "Sowers and Reapers." *New Yorker,* 22 Jan. 2001, 41–45.

Kipling, Rudyard. *France at War.* Garden City, N.Y.: Doubleday, Page & Co., 1915.

Klein, Gerda Weissman. *All But My Life.* New York: Hill & Wang, 1957.

Klein, Holger, ed. *The First World War in Fiction: A Collection of Critical Essays.* New York: Barnes & Noble, 1977.

Kleinkopf, Arthur. "Relocation Center Diary, 1942–1946." Unpublished diary, Hunt, Idaho. Idaho and Pacific Northwest History Collection, Twin Falls Idaho Library, Idaho, 1942–1946.

Knightley, Phillip. *The Eye of War: Words and Photographs from the Front Line.* Washington, D.C.: Smithsonian Books, 2003.

Koch, H. W. *The Rise of Modern Warfare, 1618–1815.* Englewood Cliffs: Prentice Hall, 1981.

Kogawa, Joy. *Naomi's Road.* Toronto: Oxford Univ. Press, 1986.

Korczak, Janusz. *Ghetto Diary.* New Haven: Yale Univ. Press, 2003 [1978].

Kruk, Herman. *The Last Days of the Jerusalem of Lithuania: Chronicles from the Vilna Ghetto and the Camps, 1939–1944.* Edited by Benjamin Harshav, translated by Barbara Harshav. New Haven, Conn.: YIVO Institute for Jewish Research, 2002.

Kuck, Loraine. *The World of the Japanese Garden: From Chinese Origins to Modern Landscape Art.* New York: Walker/Weatherhill, 1968.

Kundera, Milan. "Such Was Their Wager." *New Yorker,* 10 May 1999, 94–96.

Laffin, John. *Panorama of the Western Front.* Stroud, Gloucestershire: Alan Sutton, 1993.

Langer, Lawrence, ed. *Art from the Ashes: A Holocaust Anthology.* New York: Oxford Univ. Press, 1995.

Lanzmann, Claude. *Shoah: An Oral History of the Holocaust: The Complete Text of the Film.* New York: Pantheon Books, 1985.

Larsen, Svend Erik. "Landscape, Identity, and War." *New Literary History* 35, no. 3 (2004): 469–90.

Leed, Eric J. *No Man's Land: Combat and Identity in World War I.* Cambridge: Cambridge Univ. Press, 1979.

Lewin, Abraham. *A Cup of Tears: A Diary of the Warsaw Ghetto.* Oxford: Basil Blackwell, 1988.

Lewis, Charles A. *Green Nature/Human Nature: The Meaning of Plants in Our Lives.* Urbana: Univ. of Illinois Press, 1996.

Longworth, Philip. *The Unending Vigil: A History of the Commonwealth War Graves Commission 1917–1967.* London: Constable, 1967.

Machiavelli, Niccolo. *The Prince.* Translated by Harvey C. Mansfield. Chicago: Univ. of Chicago, 1998.

Mackey, Mike. *Heart Mountain: Life in Wyoming's Concentration Camp.* Powell, WY: Western History Publications, 2000.

Macquarrie, Hector. *How to Live at the Front: Tips for American Soldiers.* Philadelphia: J. B. Lippincott, 1917.

Magnuson, Frieda. *Out in '45 If We're Still Alive.* Bend, OR: Maverick Publications, 1984.

Mandela, Nelson. *Long Walk to Freedom: The Autobiography of Nelson Mandela.* Boston: Little, Brown, 1994.

Marcel, Gabriel. *The Existential Background of Human Dignity.* Cambridge: Harvard Univ. Press, 1963.

——. *The Mystery of Being.* Vol. 2, *Faith and Reality.* Translated by Rene Hague. Chicago: Henry Regnery, 1950–51.

Marcus, Claire Cooper. *House as Symbol of Self.* Berkeley: Institute of Urban and Regional Development, University of California, 1971.

Martin, Douglas. "Gardens Flourish Behind Razor Wire." *New York Times,* 1 Jan. 1999.

Marx, Leo. *The Machine in the Garden: Technology and the Pastoral Ideal in America.* New York: Oxford Univ. Press, 1964.

Maslow, Abraham H. *Toward a Psychology of Being.* Princeton: Van Nostrand, 1968.

McCarthy, Daniel J. *The Prisoner of War in Germany: The Care and Treatment of the Prisoner of War with a History of the Development of the Principle of Neutral Inspection and Control.* New York: Moffat, Yard & Co., 1918.

McClung, William Alexander. *The Architecture of Paradise: Survivals of Eden and Jerusalem.* Berkeley: Univ. of California Press, 1983.

McCown, Joe. *Availability: Gabriel Marcel and the Phenomenology of Human Openness.* Missoula: Scholars Press, 1978.

McHarg, Ian L. *A Quest for Life: An Autobiography.* New York: John Wiley, 1996.

Messenger, Charles. *Trench Fighting 1914–1918.* New York: Ballantine, 1972.

Messimer, Dwight R. *Escape.* Annapolis: Naval Institute Press, 1994.

Meyers, Steven Lee. "Broadway's New Feature: Cornstalks." *New York Times,* 13 Aug. 1991, B1–B2.

——. "Farmer Unearthed: He Planted the Corn." *New York Times,* 15 Aug. 1991, B5.

Mills, Susan. *Ruderal Plants in Manhattan.* Rosendale, NY: Women's Studio Workshop, 1995.

Mishell, William. *Kaddish for Kovno: Life and Death in a Lithuanian Ghetto, 1941–1945.* Chicago: Chicago Review Press, 1988.

Mitchell, Henry. *The Essential Earthman: Henry Mitchell on Gardening.* Bloomington: Indiana Univ. Press, 1981.

Monde, Danny. "A Soul on Fire." *Jerusalem Report* 15, no. 1 (3 May 2004): 34–39.

Monin, Lydia, and Andrew Gallimore. *The Devil's Garden: A History of Landmines.* London: Pimlico, 2002.

Moore, Charles W., William J. Mitchell, and William Turnbull Jr. *The Poetics of Gardens.* Cambridge: MIT Press, 1998.

Morgan, Guy. *P.O.W.* New York: McGraw-Hill, 1945.

Morison, Samuel Eliot. *The Invasion of France and Germany, 1944–1945.* Vol. 11 of *History of United States Naval Operations in World War II.* [ch. 1]. Boston: Little, Brown, 1947–62. Reprinted Castle Books, 2001.

Mosse, George L. *Fallen Soldiers: Reshaping the Memory of the World Wars.* New York: Oxford Univ. Press, 1990.

Moynihan, Michael, ed. *Black Bread and Barbed Wire: Prisoners in the First World War.* London: Leo Cooper, 1978.

Mukerji, Chandra. *Territorial Ambitions and the Gardens of Versailles.* Cambridge: Cambridge Univ. Press, 1997.

Mydans, Carl. *More than Meets the Eye.* New York: Harper, 1959.

Myer, Dillon S. *Uprooted Americans: The Japanese Americans and the War Relocation Authority during World War II.* Tucson: Univ. of Arizona Press, 1971.

Myers, Odell. *Thrice Caught: An American Army POW's 900 Days under Axis Guns.* Jefferson, N.C.: McFarland, 2002.

Nakano, Takeo Ujo. *Within the Barbed Wire Fence: A Japanese Man's Account of His Internment in Canada.* Toronto: Univ. of Toronto Press, 1980.

Nash, Grace. *That We Might Live.* Scottsdale, Ariz.: Shano, 1984.

Nash, Paul. *Outline, An Autobiography and Other Writings.* London: Faber & Faber, 1949.

National Park Service. *Cultural Landscape Report for Manzanar National Historic Site.* Seattle: Cultural Resources Division, Pacific West Region-Seattle, National Park Service, 2005.

Netz, Reviel. *Barbed Wire.* Middletown: Wesleyan Unversity Press, 2004.

New York Times. *Portfolio of the Great War in Gravure.* New York: New York Times, 1917.

Ng, Wendy. *Japanese American Internment during World War II: A History and Reference Guide.* Westport, Conn.: Greenwood Press, 2002.

Nobbs, Capt. Gilbert. *On the Right of the British Line.* New York: Charles Scribners Sons, 1917.

Nollman, Jim. *Why We Garden: Cultivating a Sense of Place.* New York: Holt, 1994.

Nova, Lily, and Iven Lourie, eds. *Interrupted Lives: Four Women's Stories of Internment during World War II in the Philippines.* Nevada City, Calif.: Artemis Books, 1995.

Nowotny, Joan. "Despair and the Object of Hope." In *The Sources of Hope*, edited by Ross Fitzgerald, 44–66. Elmsford, N.Y.: Pergamon Press, 1979.

Obata, Chiura. *Chiura Obata's Topaz Moon: Art of the Internment Camps.* Edited by Kimi Kodani Hill. Berkeley: Heydey Books, 2000.

O'Flaherty, Liam. *Return of the Brute.* Dublin: Wolfhound, 1998 [1929].

Oiwa, Keibo, ed. *Stone Voices: Wartime Writings of Japanese Canadian Issei.* Montréal: Véhicule Press, 1991.

Okihiro, Gary Y. *Whispered Silences: Japanese Americans and World War II.* Seattle: Univ. of Washington Press, 1996.

Okubo, Mine. *Citizen 13660.* New York: Columbia Univ. Press, 1946.

Onorato, Ronald. "Battlefields and Gardens: The Illusive Art of Mary Miss." In *Sitings,* edited by Sally Yard. La Jolla, Calif.: La Jolla Museum of Contemporary Art, 1986.

O'Shea, Stephen. *Back to the Front: An Accidental Historian Walks the Trenches of World War I.* New York: Walker & Co., 1997.

Owen, Wilfred. *Wilfred Owen: The Complete Poems and Fragments.* Edited by John Stallworthy. New York: Norton, 1984.

Oxenham, John. *High Altars: The Battlefields of France and Flanders as I Saw Them.* New York: George H. Doran, 1918.

Patch, Howard Rollin. *The Other World, According to Descriptions in Medieval Literature.* Cambridge: Harvard University Press, 1950.

Peel, Mrs. C. S. *How We Lived Then, 1914–1918: A Sketch of Social and Domestic Life in England during the War.* London: John Lane, 1929.

Pernitz, Adolf, and Susie Pernitz. *The Life and Times of Adolf Pernitz of the Adventures of a Young Jewish Boy.* Washington, D.C.: U.S. Holocaust Memorial Museum, 1994.

Pernitz, Susan. *Memories of a Wartime Teenager.* Washington, D.C.: U.S. Holocaust Memorial Museum, 1989.

Philps, Richard. *Prisoner Doctor: An Account of the Experiences of a Royal Air Force Medical Officer during the Japanese Occupation of Indonesia, 1942 to 1945.* Lewes, U.K.: Book Guild, 1996.

Pollan, Michael. *Second Nature: A Gardener's Education.* New York: Atlantic Monthly Press, 1991.

Poznanski, Jakub. *Dziennik z lodzkiego getta* (Diary from Lodz Ghetto). Warsaw: Dom Wyawniczy Bellona i Zydowski Instytut Historyczny, 2002.

Raver, Anne. "From Rubble, Ingenuity Sprouts." *New York Times,* 22 Aug. 2002, D1,6.

——. "Honoring Loss with the Power of Green." *New York Times,* 5 Sept. 2002, D1.

——. "Softening Gritty Urban Gray with a Little Green." *New York Times,* 1 Sept. 1996.

——. "This Stop: 65th Floor, Rain Forest." *New York Times,* 13 Feb. 2003, D1.

Reason, David. "A Hard Singing of Country." In *The Unpainted Landscape,*

Scottish Arts Council, edited by Simon Cutts. London: Coracle Press, 1987.

"Report on the Activities of Toporol. First Semi-Period, 1st December–31st May 1941." In *To Live with Honor and Die with Honor!*, edited by Joseph Kermish.

Restuccio, Jeffrey. "Natural Rhythms of Gardening Reduce Stress." *The Healing Art of Garden: A Newsletter of the Friends of Horticultural Therapy*, spring 1995.

Richarz, Monika, ed. *Jewish Life in Germany: Memoirs from Three Centuries*. Translated by Stella P. Rosenfeld and Sidney Rosenfeld. Bloomington: Univ. of Indiana Press, 1991.

Rieff, David. "Displaced Places." *New York Times Magazine*, 21 Sept. 2003, 36–42.

Riley, Robert B. "From Sacred Grove to Disney World: The Search for Garden Meaning." *Landscape Journal* 7, no. 2 (1988): 136–47.

Ringelblum, Emmanuel. *Notes from the Warsaw Ghetto: The Journal of Emmanuel Ringelblum*. Edited and translated by Jacob Sloan. New York: Schocken, 1974 [1958].

Roberts, Richard H. *Hope and Its Hieroglyph: A Critical Decipherment of Ernst Bloch's Principle of Hope*. Studies in Religion 57. Atlanta: Scholars Press, 1990.

Roland, Charles. *Courage under Siege: Starvation, Disease and Death in the Warsaw Ghetto*. New York: Oxford Univ. Press, 1992.

———. *Long Night's Journey into Day: Prisoners of War in Hong Kong and Japan, 1941–1945*. Waterloo, Ont.: Wilfred Kaurier Univ. Press, 2001.

Rolf, David. *Prisoners of the Reich: Germany's Captive 1939–1945*. London: Leo Cooper, 1988.

Rosenfeld, Oskar. *In the Beginning Was the Ghetto: Notebooks from Lodz*. Evanston: Northwestern Univ. Press, 2002.

Rosensaft, Hadassah. *Yesterday: My Story*. Washington, D.C.: U.S. Holocaust Memorial Museum, 2004.

Roskies, David G. *The Literature of Destruction: Jewish Responses to Catastrophe*. Philadelphia: Jewish Publication Society, 1988.

Ross, John R., and Reiko Katsuyoshi Ross. *Second Kinenhi: Reflections on Tule Lake*. San Francisco: Tule Lake Committee, 1980, 2000.

Roth, John K., and Elisabeth Maxwell. *Remembering the Future: The Holocaust in an Age of Genocide*. New York: Palgrave, 2001.

Rudashevski, Yitskhok. *The Diary of the Vilna Ghetto, June 1941–April 1943*. [Tel Aviv]: Ghetto Fighters' House, 1973.

Rudavsky, Joseph. *To Live with Hope, to Die with Dignity*. Lanham, Md.: Univ. Press of America, 1987.

Rudofsky, Bernard. *The Prodigious Builders: Notes Toward a Natural History of Architecture with Special Regard to Those Species That Are Traditionally Neglected or Downright Ignored*. New York: Harcourt Brace Jovanovich, 1977.

Sackville-West, Vita. *The Garden*. London: Francis Lincoln, 2004 [1946].

Sams, Margaret. *Forbidden Family: A Wartime Memoir of the Philippines, 1941–1945*. Edited by Lynn Z. Bloom. Madison: Univ. of Wisconsin Press, 1989.

Sassoon, Siegfried. *Siegfried Sassoon Diaries 1915–1918*. Edited by Rupert Hart-Davis. London: Faber & Faber, 1983.

———. *Siegfried's Journey, 1916–1920*. New York: Viking Press, 1946.

———. *The War Poems of Siegfried Sassoon*. London: W. Heinemann, 1919.

Saunders, Nicholas J. *Trench Art: A Brief History and Guide, 1914–1939*. London: Leo Cooper, 2001. Published in the U.S. as *Trench Art: Materialities and Memories of War*. New York: Berg, 2003.

Scarry, Elaine. *On Beauty and Being Just*. Princeton: Princeton Univ. Press, 1999.

Schama, Simon. *Landscape and Memory*. New York: Alfred A. Knopf, 1995.

Schlebecker, John T. *Whereby We Thrive: A History of American Farming—1607–1972*. Ames: Iowa State Univ. Press, 1975.

Segal, Charles. *Poetry and Myth in Ancient Pastoral: Essays on Theocritus and Virgil*. Princeton: Princeton Univ. Press, 1981.

Seidman, Dr. Hillel. *The Warsaw Ghetto Diaries*. Edited and translated by Yosef Israel. Southfield, Mich.: Targum Press, 1997.

Sewell, William. *Strange Harmony*. London: Edinburgh House Press, 1946.

Shade, Patrick. *Habits of Hope: A Pragmatic Theory*. Nashville: Vanderbilt Univ. Press.

Shepard, Paul. *Man in the Landscape: A Historic View of the Esthetics of Nature*. New York: Knopf, 1967.

Sherman, Mark, and George Katagiri, eds. *Touching the Stones: Tracing One Hundred Years of Japanese American History*. Portland: Oregon Nikkei Endowment, 1994.

Sherriff, R. C. *Journey's End*. New York: Penguin, 1983 [1929].

Sierakowiak, Dawid. *The Diary of Dawid Sierakowiak: Five Notebooks from the Lódz Ghetto*. Edited by Alan Adelson and translated by Kamil Turowski. New York: Oxford Univ. Press, 1996.

Slawson, David A. *Secret Teachings in the Art of Japanese Gardens: Design Principles, Aesthetic Values*. New York: Kodansha International, 1987.

Slouka, Mark. "A Year Later." *Harper's Magazine*, Sept. 2002, 35–43.

Smith, Page. *Democracy on Trial: The Japanese American Evacuation and Relocation in World War II*. New York: Simon & Schuster, 1995.

"Soldier Grows Grass, Controversy." *Register-Guard* (Eugene, Ore.), 1 Jan. 2005, B2.

Solnit, Rebecca. *Hope in the Dark: Untold Histories, Wild Possibilities*. New York: Nation Books, 2004.

Sontag, Susan. *Regarding the Pain of Others*. New York: Farrar, Straus & Giroux, 2003.

Spencer, Carita. *War Scenes I Shall Never Forget*. N.p.: n.p., 1916.

Spiegel, Isaiah. *Ghetto Kingdom: Tales of the Lodz Ghetto*. Evanston: Northwestern Univ. Press, 1998.

Stallworthy, John, ed. *The Oxford Book of War Poetry.* New York: Oxford Univ. Press, 1984.

Stibbe, Edward V. *Reminiscences of a Civilian Prisoner in Germany, 1914–1918.* Leicester, U.K.: n.p., 1919.

Stohr, Kate. "In the Capital of the Car, Nature Stakes a Claim." *New York Times,* 4 Dec. 2003.

Szereszewska, Helena. *Memoirs From Occupied Warsaw, 1940–1945.* Portland, Ore.: Valentine Mitchell, 1997.

Szpilman, Wladyslaw. *The Pianist: The Extraordinary Story of One Man's Survival in Warsaw, 1939–45.* Translated by Anthea Bell. New York: Picador, 1999.

Taft, William Howard, ed. *Service with Fighting Men: An Account of the Work of the American Young Men's Christian Associations in the World War.* New York: Association Press, 1922.

Takeuchi, Thomas, comp. *Minidoka Interlude, September, 1942–October, 1943.* Hunt, Idaho: Thomas Kaname Takeuchi Family, 1995 [1943].

Tamura, Anna Hosticka. Gardens below the Watchtower: Gardens and Meaning in WWII Japanese American Internment Camps. Master's thesis, University of Washington, 2002.

———. "Gardens below the Watchtower: Gardens and Meaning in World War II Japanese American Incarceration Camps." *Landscape Journal* 23, no. 1 (2004): 1–21.

Taverna, Kathryn, and Alan Adelson, directors. *Lodz Ghetto.* Atlas Video. Bethesda: Jewish Heritage Project, 1992.

Tavernier, Bertrand, director. *La Vie et rien d'autre (Life and Nothing But).* France, 1989.

Taylor, A. J. P. *Illustrated History of the First World War.* New York: Putnam's, 1964.

Taylor, Sandra C. *Jewel of the Desert: Japanese American Internment at Topaz.* Berkeley: Univ. of California Press, 1993.

Terkel, Studs. *Hope Dies Last: Keeping the Faith in Troubled Times.* New York: New Press, 2003.

Thacker, Christopher. *The History of Gardens.* Berkeley: Univ. of California Press, 1979.

Thomas, Dorothy Swaine. *The Salvage.* Vol. 2 of *Japanese American Evacuation and Resettlement.* Berkeley: Univ. of California Press, 1946–52.

Thompson, Ian. "Derek Jarman's *Garden*" (review). *Landscape Research* 20, no. 2 (1995): 89–90.

Thornicroft, John, director. *Ground Force* (video). London: BBC Video, 2002.

Tochihara, Tama Keiki. A Generation of Gardens: Japanese Style Gardens of the Issei in Seattle. Master's thesis, Cornell University, 2003.

Topas, George. *The Iron Furnace: A Holocaust Survivor's Story.* Lexington: University Press of Kentucky, 1990.

Tory, Avraham. *Surviving the Holocaust: The Kovno Ghetto Diary.* Edited by

Martin Gilbert. Translated by Jerzy Michalowicz. Cambridge: Harvard Univ. Press, 1990.

Toyama, Tim, and Chris Tashima. *Day of Independence* (film). Directed by Chris Tashima. Los Angeles: Cedar Grove Productions, 2003.

Trunk, Isaiah. *Jewish Responses to Nazi Persecution: Collective and Individual Behavior in Extremis.* New York: Stein & Day, 1979.

Tsuchida, Nobuya. "Japanese Gardeners in Southern California 1900–1941." In *Labor Immigration Under Capitalism,* edited by Lucie Cheng and Edna Bonacich. Berkeley: Univ. of California Press, 1984: 435–69.

Tushnet, Leonard. *The Uses of Adversity.* New York: T. Yoseloff, 1966.

Uchida, Yoshiko. *Desert Exile: The Uprooting of a Japanese American Family.* Seattle: Univ. of Washington Press, 1982.

———. *Journey to Topaz: A Story of the Japanese-American Evacuation.* New York: Scribners, 1971.

Ulrich, Roger S. "Biophilia, Biophobia, and Natural Landscapes." In *The Biophilia Hypothesis.* Edited by Stephen R. Kellert and Edward O. Wilson, 73–137. Washington, D.C.: Island Press, 1993.

———. "View through a Window May Influence Recovery from Surgery." *Science* 224 (1984): 420–21.

Unger, Michal, ed. *The Last Ghetto: Life in the Lodz Ghetto, 1940–1944* (in Hebrew). Jerusalem: Yad Vashem, 1995.

U.S. Commission of Wartime Relocation and Internment of Civilians. *Personal Justice Denied: Report of the Commission on Wartime Relocation and Internment of Civilians.* Washington, D.C.: Government Printing Office, 1983.

U.S. Holocaust Memorial Museum. *Hidden History of the Kovno Ghetto.* Boston: Little, Brown, 1997.

———. *Historical Atlas of the Holocaust.* New York: Macmillan, 1996.

Vance, Jonathan F. *Objects of Concern: Canadian Prisoners of War through the Twentieth Century.* Vancouver: UBC Press, 1994.

———, ed. *Encyclopedia of Prisoners of War and Internment.* Santa Barbara: ABC-CLIO, 2000.

Vaughan, Elizabeth Head. *Community under Stress: An Internment Camp Culture.* Princeton: Princeton Univ. Press, 1949.

———. *The Ordeal of Elizabeth Vaughan: A Wartime Diary of the Philippines.* Edited by Carol M. Petillo. Athens: Univ. of Georgia Press, 1985.

Vischer, A. L. *Barbed Wire Disease: A Psychological Study of the Prisoner of War.* London: John Bales, Sons & Danielson, 1919.

Volavkova, Hana, ed. *I Never Saw Another Butterfly: Children's Drawings and Poems — Terezin 1942–1944.* New York: McGraw Hill, 1962.

Vourkoutiotis, Vasilis. *Prisoner of War and the German High Command: The British and American Experience.* New York: Palgrave Macmillan, 2003.

Walker, Alice. *In Search of Our Mothers' Gardens: Womanist Prose.* San Diego: Harcourt Brace Jovanovich, 1983.

Warner, Samuel Bass. *To Dwell Is to Garden: A History of Boston's Community Gardens.* Boston: Northeastern Univ. Press, 1987.

Warnke, Martin. *Political Landscape: The Art History of Nature.* London: Reaktion, 1994.

Warnod, André. *Prisoner of War.* Philadelphia: J. B. Lippincott, 1916.

Weber, Thomas. *Lodz Ghetto Album.* London: Archive of Modern Conflict, 2004.

Webster, Donovan. "Bombs into Cowbells." Photographs by Hei Han Khiang. *New York Times Magazine,* 28 June 1998, 32–33.

Weintraub, Stanley. *Silent Night: The Story of the World War I Christmas Truce.* New York: Penguin, 2001.

Westheimer, David. *Sitting It Out: A World War II POW Memoir.* Houston: Rice Univ. Press, 1992.

Westing, Arthur H., and E. W. Pfeiffer. "The Cratering of Indochina." *Scientific American* 226, no. 5 (May 1972): 21–29.

Willamson, Henry. *In Spite of All Rejoicing: A Soldier's Diary of the Great War.* New York: Duffield & Co., 1929.

Williams, Duncan Ryuken. "Camp Dharma: Japanese-American Buddhist Identity and the Internment Experience of World War II." In *Westward Dharma: Buddhism Beyond Asia.* Edited by Charles Prebish and Martin Baumann. Berkeley: Univ. of California Press, 2002.

Wilson, Edward O. *Biophilia.* Cambridge: Harvard, 1984.

Witkop, Philipp. *German Students' War Letters.* Translated by A. F. Wedd. Philadelphia: Pine Street Books, 2002 [1929].

Woelfle-Erskine, Cleo, ed. *Urban Wilds: Gardeners' Stories of the Struggle for Land and Justice.* Oakland, Calif.: Water/Underground Publications, 2001.

Wolschke-Bulmahn, Joachim. "'Freiheit in Grensen'? Gardens As Places of Progress, Protection, and Persecution." In *Down the Garden Path: The Artist's Garden After Modernism,* edited by Valerie Smith. New York: Queens Museum of Arts, 2005.

Wood, Jerry E. R., ed. *Detour, The Story of Oflag IVC.* Edited by J. F. Watton. London: Falcon, 1946.

Yamada, Mitsuye. *Camp Notes and Other Writings.* New Brunswick: Rutgers Univ. Press, 1998.

Zapruder, Alexandra, ed. *Salvaged Pages: Young Writers' Diaries of the Holocaust.* New Haven: Yale Univ. Press, 2002.

Zelkowicz, Josef. *In Those Terrible Days: Notes from the Lodz Ghetto.* Jerusalem: Yad Vashem, 2002.

Zuckerman, Yitzhak. *A Surplus of Memory: Chronicle of the Warsaw Ghetto Uprising.* Translated and edited by Barbara Harshav. Berkeley: Univ. of California Press, 1993.

Zyskind, Sara. *Stolen Years.* Translated by Marganit Insar. Minneapolis: Lerner, 1981.

Illustration Credits

PAGE 2   Photograph courtesy of the Imperial War Museum, IWM HU 63694.

PAGE 3   Photograph by Simon Norfolk; reprinted from Rieff, *Displaced Places.* The original caption read in part, Mailia Husseinova "built a makeshift garden with white stones, and two summers ago she planted sunflowers that grew to drape over the roof of her tent. She says that though others in the camp think she's odd for doing so, she likes to surround herself with beautiful things."

PAGE 8   Photograph © Museum of Fine Arts, Boston.

PAGE 10   Photograph by William Wenk, reprinted courtesy of the photographer.

PAGE 11   Photograph by Finn Larsen.

PAGE 15   German engraving in John Keegan and Joseph Darracott, *The Nature of War* (New York: Holt, Rinehart & Winston, 1981), 106.

PAGE 18   Photograph by the author, 2001.

PAGE 22   Keystone View Company No. 18042. From the author's collection.

PAGE 25   New York Times, *Portfolio of the Great War* (New York: New York Times, 1917).

PAGE 26   Photograph courtesy of the Imperial War Museum, IWM Q69695.

PAGE 30   Photograph courtesy of the Imperial War Museum, IWM
           Q1163.

PAGE 36   Paul Nash, oil on canvas. Photograph courtesy of the
           Imperial War Museum, IWM Art 2242.

PAGE 38   Photograph courtesy of the Imperial War Museum, IWM
           HU 65414.

PAGE 39   (left) Illustrated London News, 12 June 1915, xx; (right) Illustrated
           London News, 8 May 1915, 595.

PAGE 40   Illustrated London News, 25 Sept. 1915, 403.

PAGE 41   Photograph courtesy of the Imperial War Museum, IWM
           Q54737.

PAGE 43   Photograph courtesy of the Imperial War Museum, IWM
           Q32111.

PAGE 44   Talbot House Archive.

PAGE 46–47.   Photographed 15 Aug. 1918. Directorate of Agricultural
           Production. Photographs courtesy of the Imperial War
           Museum, IWM Q9800 (46) and IWM Q9782 (47).

PAGE 50   From the author's collection.

PAGE 54   Photographed 20 June 1918. Australian War Memorial,
           Negative Number E02642.

PAGE 56   Photographed 3 May 1917. Photograph courtesy of the
           Imperial War Museum, IWM Q5289.

PAGE 57   Photographed 9 Feb. 1918. Photograph courtesy of the
           Imperial War Museum, IWM Q8470.

PAGE 64   Ghetto Fighters Museum/Israel.

PAGE 73   United States Holocaust Memorial Museum.

PAGE 76   Ghetto Fighters Museum/Israel.

PAGE 78   United States Holocaust Memorial Museum.

PAGE 79   United States Holocaust Memorial Museum.

PAGE 80   Yad Vashem The Holocaust Martyrs' and Heroes'
           Remembrance Authority.

PAGE 81   United States Holocaust Memorial Museum.

PAGE 82   Photograph by Studio Leo Forbert, United States Holocaust
           Memorial Museum.

PAGE 84   Ghetto Fighters Museum/Israel.

PAGE 86   Ghetto Fighters Museum/Israel. Reprinted with permission
           of the Archive of Modern Conflict, London.

PAGE 89   Ghetto Fighters Museum/Israel.

PAGE 93   United States Holocaust Memorial Museum.

PAGE 94   Photograph by George Kadish/Zvi Kadishman, United
           States Holocaust Memorial Museum.

PAGE 96   United States Holocaust Memorial Museum.

PAGE 97   Photograph by George Kadish/Zvi Kadishman, United
           States Holocaust Memorial Museum.

PAGE 98   Ghetto Fighters Museum/Israel. Reprinted with permission
           of the Archive of Modern Conflict, London.

PAGE 99   Ghetto Fighters Museum/Israel. Reprinted with permission
           of the Archive of Modern Conflict, London.

PAGE 101   Photograph by George Kadish/Zvi Kadishman, United
           States Holocaust Memorial Museum.

PAGE 104   Ghetto Fighters Museum/Israel. Reprinted with permission
           of the Archive of Modern Conflict, London.

PAGE 115   Photograph courtesy of the Imperial War Museum, IWM
           HU 57920.

PAGE 117   Drawing by Miss E. Fortescue-Brickdale.

PAGE 123   Photograph by Charles Tait.

PAGE 125   Photograph courtesy of the Imperial War Museum, IWM
           Pope-Hennesey Papers.

PAGE 129   Photograph courtesy of the Imperial War Museum, IWM
           Pope-Hennesey Papers.

PAGE 131   Hoffman, *In the Prison Camps of Germany,* after p. 96.

PAGE 132   www.Pegasus-one.org/pow/09AZ/PicOf_9AZ_Garden.htm,
           courtesy of Thelma McMurchy.

PAGE 133   Photograph courtesy of the Imperial War Museum,IWM
           C.I. Rolfe Papers.

PAGE 136   Australian War Memorial, Negative Number P00077.021.

PAGE 137   Murray Griffin, Changi 1945. Pen and ink and wash over pencil, 24.6 x 30.4 cm, Australian War Memorial (ART25053).

PAGE 141   www.edrington.com/images/Santo_Tomas_-_map_1.jpg.

PAGE 149   *Tiki Times,* 8 Jan. 1945. Ministry for Culture and Heritage, Wellington, New Zealand.

PAGES 150–151   Photographs courtesy of the Imperial War Museum, IWM G.D.H. Ross Papers.

PAGE 153   Drawing by German POW. Courtesy of Manfred "Fritz" Nassauer, U.S. soldier.

PAGE 158   Photograph by Dorothea Lange. Bancroft Library, University of California, Berkeley, BANCPIC 1967.014.

PAGE 163   Photograph by Dorothea Lange, 29 June 1942. Bancroft Library, University of California, Berkeley. Japanese American Relocation Digital Archive (JARDA). Available from the Online Archive of California, http://ark.cdlib.org/ark:/13030/ft867nb4ss.

PAGE 166   UCLA Special Collections 122, box negative #285.

PAGE 167   Jeffery F. Burton, *Three Farewells to Manzanar,* 262.

PAGE 169   Densho: The Japanese American Legacy Project is a digital archive of videotaped interviews, photographs, documents, and other materials relating to the Japanese American experience. Additional information on the project is available at www.densho.org. Photograph denshopd-p15-00045.

PAGE 170   Sumi on paper by Chiura Obata, 28 Dec. 1942.

PAGE 172   Mine Okubo, *Citizen 13660,* 150.

PAGE 173   *Gila News-Courier,* 11 Nov. 1942. Microfilm, Japanese American National Museum. The photograph was accompanied in the *News-Courier* by this description: "*Ingenuity Marks Miniature Landscape Creation:* The abode at 56-10-D is surrounded by one of the most exotic miniature landscapes found in Butte. Taking his own background and transmission into 3 different worlds, Sam Fukuda, 44, has capsuled the settings of Miyajima, Japan; San Francisco; and lastly of Gila colony. It features a fish-pond filled with Canal caught carps, catfish, and 'medaka'; and at night 2 Japanese rock lanterns glamorously illuminate all the walled-in collections of petrified rocks and cactus. Fukuda, who was formerly a landscape gardener in San Francisco, explained, 'It took me 6 weeks for gathering the materials and ideas to complete it, not saying the amount of elbow grease I put into it. And having used only the natural resources of Gila, 34.35 was about all I spent for the cement and grass seeds.' "

PAGE 174 Bancroft Library, University of California, Berkeley. Japanese American Relocation Digital Archive (JARDA). Available from the Online Archive of California; http://ark.cdlib.org./ Photograph by Francis Stewart.

PAGE 175 Painting by Henry Sugimoto, 1944. Japanese American National Museum.

PAGE 176 Japanese American National Museum.

PAGE 181 Photograph by Dorothea Lange, 7 July 1942. Bancroft Library. Japanese American Relocation Digital Archive (JARDA). Online Archive of California, http://ark.cdlib .org/ark:13030/ft1k4003bq.

PAGE 182 Photograph by Jack Iwata. Japanese American National Museum.

PAGE 185 Photograph by the author, 2001.

PAGE 187 Photograph by Toyo Miyatake. Courtesy of Archie Miyatake.

PAGE 188 Photograph by Toyo Miyatake. Courtesy of Archie Miyatake. In Tamura, *Gardens below the Watchtower,* 55.

PAGE 191 Photograph by Jack Iwata. Japanese American National Museum.

PAGE 193 Sketch by Eddie Sato, 29 Oct. 1943. Tamura, *Gardens below the Watchtower,* 63, University of Washington Microfilm.

PAGE 197 Photograph denshopd-p2-00068. Densho.

PAGE 203 From the author's collection.

PAGE 205 Photograph by the author, 2002.

PAGE 208 Photograph by the author, 2001.

PAGE 209 National Archives.

PAGE 216 Photograph by Don Smith, 1991. From the author's collection.

PAGE 217   Photograph by Don Smith, 1991. From the author's collection.

PAGE 218   Photographed 1 Jan. 1944. Australian War Memorial, Negative Number 063365.

PAGE 219   Photograph by the author, 1993.

PAGE 220   Photograph by Daniel Winterbottom.

PAGE 222   Photograph by Margaret Morton.

PAGE 227   Photograph by Sam Helphand.

PAGE 228   USHMM.

PAGES 230–231   Photographed 2 May 1918. Photographs courtesy of the Imperial War Museum, IWM C.O. 2628.

PAGE 232   Photograph by Tom Parker, 17 Nov. 1942. Bancroft Library, University of California, Berkeley, BANC PIC 1967.014.

PAGE 233   Photograph by George Kadish/Zvi Kadushin, USHMM.

PAGE 236   Chelsea Flower Show 2004 website. The designers described their garden as follows: "Nature itself demonstrates hope, constantly healing and repairing the scars inflicted on the world by mankind."

PAGE 237   Photographed 28 Jan. 1918. Photograph courtesy of the Imperial War Museum, IWM Q.10634 (in Housing V. 54).

PAGE 242   Photograph by the author, 2004.

PAGE 243   http://www.neilsperry.com/2004_webletter/oct8/home.html

PAGE 244   Photograph by Sgt. Amy Dobler, Headquarters Company, 141st Engineer Combat Battalion. *National Guard Magazine*, 19 Nov. 2004.

PAGE 245   Photograph by the author, 1981.

PAGE 247   Community Gardening Association of Bosnia and Herzegovina. Project of American Friends Service Committee.

Index